Amalia's Tale

BOOKS BY DAVID I. KERTZER

AMALIA'S TALE
An Impoverished Peasant Woman, an
Ambitious Attorney, and a Fight for Justice

PRISONER OF THE VATICAN
The Popes' Secret Plot to Capture Rome from
the New Italian State

THE POPES AGAINST THE JEWS
The Vatican's Role in the Rise of Modern Anti-Semitism

THE KIDNAPPING OF EDGARDO MORTARA

POLITICS AND SYMBOLS
The Italian Communist Party and the
Fall of Communism

SACRIFICED FOR HONOR
Italian Infant Abandonment and the Politics
of Reproductive Control

RITUAL, POLITICS AND POWER

COMRADES AND CHRISTIANS
Religion and Political Struggle in Communist Italy

Amalia's Tale

An Impoverished Peasant Woman, an Ambitious Attorney, and a Fight for Justice

David I. Kertzer

Houghton Mifflin Company
BOSTON · NEW YORK
2008

Library of Congress Cataloging-in-Publication Data

Kertzer, David I., date.
Amalia's tale : an impoverished peasant woman, an ambitious
attorney, and a fight for justice / David I. Kertzer.
p.   cm.
Includes bibliographical references and index.
ISBN-13: 978-0-618-55106-4
ISBN-10: 0-618-55106-9
1. Bagnacavalli, Amalia — Trials, litigation, etc. — History. 2. Bologna
(Italy) — Trials, litigation, etc. — History. 3. Trials (Malpractice) —
Italy — Bologna — History. 4. Barbieri, Augusto. 5. Medical personnel
— Malpractice — Italy — Bologna — History. 6. Medical laws and
legislation — Italy — Criminal provisions. 7. Negligence, Criminal —
Italy. 8. Lawyers — Italy — Bologna — History. 9. Syphilis. I. Title.
KKH41.B65K47 2008   344.45 4104121 — dc22   2007008519

Printed in the United States of America

Book design by Robert Overholtzer

MP 10 9 8 7 6 5 4 3 2 1

FOR TWO JACKS

*Little Jacob Bear and his sorely missed
great-grandfather, Jacob Dana*

Contents

Prologue

THE STORY I am about to tell may seem strange, even bizarre. No one who reads this book will have ever heard of its protagonist, an illiterate young peasant woman, much less of the seemingly hopeless battle she fought, taking on a count and assorted others of her social superiors. Nor is the reader likely to have ever heard of the nature of her complaint, of the nineteenth-century scourge — whose name was so terrible that it was rarely uttered — that was devastating remote villages in Italy, France, and beyond.

But I offer this unknown story, not because of its ability to shock, but because it offers a rare glimpse into a world that is no more. From its idiosyncratic vantage point, it allows us to peer deep into a world in transformation, a society changing with breathtaking speed.

Italy in the not so distant past was a country of huge contrasts, of nobles and peasants, of great writers and a mass of illiterates, of fabulous palaces and rat-infested hovels. Until recently, most Italians lived in poverty in the countryside while the rich and powerful lived in the cities. Civilization — *civiltà* in Italian — meant urban life. Life in the countryside was regarded as fine for the *contadini*, the peasants, but only because no one thought of them as part of civilized society. There was no romance to rural living in

Italy, no glorification of the soil or those who tilled it. Yet the worlds of rich and poor, of city and countryside, were intimately linked. Vast areas of fertile farmland were owned by the urban elite, who visited each fall to be sure that the peasants who farmed it did not hold anything back. The parish priests who tended their rural flocks were, in this respect, no different, for they too took their orders from their superiors in the city.

The old social order began to change after the explosion that was the Risorgimento. Indeed, Italy only came into existence as a unified country in 1861, and even then Rome and the region around it remained a holdout. It was only in 1870, when the Italian army literally blasted through the medieval wall surrounding the Eternal City, that Rome fell and the defeated pope, Pius IX, retreated to his Vatican palaces as a self-styled prisoner. The following year Rome became the capital of the new Italian state.

At first, not much changed in the lives of most Italians: the peasants continued to till the soil and tend their flocks in much the same way their ancestors had. True, there was now a parliament and no longer an absolute ruler. But the senators were appointed by the king, and although the members of the House of Deputies were elected, no peasant could cast a ballot. In fact, in the years after unification, the majority of Italians, the *contadini*, had scant interest in their new government other than to lament it as another source of taxes, military conscription, and support for the landlords. Few of them could read government proclamations — or anything else — nor could they understand what either their king or those in parliament said, for such speech was unintelligible to the dialect-speaking peasantry.

While at first it seemed that, to paraphrase the aristocratic protagonist of *The Leopard,* all had to change so that all could stay the same, it soon became clear that change was coming. Long-held assumptions were being questioned, not least among them the notion that the masses of people had no rights, that it was up to the privileged few to decide what was best for those beneath them.

In 1876, the historic right — closely tied to the aristocracy and committed to maintaining the old social hierarchy — fell, and the left gained control of the Italian parliament. Although far from a revolutionary force, and soon to show itself all too ready to compromise to hold on to power, the left began a series of reforms that would transform the Italian countryside. Not the least of these was the spread of mandatory schooling in the hinterland and, by the turn of the century, the first, albeit weak, rules regulating women's and child labor.

Yet the major pressure for change in those years came not from the government but from quite another source. Ever since the revolutions of 1848, European society had been roiled by a maelstrom of popular movements against the privileged classes. With the First and then the Second International, these protests mutated from a disorganized series of abortive anarchist uprisings and associated millenarian delusions into a rapidly expanding and increasingly powerful socialist movement. In northern Italy in the last two decades of the century, tens of thousands of workers and peasants formed local cooperatives and leagues, demanding a transformation of society. When they began to coalesce into a nationwide socialist party in the 1890s, the elites began to get nervous. The peasants, who had for centuries seen themselves destined to spend their lives toiling for their wealthy landowners, began to question their fate. Rural strikes spread and outrageous — or so they seemed to the *padroni* — new demands were made.

The tale of Amalia Bagnacavalli is the story of people living amid this historic upheaval. Her story can scarcely be imagined any earlier in Italian history. It would have been inconceivable that an illiterate peasant woman could take legal action against one of Bologna's foremost aristocrats and one of the major urban institutions of her time — the Bologna foundling home. For all this to take place, a host of major changes had to appear. There had to be an established legal system that would allow such a suit to be filed and pursued. There would have to be a crusading lawyer who, motivated by a new ideology and by social ambitions unleashed by the loosening of aristocratic control, would champion her cause. And there would have to be a change in legal philosophy in the courts, with lowly workers seen as having certain basic rights.

The setting — the foundling home and the vast network of babies and wet nurses spread throughout the hinterland it oversaw — may seem to be an unlikely one for a story of dizzying social change. On the face of it the system, established centuries earlier, remained remarkably stable. Yet as a backdrop it offers some special advantages. In an Italy then poised between two epochs, nothing more dramatically illustrates the human dimensions of the relations of city to country, of rich to poor, than the foundling homes. For centuries they had taken in hundreds of thousands of babies abandoned by their parents at birth. In the days before safe artificial feeding, the survival of this mass of unfortunates depended on a peculiar system that involved renting out the bodies of peasant women. For these women in the desperately poor communities of the rural periphery, survival depended on being able to take in babies from the city's foundling home and getting paid for lending the infants their breasts. The cities sent thousands and thousands of these unfortunate "creatures," as they were called, into the countryside, pumping large amounts of money into the rural communities along with them. In the poorest villages in the late nineteenth century, thousands of women took in such children, like their mothers and grandmothers before them.

What follows is the story of one of the women who went to collect such a child, who sought some modest income by offering her breasts to one of society's neediest. It is at the same time the story of the upending of a well-established social hierarchy. It is the tale of a wholly unexpected triumph of the poor against the rich, of an illiterate peasant woman against a powerful male elite. It is a story that seeks to bring another time alive, and with it another world, yet its themes of human tragedy and triumph are timeless. It is the story of a rural woman whose life was ruined and the man from the city who would not stop — or so it seemed — until he had seen justice done.

Amalia's Tale

CHAPTER 1

An Unexpected Visitor

AUGUSTO BARBIERI COULDN'T imagine what would have brought in the woman who sat across the desk from him. He had opened his office in Bologna only a few years earlier, in 1886, and at twenty-eight had little experience with clients of any kind. Yet he knew that a visitor like this one was unusual.

If he felt a bit taken aback by the roughly dressed woman, she must have viewed him with even greater discomfort. Although he was not wealthy, the young lawyer took pride in the way he looked and in having his office reflect the importance of his social position. He wore a dark, three-piece woolen suit. Ponderous law books stood neatly in glass-paned wooden cabinets behind his heavy antique desk. Yet, although the woman came from another world, it was a world he knew something about. From her dress and the way she walked, anyone could tell that she was a peasant. And because he himself had come from the mountains outside Bologna and moved to the city as a child, he had no trouble identifying her distinctive dialect. Should he ask her to sign her name, he knew, she would simply blush and shake her head.

That is, she would have blushed if she were not already so red, for her face was covered by a rash. And though he expected her to

feel ill at ease in the unfamiliar surroundings, she seemed excep-
tionally uncomfortable in the open-backed wood chair.

While having an illiterate peasant woman in his office came as a
surprise to him, it was not unwelcome. The young lawyer had built
his reputation, at least among his small circle of colleagues, as part
of a band of an enlightened elite whose mission was to transform Italy into a modern country. For too long, they thought, the
Italian peninsula had been in the control of reactionary forces —
the church most of all, but also an assortment of retrograde aristocrats. Ever since Napoleon's troops had brought the ideas of the Enlightenment to Italy at the turn of the nineteenth century, there
were those who dreamed of a day when the old regimes would be
swept away and Italy unified under secular rule. This movement —
the Risorgimento — culminated in the proclamation of the Kingdom of Italy in 1861, when the old order crumbled and the power of
the church was dealt a severe blow.

By the time Amalia entered Barbieri's office, the offspring of Italy's Risorgimento had divided into two broad political camps: the
right and the left. Both were considered anathema by the church,
which refused to recognize the legitimacy of the new state and
called on good Catholics to boycott it. That portion of the old aristocracy who saw change as desirable, or at least inevitable, natu-
rally congregated on the right, along with other large landowners.
The left, to which Barbieri belonged, brought together a wide range
of groups, from those who rejected the Savoyard monarchy and
demanded a republic to those who had made peace with the monarchy but believed not in the authority of the Roman Catholic
Church, but in a new god, the god of science. It was to this moderate camp that Barbieri belonged. Life could be improved for everyone, he and his colleagues believed, and they saw it as their mission
to better the lot of society's unfortunates. The educated elite had a
duty, they thought, to do away with the vestiges of medieval society
and with the power of those who had profited from it: the church
and the aristocracy.

Two years earlier, Barbieri had published a weighty tome on the proper use of government: to improve the public good. He devoted much of it to problems of public education, public health, and protecting the working class, railing against the evils of class privilege and calling for a society where people gained rewards based only on their merits. The new science of social statistics would help reveal society's ills, he believed, and the application of scientific methods would show them what needed to be done. Old institutions would have to embrace these new principles or be replaced.

The woman who faced him certainly seemed to embody the social ills he had written about, an impression that only grew when he heard the story she was about to tell.

Barbieri wondered how she had chosen him from all of the city's lawyers. There were likely no attorneys where she came from, and, he could safely assume, of the world of the law and the courts she knew nothing. But, as he was to learn on that day in early August 1890, she had recently experienced such a traumatic turn of events that it seemed to her that she was scarcely the same person she had been just a few months earlier.

It took her a long time to tell her story, but Barbieri could be a good listener and was more than willing to put off the little work he had to hear what she had to say.

Her name, she said, was Amalia Bagnacavalli. She lived in a little hamlet called Oreglia, part of the larger mountain town of Vergato, whose hamlets lay scattered across a vast area. With her lived her husband, Luigi, their one-year-old daughter, and Luigi's family. Amalia's marriage had meant a step down for her: while her parents owned the land they farmed, her husband's family had no land of their own. These distinctions meant something to the people of the mountains, even though life was difficult for them all, for the soil was rocky, the growing season short, the parcels the peasants owned small.

Winters were the hardest time. Supplies put in storage the previous fall dwindled, and the new crops were still far off. That winter, just as their stocks sank to their lowest point of the year, Luigi's parents urged Amalia to help out in a way that she had never been able to before. All the families they knew looked to the foundling home in Bologna in times of need. In exchange for taking in foundlings, they received monthly payments that for many provided the only cash they had. Most generous of all were the payments made to the women who could nurse the newly abandoned babies. The foundling home would not allow a woman with a child under age one — and so nursing her own child — to take a foundling to nurse. But Amalia's baby, Adele, had just passed her first birthday.

Amalia had never traveled outside the Oreglia area and had never seen a town of more than a few hundred people. To get a foundling meant going to Bologna, twenty miles away and separated by a road that this time of year was often impassable. Blocked by snow in the coldest months, the road snaked along the Reno River, whose swollen waters regularly flooded it in the spring.

Fortunately, three years before Amalia's birth, the train line running south from Bologna to Tuscany opened to great fanfare. She had often seen trains pass but had never been on one herself, or for that matter ever traveled anywhere except by foot or, on rare occasions, in a wagon or on a mule. That March morning she walked to the tiny station a few kilometers from her home and gave the stationmaster five lire for a ticket to Bologna. Handling the coins was itself a new experience, and, as Barbieri knew, the money seemed like a sizable sum to her. Even if she had been lucky enough to be hired for a week to do farm labor, she would barely have been paid that much. Her mother-in-law had given Amalia the money for the one-way fare, telling her that the foundling home would pay for her return.

That Amalia would travel by herself, without her husband, was not surprising, for her trip to the foundling home was firmly part of a world of women's affairs that had existed for centuries. Although peasant life in northern Italy was in some ways patriarchal, there was a sharp separation between the spheres of men and women. In the women's sphere, women ruled. For a young woman like Amalia, it was Luigi's mother, her own mother-in-law, who controlled her daily life. Luigi himself would keep his distance from any affairs involving infants — although, as it would turn out, he would soon be involved in dealings with the foundling home that he could never have anticipated.

When Amalia got off the train in Bologna, she could only have gawked at the massive city wall in front of her. Built in the 1300s to defend Bologna from its medieval enemies, it was a towering sign of the boundary separating the world of the peasants from the world of civilization. Amalia spotted the towering gate that would allow her to pass into the city. As she approached it, she encountered the two officials who always stood watch there, one who wore a normal suit and hat and the other a police uniform, a sheathed sword hanging from his waist. The men stood guard, eyeing peasants such as Amalia with particular care, looking for signs of a telltale bulge in their clothes. They knew all the tricks that the peasant women used to sneak in goods for the market in their billowing blouses. Had they suspected something, they would have ushered Amalia into a nearby booth, where a female guard would have had her disrobe.

The wall no longer served any purpose militarily, but it still proved valuable to the city fathers. No one could bring goods in without paying a tax, a medieval practice that had somehow survived in the modern Italian state and which even then provided the city with the bulk of its annual budget. For the peasants outside, seeking to sell their fruits and vegetables in the city, nighttime offered a chance to try to scale the wall in those vulnerable spots where an athletic young man might have a chance. Other peasants built secret compartments in their donkey-drawn carts, hoping to avoid the duty on at least some of their goods.

Amalia, carrying no basket, her clothes showing no evidence of forbidden fruits, would not have been stopped. Having no clear idea of where to go, she must have asked a woman nearby for directions. At that time of year, Bologna's *popolane* — women from the poorer classes that dominated the city's population — typically wore heavy dark coats over smocks that went all the way down to their sturdy shoes. These women covered their heads with a simple kerchief (if they covered them at all), for hats were for women of greater means. A poor woman wearing a hat would be ridiculed for her pretensions.

Along the side of the medieval canal that ran through the city, a sickening smell wafting from its dark, sewage-laced waters, dozens of women lined up shoulder to shoulder. Oblivious to the rest of the world, they dunked their bed linens and underwear in the murky water and then beat them on the brick shelf that lined the canal. All along the canal crude wooden stakes were sunk into the ground, a rope running between them. The white sheets that the women hung to dry from the ropes stood out against the dark buildings behind them. When she returned to the city a few months later to meet Barbieri for the first time, Amalia would see these same women in a slightly different position. Beneath the spot where they had stood before was a second, submerged shelf, which made their work easier in the warmer months — although, as Barbieri knew, it put them at increased risk of infection from the many diseases carried by the putrid waters.

Men passed by in small donkey-pulled carriages, sitting on the wooden slat-backed bench that stretched between the two large wooden wheels, most wearing dark capes draped over their shoulders and round black hats with wide, flat brims. Even the poor took pride in how they looked. A man would rather appear every day in his one good, clean suit, although it had been patched dozens of times, than wear one marked by a single stain. Beneath the porticoes over the city's sidewalks gathered people who were clearly of another class altogether. Some men wore suits with vests and high-collared white shirts, their dapper look completed with bowler hats. The women of the more comfortable classes paid even more attention to their appearance, dressing in elaborate, light-colored suits and huge hats, often with a smartly tied silk kerchief around their neck and an umbrella hooked on arm. Their form-fitting clothes, hugging their bodies from their chests all the way down their legs, stood in sharp contrast to the loose dress of the poor.

Those who could do so tried to leave their homes during the day, for the great majority of Bologna's hundred thousand residents lived in dark, dank apartments. Filled with smoke from the charcoal braziers that warmed them, they were rank from the stench of the sewage and night water. It was March, and the *popolani* had made their way once again through the winter, which they called "the onion months," in rueful reference to the cheap, easily preserved ingredient that flavored the polenta that was all they had to fill their stomachs. They were damp months, the fog often so thick that it was impossible to see across the street, months when work was short, the nights were long, and those families that had enough charcoal to heat their homes were considered lucky.

But what must have struck Amalia was not this poverty but the magnificence of what she saw around her. She had never seen buildings as splendid as the massive, ornate stone structures that lined the road and never seen porticoes like the ones she walked under. She could not have passed through the city gate without seeing something she had never encountered before, a steam trolley, which had begun service in Bologna seven years earlier, its route circling the walls. Inside the city, an endless procession of horse-drawn carriages rumbled down the streets, each with an umbrella fixed to the front seat to protect its driver from Bologna's frequent rain. Running down the middle of the cobblestone street that led from the city gate toward the main piazza, open-sided trolleys raced by, each pulled along its steel track by two horses.

At nearly every corner, a woman would sit on a stoop before a blackened brazier, the heat visible as waves and smoke, with a pile of thick chestnut pancakes to sell to hungry passersby. Men and women carrying large wicker baskets sold an assortment of other treats. One such man, a well-known figure in Bologna, wearing a tall top hat and carrying an outsized basket, attracted more attention than the rest, not only because his sugared *focacce* were a powerful lure for the hungry, but because he was famous for regaling all who would listen with stories of his friendship with the queen.

If Amalia noticed a special excitement in the air, it was not just people's relief at making it through another winter. Something stupendous was coming to Bologna, and people could talk of nothing else. Every wall, it seemed, was plastered with large, colorful posters announcing the imminent arrival of Buffalo Bill's Wild West show, which would play for eight days to standing-room crowds. Europe had been abuzz with reports of Buffalo Bill's extravaganza ever since his first visit to England, three years earlier. It was hard to forget the image of the show's command performance for Jubilee Day, when the kings of Denmark, Greece, and Belgium crowded into a small stagecoach next to the Prince of Wales — and future king of England — with Buffalo Bill at the reins, fending off a mock attack from a threatening band of whooping, feathered Indians. Buffalo Bill had returned to Europe in 1889, bound first for the Paris Universal Exposition, where over ten thousand people, including the French president, crowded into the show's opening performance. From there the show made its way to southern France and Spain before heading for Rome, where the cowboy entrepreneur was received by the elderly Pope Leo XIII.

Buffalo Bill Cody, an iconic figure in his buckskin suit on his white horse, was now coming to Bologna with scores of Indians; well over a hundred horses on which they performed their savage, bare-chested acts of derring-do; a dozen buffalo; a handful of elk and Texas steer; and the famed twenty-nine-year-old sharpshooter Annie Oakley. Those lucky enough to see the show were in for another special treat. They would be the first Italians to eat popcorn; polenta, it soon became clear, would not be the only item in the Bolognese diet to owe its origin to the New World's corn.

But not everyone in Bologna that day was in such a fine mood. In front of the cathedral, groups of families clutched their belongings, the women dressed much like Amalia and speaking a dialect similar to her own. Coming from mountain towns like hers, they too sought a way out of their misery. Their neighbors had told them of the opportunities in the New World open to those who had the courage to seize them. Having many hours to wait for the long, overnight train ride to Genoa, where they would set sail, they went to the cathedral, hoping that the archbishop might himself bless their children before their departure.

Ever since the agricultural crisis had engulfed Italy, along with much of Europe, a few years earlier, the number of people leaving the country had increased dramatically. Around the turn of the century, the United States became the Italians' favored destination. Indeed, in the first decade of the new century, Italy, with a population of 33 million, would see a staggering 2.4 million of its people set sail for the United States and Canada. For now, however, South America beckoned, and Brazil, which had abolished slavery two years earlier, was just then surpassing Argentina as the destination of choice.

The huge headquarters of Bologna's city government, the *palazzo comunale*, loomed in the city's center. Built in the thirteenth century to be impregnable to attack, it remained an awe-inspiring sight. Its massive front portal looked out on the vast central piazza, recently renamed Piazza Victor Emmanuel to honor Italy's royal founder. On the side of the piazza nearest the train station was a fountain topped by the giant naked figure of a muscled Neptune, his trident in hand, crafted by Giambologna three centuries earlier. The concrete nymphs circling the base of the statue could not have failed to attract Amalia's attention — nor been more appropriate to her mission — for their fingers squeezed streams of water from their breasts.

The piazza was always filled with people, some striding purposefully, others tarrying to listen to the knots of gesticulating men, whose endless debates provided amusement from morning to night. Amalia would have been struck by another odd sight, as men wearing dark suits, ties, and hats rode by on bicycles, a recent invention that had yet to reach the mountains.

On the far side of the piazza loomed a church so large that all of the churches Amalia had ever seen in her life could have been comfortably placed in one of its smaller corners. Construction had begun on San Petronio in 1390, its mammoth size and splendid art designed to impress the rest of the world with Bologna's grandeur. But its marble façade was never finished because, at least according to the story believed by all *bolognesi*, the pope had put a stop to it, angry that Bologna was trying to build a church more impressive than his own. Its elaborate pink and white marble façade barely extended above its three beautifully sculpted portals. The upper two-thirds had been left unfinished, the simple brown tiles punctuated by regularly spaced holes intended to hold a façade that never came.

Throughout the piazza scruffy boys, like none Amalia had ever seen, scurried about, scattering the ever-present pigeons and begging cigarettes from men who angrily shooed them away. Others, smaller children dressed practically in rags, ran through the piazza shoeless, although the weather was far from warm. Mendicants of every sort surrounded the church entrance, some missing limbs, some with a crutch or two, some blind, all hoping to find a good Christian in a charitable mood. It was but a short walk now to Amalia's destination, an institution known as the Bastardini, the home of the "little bastards." Within its walls Amalia's life was about to take a fateful turn.

CHAPTER 2

The Fateful Day

❧

LTHOUGH AMALIA COULD NOT have known it, Bologna's
foundling home had already come to Barbieri's attention,
attracting his righteous wrath for its antiquated practices.
His book on proper administration used it as a prime example of
why the city's old medieval institutions had to be placed on a more
scientific footing.

By the nineteenth century, foundling homes were scattered
around much of Europe, but they had begun in Italy. According to
some historians, the first such home was founded in 1198 on the orders of Pope Innocent III himself, horrified, it was said, by the
numbers of bloated bodies of dead babies pulled out of the Tiber in
fishermen's nets. Embarrassed that Rome, the capital of Christen-
dom, should have its image blighted by such a sight, the pope ordered the construction of a home where such unwanted newborns
could be left. Even if they did not live long, he reasoned, at least
they would be properly baptized and so find heavenly comfort.

Bologna's foundling home opened in the fifteenth century, growing out of a Benedictine convent that had begun taking in foundlings two centuries earlier. By the 1600s, ecclesiastical authorities
were instructing the local officials and parish priests to be on the
lookout for pregnant, unwed women and to report them to the

foundling home. Their main fear was that such women, facing disgrace, would try to conceal their pregnancies by procuring an abortion or killing their babies right after birth. But the authorities were also on guard against another evil, and the police were ordered to find any unwed women who tried to keep their babies. The very sight of an unmarried woman with a baby was regarded as an outrage to public morality, one that could not be tolerated in the Papal States.

The popes had served as temporal rulers — "pope-kings," as they came to be called — over central Italy since the year 754. The amount of territory they controlled waxed and waned with the vagaries of the popes' alliances with more militarily powerful forces. At the center lay Rome. There the warring noble families saw no prize greater than the papacy itself, and for centuries they fought over the honor and power that came with placing one of their number on St. Peter's throne. Bologna became part of the Papal States only in the early 1500s, when it was conquered by the army of Pope Julius II. With brief interludes caused by assorted uprisings and invasions, papal rule lasted in Bologna until the pope's forces were driven out in 1859.

With the unification of Italy two years later, the foundling home was placed under the authority of a board responsible for all of the city's hospitals. Until then an essentially private institution, it became public, the proceeds from its endowment now supplemented by taxes collected throughout the province.

The home's new directors faced the same challenge as their predecessors. The only way to keep the hundreds of babies who flooded in each year alive was by placing them at the breasts of women who were willing to nurse them, for it was only with the introduction of pasteurization and supplemental formulas in the twentieth century that animal milk could be used safely. Year after year, half the abandoned babies died before reaching their first birthday, a death rate that was more than twice as high as that found in the general population. As one social reformer of the time put it, they might as well place over each foundling home's door the motto: "Here babies come to die at public expense." Or, as Thomas Malthus wrote almost a century earlier: "If a person wished to check population and were not solicitous about the means, he could not propose a more effective measure than the establishment of a sufficient number of foundling hospitals."

The babies were known as *bastardini* for good reason, for they were all born to unwed women, women whose anonymity the system was designed to protect. It was strictly forbidden for married couples to abandon their babies while, for centuries, unwed women were required to give them up. Times had now changed, with the demise of the Papal States, and police were no longer sent to seize babies from those unwed women who wanted to raise them. But such was the shame of bearing an illegitimate child that few women were willing, or able, to do so. Even when an unwed mother might herself want to keep her child, her family, threatened by disgrace, would rarely agree to it.

Amalia's town, Vergato, was typical of the mountain communities near Bologna, for it was filled with foundlings of all ages, the legacy of a centuries-old tradition of taking such children in. Not only did foundling home officials have to find wet nurses for Bologna's abandoned infants, they also needed to find families to care for the children until they reached their fifteenth birthday. Following a belief common throughout Italy, it was thought best for the foundlings to grow up in the countryside, where they would learn the skills of peasant life that would prepare them for an independent future. Keeping them in the foundling home was inconceivable — there were thousands of them — and placing them in homes in the city was considered a bad idea. In the city the children, already suffering from the disadvantage of their birth, would be all too easily corrupted and led into a life of crime and moral degradation. As a result, the foundling home oversaw a vast network of thousands of rural families, each given a monthly stipend. In Oreglia, almost a quarter of the households were getting these payments from the home. Together these were by far the largest public expenditure for social welfare in Bologna, money that came for the most part from taxes paid by the towns and cities of the province.

When Amalia was ushered into the inner courtyard of Bologna's foundling home, she entered a world apart, a world of newborn babies and the women who nursed them. Here, in fact, was the perfect setting for Barbieri's theories of good governance, for nowhere in the new Italian state was there a closer link between science, government, and social welfare.

Amalia could not enter the large hall where the dozens of babies were kept and where ten women, held in a kind of imprisonment, nursed them until an outside wet nurse could be found. For two hundred years, in order to ensure that it had enough women to nurse the babies there, the foundling home dragooned poor unmarried mothers, a practice found elsewhere in Italy as well. No baby could be left at the Bologna foundling home without a payment of 25 lire. Any woman who could not afford the fee was forced to spend at least two or three months there, nursing two, three, or more babies at a time. In the course of these months she might nurse dozens of different babies. The one baby she was forbidden to nurse was her own.

During their time in the foundling home, such women were not allowed any visitors, nor could they leave the building by themselves. As a matter of good medical practice, the officials arranged for the women to get some fresh air periodically, but on these special occasions they were accompanied by chaperones and escorted outside the city walls to avoid unwanted attention.

Before the sixteenth century, the line separating the married from the unmarried was often blurred, and children's "legitimacy" was not a real issue. But all this changed in the sixteenth century when the church, fighting off the new threat of Protestantism, tightened its strictures on marriage. Illegitimacy was stigmatized, and unwed women who got pregnant faced ruin. What made matters worse was the church's belief that the women alone were responsible for their pregnancies. Except where violent rape could be proven — and the standards of proof were very high — the authorities were not to ask about the babies' fathers. The protection of men from such paternity searches — justified by the need to protect the family, for it was assumed that many of them were married — was one of the many papal laws that had been kept by the new Italian state.

When Amalia walked through the courtyard, she would have seen none of these women. She might, though, have glimpsed others who crowded into one of the palazzo's wings. Two hundred women, ranging in age from the postpubescent to the senile, lived there, women who had themselves begun life in these halls. Just as the foundling home officials sought to protect the honor of unwed mothers, they also felt responsible for the honor of the girls abandoned there. Monthly payments to families caring for foundlings stopped on the child's fifteenth birthday. Boys were then on their own, but girls still had to be protected. The ideal, for the foundling home, was for each girl to remain in the household that had been caring for her, earning her keep by helping the other women with their work. But her ultimate fate depended on marriage, which the foundling home promoted by providing a dowry. Yet, even with a dowry, some never succeeded in finding a mate. To guard the honor of these unfortunate women, the foundling home took them back. As a result, some in the foundling home's conservatory had been living there for over sixty years, the cost of their upkeep offset by the work they did, making the foundlings' clothes and bed sheets.

Amalia may have noticed one of these old women bringing laundry through the courtyard, but her attention was drawn elsewhere. Ushered into a separate room, she was told to wait. Before long, a man whom she would later learn was Dr. Pinzani came in. Amalia clutched the pieces of paper she had guarded carefully since leaving her home earlier in the day and nervously handed them to him. With all of the women in Oreglia who had made this trip in the past, there had been no lack of neighbors to advise her on what she would need. To be given a child, a woman had to bring a medical certificate from her doctor, certifying not only her own good health and the good quality of her milk but her husband's health as well. She also needed a certificate of her good morals. In years past, this was provided by the local parish priest, but now, with the end of the Papal States, it was issued by the town office. Finally, she needed certificates to prove that her own baby had either died or was now over twelve months old.

The doctor told her to lie on the examining table. He looked into her eyes, then down her throat. He felt her glands and then, to her embarrassment, lifted up her dress and examined her private parts. For centuries, those seeking a wet nurse were warned to look closely for any sign of syphilis in the woman, and the doctor wanted to be careful. As a British treatise on midwifery put it in 1673: "She must be very healthful . . . hath no spot, nor the least suspicion of any venereal distemper . . . no scab, itch, scald, or other filth of the like nature."[1] Satisfied by what he saw, the doctor told her to lift off her homemade wool dress, and he carefully felt her breasts. He stared at her nipples, then squeezed each breast until the milk squirted out. Amalia nervously wondered whether the doctor was satisfied. She knew from her neighbors that she was the right age, for the foundling home preferred young women, but she had also heard that women who had been nursing their own baby for as long as she had were thought to have old milk. The foundling home favored those women whose own children had died in the first months of life, as their milk was the freshest. This was another reason that it was easier for the foundling home to find good wet nurses in the winter, for winter was a time when more babies died, the victims of the respiratory ills that plagued the mountain families' frigid homes.

Told to put her clothes back on, Amalia could hardly have felt more ill at ease. The doctor called in a nurse and spoke to her in a voice too low for Amalia to hear. They then walked out the door, leaving Amalia alone, staring at the walls, although for how long she could not have said. Had a clock stood in the examining room, she would still not have known, for she could not tell time.

At last the nurse and the doctor returned, the nurse holding a female infant wrapped in swaddling clothes. At the first sight of the baby, Amalia, who had imagined this moment for months and wondered what the new baby would be like, was horrified. She looked nothing like her own daughter, Adele, who had always been the picture of health. With a sickening feeling, she realized that something was wrong with the scrawny, whimpering infant the nurse held out to her.

Amalia told the doctor that she didn't want the baby. But the doctor replied that she had no choice. If she thought she was too good to take her, he said, someone else who wasn't so picky would soon come along. If Amalia did take the child, the doctor added, she would get 9 lire every month. Otherwise, she would get nothing.

Amalia couldn't face going home empty-handed even if she had the money to buy a return ticket. As it was, she didn't know what she would do if she had to leave without getting the fare from the foundling home.

She again begged the doctor to let her take another baby, a healthy one, but again he refused. Reluctantly, she reached out and took the crying infant.

The nurse admonished Amalia to take good care of the child. She was never again to nurse her own baby, for her milk was now meant for the foundling alone. The nurse also showed her the lead medallion around the baby's neck; it was tied by a string in such a way that it could not be removed. On it was her name, Paola Olivelli, along with the year she arrived at the foundling home and the number that identified her in its records. The nurse warned Amalia never to take the medallion from the baby's neck.

That Paola had a last name at all was a sign of the changing times. Before the nineteenth century, most foundlings in Italy were given only a first name; if they did have a surname, it was simply the same name given to all the babies. Following this practice, for centuries Bologna's foundlings were called Degli Esposti (*esposti* being the Italian word for "foundlings"), and hundreds of thousands of babies abandoned at the Naples foundling home were likewise named Esposito. The babies at Milan's huge foundling home were called Colombo (after the *colombo,* or "pigeon," the symbol of the home, whose sculpted image adorned its crest). The legacy of this practice — and a testament to the massive scale of infant abandonment in Italy in the past — is that Esposito and Colombo are the fourth and seventh most common surnames, respectively, in all of Italy today. It was only in the nineteenth century that moralists began to worry about the stigma foundlings suffered by having their lack of parentage so publicly on display. A campaign began to give each child a distinctive last name, which was no small matter in a place like Milan, whose foundling home staff in the first years of the new Italian state had to invent over fifty-five hundred surnames each year.

It was only when they were on the train headed home that Amalia first took Paola out of her swaddling to examine her more carefully. What she saw made her shudder. The baby's body was malformed, her chest strangely twisted. And something else was wrong. At the foundling home Amalia had noticed that Paola's eyes seemed suspiciously filmy. Now that she got to look more closely, Amalia realized that the baby was blind.

CHAPTER 3

The First Signs

B ARBIERI WAS MESMERIZED by Amalia's story and getting
used to her thick country accent. Because Monghidoro, the
town of his birth, was not far from Amalia's hamlet, this was
easier than it would have been for many of his colleagues. Barbieri's
father, a notary, had been one of his town's most prominent citizens, presiding over land sales, wills, and assorted other transac-
tions. Although his family had moved to Bologna when Barbieri
was young, much of his business continued to come from his old
mountain town, and they still owned land there.

Amalia continued with her account.

When she returned home that evening, she said, she found everyone there: her husband, Luigi Migliorini, who at thirty-two was
nine years older than she, her little Adele, Luigi's parents, and
Luigi's two brothers and sister, all of whom worked on the farm.
The next day Amalia's own family, who lived nearby, got to see the
baby from Bologna. For Amalia's father, the child could only bring
back painful memories, for he too had begun life at the Bologna
foundling home.

The two households were closely bound. Before Amalia married
Luigi, her older brother, Alfonso, had married Luigi's sister, Elisa,
and a year before Adele was born to Amalia they had had twins.

Following tradition, at his marriage, each man had brought his bride to live in his parental home, so Amalia and her sister-in-law had, in effect, swapped houses.

Barbieri could visualize the kind of dark dwelling where Amalia lived. He knew that to make it through the winter, Amalia's family relied on the chestnuts they gathered from the forest in the fall, together with whatever corn was left from the harvest. The vegetables they grew — the cauliflower, tomatoes, and artichokes — would have been long gone by the time that Amalia returned home. No doubt, Barbieri thought, they had their own little chicken coop, which Amalia and the other women tended, but they would trade their eggs for more pressing needs and eat the chickens only on special occasions. They would also grow grapes for white wine, but they would not permit themselves the luxury of drinking it without adding water to make it go further. The watery wine helped them get down the polenta and the stale dark bread. Barbieri knew, too, that Amalia would never eat her meals at the table. Among the peasants, only the men sat while the women served, the patriarch at the head of the table. After supper on cold nights, they would all move into the barn, the heat of the cows helping to keep them warm as the women spun hemp and wool into thread and then wove the family's clothes.

Amalia's house was made of local stones, chosen so that they could be placed one on top of the other using the minimum amount of mortar, the windows kept small to protect against the winter cold and summer heat. Huge slabs of flat-topped rock formed the floor, and a steep wooden staircase led to the room above, where even Amalia could not stand up straight under the slanted ceiling.

Although a few one-room schools were scattered around Vergato, Amalia had never been in one. When she was ten years old, parliament passed a law requiring all children to attend three years of elementary school, but none of Vergato's schoolhouses was near her home.

Amalia had hoped that taking in a foundling would give her

more status in her husband's household and make her life easier, but she soon realized her mistake. The baby was doing poorly. Not only did she cry all the time, but she would barely suckle at Amalia's breast — a painful contrast to Adele, who had always nursed happily. Worried that her milk might dry up, Amalia began nursing Adele again. And while Adele napped easily and slept through the night, Paola rarely napped and kept waking up, sobbing, at all hours. Amalia thought that if she could just get her to eat something, the baby would start sleeping. She tried to get Paola to swallow some bread soup. When this did not work, she made some pancakes with chestnut flour, chewed on them, and then extracted the mush from her mouth, put some on her fingertip, and tried to get the squalling baby to swallow it. Nothing worked.

With all the women nearby who were experienced with foundlings — and some had nursed three, four, or even more — Amalia hoped to find some advice. But the women could only commiserate with her on her bad luck.

Things soon got worse. Not only wasn't Paola eating, but her nose was constantly running and, more worrisome still, began to emit a strange yellow fluid that ran down her lip. At the same time, Amalia noticed that the baby's breath had a pungent smell. One day, when Amalia was changing her, she noticed strange tiny white sores, about the size of pinheads, on her backside. Touching them, she was surprised how hard they felt. Soon a red rash appeared around the sores and quickly spread along the inside of Paola's thighs. Alarmed, Amalia decided to take Paola to the doctor.

If Barbieri considered himself a champion of the oppressed, the bearer of scientific enlightenment to a benighted society, Carlo Dalmonte, the town doctor of Vergato, was his rural counterpart. What he discovered when Amalia brought him the baby stirred all of his righteous fury.

Each rural town had one or two doctors on the payroll who provided free medical care. In fact, half of Italy's physicians at the time were rural town doctors, normally with three-year terms. Poorly paid, they tended to come from the lower middle classes of rural society and to mix with others of similar standing — schoolteachers, parish priests, and the like. In 1875, just two years after finishing his medical degree at the University of Bologna, Dalmonte had been appointed Vergato's town doctor, a position he held for the rest of his life.

He was now an old hand at dealing with local wet nurses. It had not taken long for him to see the suffering that the foundlings were bringing to the mountain families. Soon after he took up his position, two young women came to him in the same month with symptoms of syphilis, which they had contracted from their foundlings. Incensed, he sent what would turn out to be but the first of many complaints to the authorities.

Because a certain number of the foundlings' mothers had syphilis — it was especially prevalent among Bologna's prostitutes, who were among the foundling home's most loyal patrons — it was far from uncommon for a foundling to be born with the disease. Soldiers who were stationed temporarily in Bologna were a common source of women's infections, as were other men who visited prostitutes and passed the disease on to their lovers.

Over the next few years, the young Vergato doctor continued to complain about the foundling home, outraged by the parade of local women infected by their diseased foundlings. In 1883 he contacted the provincial health board, protesting that although he had written three years earlier, the foundling home had done nothing to improve its procedures. He recounted the latest case: a woman had taken a sick baby back to the foundling home and been given another baby to nurse. The first baby died of syphilis, and the wet nurse soon showed its early signs herself, subsequently infecting the healthy second baby as well. Dalmonte urged the authorities to address the foundling home's negligence, which, he lamented, had already caused incalculable suffering.

The health board forwarded the complaint to the foundling home, and two months later its doctors replied at length. They suggested that Dalmonte's diagnostic skills could not be trusted and that it was not uncommon for peasant families to blame the foundling home for a disease that they contracted from their own immoral behavior. Admittedly, the doctors added, some women did contract syphilis from their foundlings, but they could do nothing about it. Often, the babies showed the first signs of syphilis at only two or three months or even later. Were the foundling home doctors to wait that long before sending the infants to wet nurses, they would need a headquarters ten or twenty times larger than the one they already had. Even with such palatial quarters, the number who would die before getting to be nursed was so horrifying that such an answer was unthinkable.

In 1887 Dalmonte again addressed this problem, reacting to the national health ministry's new guidelines on syphilis. At a meeting of the Vergato health board, he argued that it was dangerous to rely, as the guidelines suggested, on medical testimony that the mother of an infant had been free of syphilis when deciding whether the baby was at risk. Medical science knew, he argued, that syphilis could be passed down to a child directly through the father's sperm just as easily as it could through the mother herself. In this, Dalmonte shared the opinion of most medical experts of the time, an error that was finally laid to rest only in the twentieth century.

When Amalia took little Paola to see Dalmonte in April 1890, he stretched out her lip and saw the ulcerated sores. Muttering to himself, he told the frightened Amalia never to nurse the baby again, and he made her promise to take Paola back to the foundling home without delay.

Amalia left the next morning, April 11, for Bologna, retracing her steps of eighteen days earlier. This time, the woman at the foundling home gate took her to a different room, where she was soon joined by a different doctor than the one she had met earlier. Emanuele Bruers, the assistant foundling home physician, took a quick look at the baby, who in addition to her other problems had now not been nursed for twenty-four hours. Amalia pulled from her dress Dr. Dalmonte's paper and handed it to him. Bruers read the sheet, then told her that she shouldn't nurse any baby for at least a month. Every morning, he instructed her, she should look for any sign of a sore on her body, especially around one of her nipples. If she saw something, she was to come right back. Frightened and confused, Amalia hurried to the train station for the long trip home.

Barbieri remained a patient listener, realizing that the point of Amalia's story, the reason for her visit to his office, was about to be told.

Not having the screaming baby anymore was a big relief, Amalia admitted, but the first days back she could not get out of her mind the image of the angry Dr. Dalmonte, cursing the foundling home and telling her that she was a fool to have taken such a sickly child. She thought too of the icy Dr. Bruers, who had said she had done well to bring the baby back but warned her to watch for any strange sores.

All this meant that for the next several days Amalia had a hard time thinking of anything else. Whenever she could get away from the gaze of her in-laws, she snuck a peek under her dress to be sure that all was well.

All did go well for the first three weeks, and she was beginning to think less often of Paola and the two doctors, when one morning, shortly after she woke up, she felt something a bit odd around the nipple on her left breast. As soon as she could she went outside, found a place where she could not be seen, and unbuttoned her blouse. On the deep brown skin of her nipple was an odd little depression. She pressed it a bit, but it didn't hurt. In fact, she told Barbieri, if she didn't touch it, she couldn't feel anything at all. She remembered what the foundling home doctor had told her, but surely, she thought — or at least hoped — this was not worth mentioning. The doctor would laugh at her if she made the long trip to Bologna just for this.

Although Amalia tried to ignore the mark on her nipple, she couldn't resist looking at it whenever she was alone. She kept trying to convince herself that it was harmless, but one day it began to get bigger, and in the place of the depression a small hard growth took shape. She left the house, found a place she could be alone, and looked at it carefully. It was just above the tip of her protruding nipple, round and hard around the outside, with a depression in the center and a strange light grayish color.

Amalia was frightened, but she kept hoping that the strange sore would go away. She could not face going back to the foundling home, where the grim doctor would make her remove her dress and handle her breast. For many days more she waited. Finally, desperate to confide in someone, she told a friend. She should see the doctor right away, her friend advised, suggesting that rather than go all the way to Bologna she return to Dr. Dalmonte.

When was this? asked Barbieri.

Amalia extracted a piece of paper from her dress and handed it to the lawyer, as the doctor had advised.

Barbieri looked at the sheet and read it quickly, noting the date, June 15, 1890, and the signature at the bottom: Carlo Dalmonte, town doctor, Vergato. It was a medical certificate of a diagnosis of syphilis. Having examined Amalia Bagnacavalli on this day, the doctor had written, he had detected the growth of an initial syphiloma on her left breast. He also stated the cause: Amalia had been given syphilis by the foundling Paola Olivelli.

Barbieri looked up again. What had the doctor told her? he asked.

He said, Amalia recalled, that the baby had given her syphilis and that she should return to Bologna for treatment. He told her not to return to the foundling home, because, he said, the doctors there would be no help. Instead, he told her about a special hospital where they knew how to take care of people like her. Amalia replied that she had no money, but the doctor said that she should borrow what she needed from her family and that he would help her get the foundling home to pay, because it was their fault. She hadn't gone to Bologna right away because she had to find the money and couldn't keep asking her mother-in-law to take care of Adele, but she went as soon as she could.

It was Amalia's third trip to Bologna in two months. If she now had more confidence about getting to the city, she dreaded going to the hospital. Everyone knew that hospitals were places where people went to die.

From the train station it took Amalia a half hour to get to Saint Orsola Hospital, walking along the outside of the city wall. The clinic had not been there long. When the popes ruled Bologna, it was on the grounds of the women's prison. Police regularly rounded up prostitutes suspected of having the disease and took them there, forcing them to remain until they were pronounced cured some months later.

By the time Bologna officially became part of Italy, the city had come under the laws of the Savoyard kingdom and its ruler, King Victor Emmanuel II. Among them was the law regulating prostitution, which called for the establishment of a *sifilicomio,* a clinic for the treatment of syphilis, in each city. Any prostitutes showing signs of the disease were to be arrested and taken there. Even in its new incarnation under the Italian state, conditions were grim, and the prostitutes occasionally rebelled, as they had in 1876, when they destroyed a good part of Bologna's clinic to protest the fetid food.

Government officials required each prostitute to register with the local authorities and keep a booklet with her at all times containing the stamps of the required biweekly medical visits. So important were these that Professor Pietro Gamberini, the director of Bologna's syphilis clinic, devoted an entire chapter of his 1869 *Manual of the Diseases of Women's Sexual Organs* to the best techniques for examining the sexual organs of prostitutes. He paid special attention to the stratagems that the women used to conceal the evidence of their infection. In 1886 Gamberini reported that over the previous twenty-three years, almost six thousand of the admissions to Bologna's *sifilicomio* were prostitutes, the great majority of all women admitted, although this huge number included some who had come in more than once. He calculated that thirty-five hundred different prostitutes had been treated there in all.[1]

A French doctor who ran a similar clinic offered a harrowing view of the women who crowded its halls. Horrified by the first symptoms of syphilis spreading through their bodies and unable to sleep, these young women, said Dr. Buret, spent months trying to drown their fears by guzzling torrents of alcohol and calmed their nerves by smoking an enormous number of cigarettes. By the time they were brought to him, he wrote, they were "foul patrons, whom nothing could defile, either physically or morally — walking masses of rottenness." They would no sooner pass through the doors of his examination room, he reported, than his nostrils were assaulted. "A peculiar odor makes you retch," he wrote, and "the diagnosis is already made. It would be difficult to describe the sight which presents itself to the physician. The genitalia, hidden by the syphilides, sometimes no longer present a human form." Yet, he reported, a rigorous program of mercury treatments could heal the women within three or four months, sometimes sooner.[2]

Amalia had no experience with prostitutes and did not know just who the women in the clinic were, but they looked like no one she had ever seen in Oreglia. Even beyond the women's strange clothes and exotic hairstyles, there was something odd about them. Their skin was a strange color, tinged a ghastly gray.

Barbieri had himself read about just such discolored unfortunates. He had followed the debates on prostitution over the past years, as he and his fellow crusaders argued over the best way to regulate the oldest profession. In his book written two years earlier, in fact, he had cited a report on prostitution in Bologna written by the director of the syphilis clinic that Amalia had entered, Dr. Gamberini himself.

The strange gray tint of the women's skin, despite the fact that few of them were older than thirty, came from the mercury that the doctors gave them, injecting it with a syringe, or applying it on their skin as an ointment, or making them drink it as a potion. Amalia was shocked by the young women's toothless gums, another side effect of their treatment. And this, Barbieri knew, was often the least of their problems.

Amalia presented the sheet that Dalmonte had given her to a nurse in the clinic. She led Amalia into a room with a long, tall table and told her to lie down. A doctor entered and asked her to lift up her dress and her underclothes. He then told her to spread her legs out on the supports that flared out from the table, the ends shaped like slippers into which he placed her feet. Humiliated, Amalia did as she was told. He poked something cold into her. He then pulled at her this way and that, before telling her to get down off the table and to sit in a chair. He had her lift up her blouse and carefully examined each of her breasts, pressing down hard on the chancre on her left nipple.

Because Amalia was not a prostitute, she was free to go, but the doctor told her that she had syphilis and should be treated. She protested that she had no money, but he explained that there were many women like her who had been infected by nursing foundlings, and that she shouldn't worry because the foundling home almost always paid for their treatment.

Amalia went home, dreading having to tell Luigi, her husband, what had happened. Even worse was the prospect of telling his parents. And it would not be long, she realized, before everyone in Oreglia would know what had happened to her.

For a while, though, she felt fine. The chancre on her breast began to go away and she hoped that the doctor was wrong, that maybe it wasn't really syphilis, or that if it were, the disease had just gone away. But then one morning she woke up in the middle of the night scratching her chest, and by the time she got up and lit a lantern she could see that she had a rash on her body and her face.

Amalia was again frightened, and more frightened still at the thought of having to return to the syphilis clinic in the city. She decided to see Dr. Dalmonte, hoping he could help her.

This visit proved to be a turning point in Amalia's life, for it launched her on a path that led to Barbieri's office. For ten years Dalmonte had been waging his hapless battle against the Bologna foundling home but was dismissed by the city doctors and state officials as an ignorant country quack. When Amalia went to see him in mid-July, complaining of the rash, he decided that something more had to be done. Vergato's latest victim would be his weapon. Dalmonte urged her to get a lawyer and sue.

She hardly knew what to make of this idea, for the world of lawyers and courts and suits was the world of the rich, not the world she knew. But the doctor insisted. If she would listen to him, he said, she had a good chance of getting more money than she had ever dreamt of having.

Amalia protested that she could never pay for a lawyer, even if she had known how to find one. Dalmonte explained that if they could find a sympathetic attorney, the lawyer could help her get the judges to provide her with free legal help. If she won, the foundling home would pay him. If they lost, she wouldn't owe the lawyer anything, and she would be no worse off. When she seemed to shrink from the thought, Dalmonte told her to think of her family. Syphilis was a serious disease; its effects could be disastrous. And it was all the foundling home's fault, he said. They were the ones who should pay.

The doctor told her he would give her something she could use to get the court to help her. He drafted a new statement, again offering his diagnosis that Paola had syphilis, but this time he added a specific accusation: according to his humble opinion, he wrote, the foundling home doctors should have seen the signs of congenital syphilis in the baby before they gave her to Amalia. It was, in short, their negligence that had led to Amalia's sorry plight.

He told Amalia that he would hold on to the page for the moment while he tried to learn what lawyer in Bologna might be willing to take her case.

As Amalia finished her story, Barbieri again wondered how the Vergato doctor had come up with his name. He could only guess that a friend of Dalmonte's had read his book and been impressed by either his call for protecting women from exploitation or his argument that courts should hold employers responsible for the harm they did to their workers.

Amalia had by this time spent a good part of the day in the lawyer's office, telling her story. Now she needed to get on the train to return home, for she had nowhere to stay in the city. Barbieri had much to think over before deciding whether he would take her case. He told Amalia that he would let her know his decision in a few days.

CHAPTER 4

Suing the Count

ALTHOUGH IT MIGHT NOT have been clear to Amalia at that first meeting, Barbieri was immediately attracted by the idea of championing her cause, appreciating its David vs. Goliath possibilities. To sue the foundling home meant suing the board of the hospitals of Bologna, which oversaw it. And to sue the hospital board meant, legally speaking, to sue its president, Count Francesco Isolani, one of Bologna's leading noblemen. The contrast between the two could hardly have been greater. On one side was an illiterate peasant woman from the mountains and, as the case began to take shape in his mind, her valiant champion, a young, recent migrant to the city himself. On the other side stood Isolani, the scion of one of Bologna's greatest aristocratic families, whose ancestors had held sway in the city for centuries.

Bologna's noblemen had suffered a blow when Napoleon and his troops entered the city in 1796, ushering in a period of French occupation that lasted almost two decades. The French found in Bologna a society ruled by a small number of nobles and the church, a retrograde society of medieval stamp. One observer — albeit with some exaggeration — described the city and its hinterland as composed of "60 or 70 tyrants and 260,000 slaves."[1] While French reforms produced an increase in the amount of land held by a new class of bourgeoisie, the aristocracy never lost its control. With the restoration of the Papal States in 1814, much remained unchanged.

The aristocrats faced what turned out to be a more enduring challenge to their power with the fall of papal rule in Bologna in 1859 and the founding of the Kingdom of Italy two years later. But far from being consigned to history's dustbin, the Isolani family, along with many of their peers, made the transition to the new regime with remarkable aplomb.

Francesco Isolani had the distinction of being the last graduate of the University of Bologna while both city and university were under papal rule, receiving his degree in June 1859, just a few days before the papal troops and the cardinal legate were driven from the city. He did his best to keep the family's grip on political power under the new conditions, becoming mayor of one of the rural towns where his vast landholdings lay and winning office in the city, province, and national governments as well.

The count further cemented his position by marrying Letizia Tattini, herself the daughter of a count and whose mother, the marquise Carolina Pepoli, was part of Bologna's most prominent noble family. As lively and loquacious as her husband was reserved and taciturn, she delighted in her role as grand dame of Bolognese society, and the salon in the Isolani palazzo became an obligatory stop for anyone with a claim to nobility or to artistic or literary standing. She also fashioned herself as a patroness of the poor, devoting many hours to Bologna's chapter of the Red Cross, whose board her husband headed.

Francesco Isolani was also president of the board of Bologna's large hemp manufacturing company and president of one of the city's major banks; his younger brother served as president of another. Seventeen years before Barbieri encountered him, Isolani had been elected to the Bologna city council, and for the previous fifteen years he had been deputy mayor in charge of the city police. Elected to represent Bologna in parliament for the first time in 1876, he had completed his third and final term on practically the same day that Amalia met Barbieri.

Yet Isolani had but a modest reputation in Rome, to put it charitably. Serving for years in parliament without once taking the podium to speak — and in fact rarely bothering even to go to Rome for the sessions, which interested him little — he was described in the massive 1896 volume about all the members of that body as "a man of mediocre intelligence."[2]

Although the count's presidency of the Bologna hospital board was only one of his many charitable activities, in some ways it was the one that most defined him and captured his deep sense of noblesse oblige. By 1890 he had been president for fourteen years. Each day he was in town — when not at one of the family's rural estates — he walked the few minutes it took to get from the Isolani palace in the center of the city to the central office of the hospitals, skirting, as best he could, the teeming produce market between them.

He could not pass through these markets without some feeling of dread, for times were not good. Just a few years earlier, the agricultural system that was the source of Bologna's prosperity had reached a crisis. Recent innovations in transportation — efficient freight trains and steamboats — were leading to ruinous foreign competition, especially from the United States. Agricultural wage laborers were finding that instead of 200 days of work a year, they were lucky to get 120. Men like the count were increasingly being told that their traditional ways of doing business — and their reliance on agriculture and land as the primary sources of their wealth — were outmoded, that if they did not take up more modern economic activities they would be ruined.

To make matters worse, the crisis was only feeding the city's reputation as a hotbed of insurrectionary activity. Bologna's anarchists — linked to the First International — had repeatedly plotted revolts against the Italian monarchy in the 1870s. An uprising in 1874 brought the aging and infirm Russian anarchist leader Mikhail Bakunin to the city. Like a similar anarchist attempt in Bologna the previous year, it ended in miserable failure, and Bakunin barely escaped. By 1880, a number of the anarchists' leading lights acknowledged the folly of their belief in the peasants' insurrectionary potential and turned to the socialist movement, which began growing rapidly. Italy's first socialist member of parliament, Andrea Costa, who took office in 1882, was from the Bologna area and indeed had been one of the leaders of an abortive anarchist uprising in 1873. Over the course of the 1880s, the Bologna countryside proved a fertile recruiting ground for the socialists. Peasants banded into militant leagues, and the rural strikes they organized inspired fear among the landowners.

Isolani's hospital board was itself fairly new, a product of the reorganization of health and welfare activities that had come with the end of the Papal States. With its vast network of rural families caring for Bologna's foundlings, the foundling home was the largest institution under Isolani's aegis, larger than any of the city's hospitals. It was also the one that caused him the most aggravation. Not only did the home have to find a wet nurse for each of the hundreds of babies abandoned there each year, but each month it also had to send payments to the thousands of rural families who cared for the institute's charges while making sure that the children were all being properly cared for. The greatest concern to the foundling home in this surveillance was preventing fraud, as it was far from rare for foster families to try to keep collecting their monthly payments long after the foundling in their care had died.

But of all the headaches that the foundling home caused the count, the worst came from the seemingly endless number of young rural women who, having contracted syphilis from the foundlings they were given, blamed the hospital for their misery. These complaints were leading to increasingly irksome inquiries from the central government about why the hospital board could not resolve the problem. It was small comfort to Isolani that the situation was even worse in some other Italian cities: in Milan, he knew, dozens of wet nurses were infected by the foundling home's babies each year, but for some reason, there no one seemed to care.

That syphilis could be transmitted through wet-nursing had been known practically from the time that the disease first appeared in Europe, and it was mentioned in a Latin medical text of 1498.[3] The constant contact of the babies' mouths with their nurses' nipples put the women at extreme risk. As the nineteenth-century French syphilologist Alfred Fournier put it, "Nothing is so dangerous to its surroundings as a syphilitic infant."[4] With syphilis so widespread — it is estimated that 10 percent of all the men in Europe's cities had the disease — foundling home directors were desperate. In Lyon, France, where in the 1880s foundlings were infecting about fifteen wet nurses each year, they had set up a special section of the hospital just to deal with all of the women who became ill.[5] At a Russian medical congress in January 1891, a government doctor reported that in the last three years for which they had statistics, they had treated 136 wet nurses in Moscow who had contracted syphilis.[6]

Making the problem worse, these women often caused wider contagion in their isolated hometowns. Medical journals were filled with dramatic examples. One, albeit extreme, instance concerned a syphilitic baby in southwestern France who infected his wet nurse. When she became sick and her milk dried up, some of her neighbors tried to nurse the baby for her. They too soon found sores on their breasts, and before long their own small children erupted in syphilitic sores of their own. Meanwhile, to help the ailing women, their relatives and friends lent their own breasts to the infants, and soon they and their children had the disease. In all, it was reported, over forty women and children had gotten syphilis from a single syphilitic infant. At a public health conference in 1875, a doctor from St. Petersburg, Russia, reported that in one peasant community in his district, eight women who had served as wet nurses in the city's foundling home returned to their own homes with syphilis and ended up infecting sixty people.[7]

Italy had the dubious distinction of being the site of the earliest known cases of syphilis in Europe. In September 1494, the young French king Charles VIII led his army south through the Italian peninsula, seeking to conquer the Kingdom of Naples. Accompanying his 26,000 troops were 500 prostitutes. After a short siege of Naples, Charles triumphantly entered the city and proclaimed himself ruler of the kingdom. But he soon learned of a threat to his supply lines from troops loyal to the pope and so ordered a hasty retreat. It was then that he first heard of a terrible new disease that was spreading rapidly among his soldiers, a strange kind of pox that was devastating his army. Although the noble family that then ruled Bologna had allowed the French king to march through its territory on the way to Naples, once reports of the horrible contagion reached them, they refused to let the king return. But such measures failed to restrain the new disease, and by 1496 people were dying in the most horrible ways imaginable from Palermo to Milan. The French king himself was not spared, suffering an agonizing death at the age of twenty-eight.[8]

For four centuries thereafter syphilis was the scourge of Europe. Its victims experienced not only terrible physical punishment but, given its association with illicit sex, social stigma as well. Clergymen and moralists pronounced their suffering to be richly merited divine punishment.

In retrospect, the nineteenth century was something of a high-water mark for syphilis in Europe, although not because the disease was necessarily more prevalent and certainly not because it was more virulent, for people's ability to survive increased over time. When syphilis first appeared, its sufferers often died within a few months. But as with many microbes, in time mutations arose that allowed those infected to survive longer, so ensuring the continued life of the pathogen itself. What seemed so notable about the nineteenth century was how common the disease had become among Europe's artistic elite. The men who were rumored to have suffered from the disease — Ludwig van Beethoven, Franz Schubert, Robert Schumann, Charles Baudelaire, Gustave Flaubert, Guy de Maupassant, Vincent van Gogh, and Oscar Wilde, to name only a few — were the artistic luminaries of the age. Just a year before Amalia's first syphilitic sore erupted, the forty-four-year-old philosopher Friedrich Nietzsche visited Italy and on a street in Turin suffered his first fit of public madness, one of the common products of the disease.

It was also in the nineteenth century that doctors argued heatedly over the nature of syphilis and how modern science should treat it. Among the most prominent of these was Philippe Ricord, who was born in Baltimore in 1800 but moved to Paris as a young man and ended up with a practice that catered to syphilitics of the French elite. Derided by an eminent Boston physician who had trained in Paris as "the Voltaire of pelvic medicine," Ricord was in such demand by his upper-class clientele that he had five different waiting rooms in his house. He made his reputation by demonstrating that syphilis and gonorrhea were two distinct diseases — a point that had been argued for centuries. He did this, in the scientific spirit of the day, by injecting 2,500 people — including many Paris prostitutes — with gonorrheal pus, showing that they subsequently developed gonorrhea, not syphilis.

In 1879 the German doctor Albert Neisser identified the bacterium gonococcus as the cause of gonorrhea. But Neisser's reputation suffered after an experiment he devised in 1895. Believing that an injection of syphilis serum could confer immunity to the disease, he inoculated young German prostitutes — the youngest only ten years old. When the girls came down with the disease, the public was outraged.[9]

In late-nineteenth-century Italy, syphilis was viewed as a public health crisis of the first order, one that modern medical science needed to address as vigorously as possible. Prompted by widespread reports of the spread of syphilis through wet-nursing, in 1887 the government health ministry issued regulations aimed directly at the problem. When Count Isolani received a copy from the prefect, he called for a review of the Bologna foundling home's procedures.

Most of the babies left at the foundling home, the doctors responded, were brought in a day or two after birth by the midwives who had delivered them. The midwives could not leave the infants without filling out a form indicating whether the baby's mother had shown any sign of syphilis.

Unfortunately, the doctors reported, this had not solved the problem. During the previous year, of the babies arriving with certificates stating that their mothers showed no sign of syphilis, seventeen had developed the disease, and seven of these had infected the women nursing them. Of the twenty-nine babies left with certificates indicating a suspicion of maternal syphilis, four had developed the disease. In short, more syphilitic babies came from mothers who were certified as not having the disease than from those certified as having it.

In addition to the babies that the midwives carried in, others — about a quarter of the foundling home's total — were brought in directly from the maternity hospital. That Bologna's maternity hospital was just across the street from the foundling home was no coincidence. As one of the men responsible for Milan's foundling home put it, the institutions were "two branches of a single trunk of the tree of goodness."[10] A respectable married woman would never go to a hospital to give birth. Only those who wanted to conceal their pregnancy and their child had any reason to go there. Begun only a few years before the Papal States fell, Bologna's maternity hospital, paired with the foundling home under a common administration, came under Isolani's authority. The maternity hospital's regulations specified that only unwed women would be admitted there, and only after they entered the eighth month of their pregnancy.

The count had not waited for the 1887 government directive to look into the problem. Nine years earlier, shortly after he had become president of the hospital board, he had asked the foundling home's medical director to determine how widespread the problem of syphilis was. The answer was sobering: in the previous ten years, 276 foundlings had been struck by syphilis. And the more recent reports revealed an even more worrisome pattern: during the 1880s, 34 former wet nurses had approached the hospital claiming that they had been infected with the disease.

While pondering the 1887 directive and the doctors' reply, the count found himself facing a growing number of complaints, some brought by rural mayors and, in a worrisome development, one or two by lawyers threatening to sue on behalf of their syphilitic clients. Yet Isolani did not seem to be unduly worried, paying off one woman with the pathetic sum of 15 lire and, in other cases, simply informing the complainants that, whatever had happened to them, neither the foundling home nor the hospital board was responsible for their plight.

In the aftermath of Amalia's visit to his office, Barbieri mulled over what he should do. A man of strong convictions, he liked to see himself as a champion of more scientific government, a protector of the poor. But he was also deeply ambitious.

He was part of that class in the new Italian state that was trying to assert its right to preeminence; his family was typical of those who saw in Italian unification its chance of coming into its own. It was just these people who were among the most enthusiastic champions of overthrowing the old regimes, which had divided the Italian peninsula into a patchwork of duchies, kingdoms, and foreign dependencies. The lands ruled by the popes, the Papal States — stretching from Rome to Bologna — had epitomized the old ways, forming a large crescent across the center of the Italian boot.

The children of Italy's middle class felt that they had to prove themselves equal in moral worth and social status to the old elites, but for Barbieri this drive went much deeper. When he was fourteen years old, his father was tried and found guilty of illegal financial dealings. Eight years later, when he was about to launch his own legal career, his father was convicted of fraud by the Bologna Court of Appeals. So embarrassed was Augusto that, years later, when his father died, he refused to accept his inheritance.

Barbieri allied himself with a group of other ambitious young men in Bologna associated with the moderate left; their meeting place was the local office of the newspaper *La Patria*, for which Barbieri wrote occasional articles. In fact, in these first years of his career, he spent more time on his journalism and his fervid debates with other young progressives than on his law practice. In addition to writing for *La Patria,* he contributed articles to newspapers in both Rome and Milan.

It was a time of fierce polemics, aimed at least as much at other groups on the left as targets on the right. Barbieri and his compatriots felt especially threatened by the socialist movement, which was then spreading rapidly, stirring hopes of a new utopia among the peasantry as well as among the burgeoning urban working class. Although Barbieri and his friends saw themselves as champions of society's unfortunates, they were convinced that it was the educated men of their class who should properly rule. As a result, they viewed the socialists as a threat, not only to their economic and political position, but to their moral standing as well. They spent much of their free time in the tiny newspaper office, notwithstanding its unfortunate location — its entryway wedged between a public urinal and a horse meat butcher shop. Enveloped in a thick cloud of cigarette smoke, they furiously argued over the latest political news, shouting to make themselves heard, arms gesticulating madly.

These were heady times of historic change, when it was exciting to be a young man who could hope to displace the old elite and take a privileged position in a dramatically changed order. At twenty-eight, Barbieri was already a published author; he had a pregnant wife who would soon produce a sibling for their two-year-old son; and he was part of a circle of politically ambitious reformers. It was time to take the plunge. Championing Amalia's cause could, if handled right, he convinced himself, make his reputation as one of Bologna's up-and-coming lawyers.

He would first need to have a formal contract drawn up. Because Amalia seemed reluctant to make another trip to Bologna and because he would need to involve her husband as well, he located Vergato's notary and sent him instructions. On August 16 the notary, Antonio Polami, sent a messenger with a note for Amalia. She and her husband, Luigi, were to come and see him the next morning. Amalia, who had been waiting to hear from Barbieri, was anxious to receive his response.

In his office, Polami showed Amalia and Luigi the document that he had carefully prepared according to Barbieri's specifications. Amalia Bagnacavalli, it read, with the permission of her husband — women in Italy were not allowed to take legal action without obtaining their husbands' consent — and Luigi Migliorini in his own right authorized Barbieri to represent them in all matters pertaining to actions taken before the judicial authorities regarding their case against the foundling hospital of Bologna. They were not to take any action without his approval.

The notary read the document to the couple and asked them if they could sign their own names to it. Luigi said he could but that Amalia could not. At the bottom of the document Luigi laboriously signed his name. Amalia's suit against the foundling home, the hospital board of Bologna, and its president, Count Francesco Isolani, was about to begin.

CHAPTER 5

The Mercury Treatment

W HEN THE COUNT sat down at his desk in his hospital board office that Wednesday, September 10, 1890, he found a letter bearing the wax seal of the Civil and Criminal Tribunal of Bologna. It had been delivered earlier in the day to the doorman of the palazzo, who had carried it up the marble staircase to Isolani's office. Such correspondence never augured well.

The count sliced open the envelope and extracted the page. From the court's commission on legal aid, it informed him that one Amalia Bagnacavalli, of Vergato, had applied to the commission to be granted legal assistance by the court to bring suit against the hospital board of Bologna. It did not describe her claim except to say that it concerned damages as defined by articles 1151 and 1152 of the civil code. Isolani was told that he had the right to attend the session of the commission where the application would be considered, at 1 P.M. on the seventeenth of the month. At that time, he could voice any objections he might have, challenging either the woman's claimed lack of financial means or the merits of her case.

It was not a good start for the count's day. That it was an impoverished woman from the mountains who was bringing the action left him in little doubt about the nature of the case. His certainty grew when he recalled that those two articles of the civil code spelled out employers' responsibilities for employees who were harmed as a result of their work. Although the law was not always enforced, it held employers responsible for injuries to their workers that stemmed from the employers' negligence.

Although Amalia's case would take a path very different from all the others he had faced, the count followed his customary routine with such matters. He called in the hospital board's lawyer, Odoardo Ferrari, gave him the document, and told him to attend the hearing and report back.

On the following Wednesday afternoon, Ferrari was ushered into the room in the courthouse where the members of the commission sat around a table for their weekly meeting. He knew nothing of any Amalia Bagnacavalli, he told them, much less of any reason to believe that she had been harmed by the foundling home. However, he could attest to the fact that the foundling home took great care in placing its babies with rural wet nurses, and that even in the unlikely event that this woman had suffered any harm from the baby she had been given, it was certainly not the foundling home's fault. Surely it was contrary to the public interest, he argued, to encourage a woman such as this to bring legal action against the hospitals of Bologna. It would simply waste the precious resources of that charitable organization. The president of the commission thanked Ferrari for taking the time to share his thoughts with them, and the lawyer departed.

The unwelcome news was not long in coming, for at the commission's next meeting, the matter was put to a vote. The commissioners decided that the woman from Vergato should be granted legal aid, allowing her to bring suit without paying the usual court costs. The court itself would not pay for her lawyer, but the commissioners knew that the ambitious young Augusto Barbieri had taken on the case, and they presumed that he thought he could win, or at least use the threat of the suit to extract payment from the hospital.

Barbieri wasted no time in plunging ahead, and when Isolani arrived at his office on Friday, October 10, he had another official envelope on his desk, this one also adorned with the crest of Bologna's Civil Tribunal.

Amalia Bagnacavalli, with the authorization of her husband, Luigi Migliorini, the summons began, hereby notified the foundling home and the hospital board, in the person of Count Francesco Isolani, that the count or his representative was to appear before the tribunal within ten days.

It then spelled out the charges: On March 24, Amalia had gone to the foundling home and been given a syphilitic infant. After two weeks of nursing, she herself contracted the disease. Under article 1151 of the civil code, the complaint concluded, the foundling home bore responsibility for the damage done to her, and Count Isolani, as president of the hospital board and therefore responsible for the foundling home, should compensate her for the harm she had suffered.

Again, an annoyed Isolani summoned the board's lawyer. Ferrari explained that he would have to talk with the woman's lawyer to see if they could agree on how to proceed.

On October 25, Ferrari reported that he had met with Barbieri, who was clearly taking the case very seriously. Barbieri wanted to show that the foundling home made a regular practice of giving syphilitic babies to healthy wet nurses and that, as a result, healthy peasant women were being infected with deplorable frequency.

The implications of the case for the hospital board, Ferrari warned the count, were dire. Should Barbieri prove successful, every time that a wet nurse got syphilis the hospital would be expected to pay for the damage she suffered. The costs could be ruinous.

While all this was going on in Bologna, Amalia remained home in Oreglia. Since she had first gone to see Barbieri, things had only gotten worse. Within days of their initial meeting, her seventeen-month-old daughter, Adele, had begun acting listless, and the normally happy baby would not stop crying. A few days later, Amalia noticed a sore on Adele's lower lip. Three weeks after that, while Amalia was changing the baby's soiled clothes, she smelled an odd odor and saw that Adele had horrible sores around her genitals. The next day the sores, now further inflamed and oozing a thick, fetid pus, began to bleed. On October 17, just as Barbieri was having his first meeting with Isolani's lawyer, little Adele took her last breath. She was the first member of Amalia's family to die of syphilis.

When Barbieri added Adele's death to the list of complaints against the hospital, the foundling home authorities reacted angrily. If Amalia had given Adele syphilis, they would argue in their brief to the court, it was her own fault. The foundling home gave babies only to women whose own newborns had either died or already been weaned. To be given a baby, the woman had to promise that she would never nurse her own child again. When Amalia had taken Paola that March, she too had made this pledge. Yet if Adele got syphilis from her mother, she must have gotten it by nursing at her breast. The fact that the baby's first sore had appeared on her lip made this clear.

If, from the hospital authorities' perspective, Amalia had shown reckless disregard for her family's health and was herself responsible for much of her misfortune, it was nowhere clearer than in the sad story of what happened to her husband, Luigi. When Dr. Dalmonte first told Amalia that she had syphilis, he warned her not to have sex with her husband until she was cured. Because he diagnosed her illness before the secondary, highly infectious, stage of the disease had begun, had she heeded his advice, it is likely that Luigi would have escaped infection. But Amalia did not, or perhaps could not, follow this advice. In early September, shortly after Adele's first sore appeared, Luigi was horrified to find a huge sore on the tip of his penis. Soon the infection spread through his groin and burrowed into the nerves. Luigi found each step he took painful.

Amalia had already begun her treatments at the syphilis clinic in Bologna, and now Luigi joined her. They were both given mercury ointment to apply to their sores and an iodine mercury solution to drink. One of the side effects of the mercury was intense salivation, so much so that there was a time, as one expert recalled in 1904, that "the beneficial effect of this drug was estimated by the pints of saliva which dribbled from the patient's mouth." By the late nineteenth century, most syphilologists thought it important to minimize the dosage, although this did not wholly eliminate many of mercury's side effects: stomach ills, nausea, liver and kidney failure, and loosened teeth.[1]

As far as Luigi could see, the treatments only made things worse. He felt sick from the mercury, and bleeding sores soon formed on his lips and in his throat. Within another month, painful sores spread all around his backside. He was feverish and had horrible headaches at night. His whole body ached.

The effects of the medical treatments of the day — mainly involving the noxious mercury in its various forms — were so unpleasant that it is no surprise that a variety of competing folk remedies arose. Some reflected the belief that to do battle with such a horrid disease required similarly horrible cures. Such was the apparent basis of the belief that one could get better by ingesting a particular kind of live Guatemalan lizard each day for a month. But there was also some popular support for the contrary theory, that the only way to fight such a hideous disease was by finding a comparably attractive remedy. One such claim was that a man could be cured of syphilis by having sex with a virgin.[2]

By the time the trial opened in November, Amalia's life had become a tale of woe. Her only child had died. Both she and her husband were now covered with sores and could walk only with difficulty. Amalia suffered from regular bouts of fever, her bones and joints ached, she had trouble sleeping, and she had a sore throat and constant stomach pains. Even worse than the sores on their bodies was the shameful mark that pronounced their condi-

tion to the world: their skins were now the awful gray color produced by mercury. Unable to work in the fields, they had to rely on
their families' aid. Since it was shortly after harvest season, supplies
still allowed the Migliorini and Bagnacavalli families the luxury of
helping them. But as they looked ahead to the winter, the couple
wondered how they were going to survive.

CHAPTER 6

The Trial Begins

TESTIMONY IN THE CASE of Amalia Bagnacavalli v. Count Francesco Isolani began in the imposing courtroom of the Tribunal of Bologna promptly at 10 A.M. on Thursday, November 20, with a parade of witnesses from Vergato. The court, agreeing with Barbieri that the view of an outside medical expert would be helpful, named Professor Giuseppe Ravaglia, of the University of Bologna's medical faculty, as its special consultant. As the first witnesses were called to the stand in Bologna, Dr. Ravaglia was busy collecting the material he needed for his report, which he would submit a few months later.

Barbieri prepared his case with great care. He had arranged for Vergato's mayor, Ulisse Bettini, and the town secretary, Ettore Soldati, to make the train trip to the city to be present for the opening of the trial, along with Carlo Dalmonte, the town doctor, and several of Amalia's friends and neighbors.

Bologna's massive brick and sandstone courthouse stood not far from the foundling home. Built in the sixteenth century based on a design by Andrea Palladio, one of the foremost architects of the Italian Renaissance, it had a large central courtyard and huge stairway. Its name, the Baciocchi Palace, derived from its last private owner, Felice Baciocchi, who rose from humble origins to the aristocracy by marrying Napoleon's sister Elisa.

Barbieri was familiar with the building and the courtroom. In order to become a lawyer, he not only had to complete his law degree and pass both an oral and a written exam, but was required to clerk for two years in a local law office and spend a year of that time sitting in on trials in the Baciocchi Palace.

Amalia and Luigi, by contrast, would never feel comfortable in any courtroom. The massive building, with its grandiose stairway composed of two elliptical ramps lined with allegorical stucco statues, represented a world distant from their own. As they sat now in the neoclassical dark wood–paneled courtroom, they felt acutely out of place. At the front of the room was the imposing wooden judges' bench with three seats, each with a lectern. For the testimony phase of the trial, only the middle seat would be occupied, the judge wearing a black robe with a white ruffled triangular jabot — a kind of judicial bib — and a round black beret with a white ribbon around its base. Italian judges did not wear wigs. Rising from the front corners of the judges' bench were tall, domed brass lamps, which had recently been converted from gas to electricity. Directly in front of the judge was a table where each witness would sit while testifying. To the judge's right was a cloth-draped podium where the lawyer stood when examining witnesses, his notes in front of him. To his left sat the court stenographer. Separating all this from the rest of the courtroom was a brass rail, behind which was the counsel table, with seats for Barbieri, Amalia, and Luigi, as well as for Ferrari and his colleagues. The lawyers all wore black robes. Behind them were several other rows of seats where the witnesses awaited their turn.

Barbieri took his position behind the podium, opened his notebook, and called his first witness.

The mayor took the stand, giving his name, Ulisse Bettini, his age, forty-seven, and his occupation, engineer. At the time Amalia got the baby from the foundling home, said the mayor, he could not say from his own firsthand knowledge if she was healthy, but on July 1, when he received Dalmonte's report that Amalia had contracted syphilis, he had made it his business to launch his own investigation. After talking to various people who were in a position to know, Bettini said he was convinced that Amalia had previously been in excellent health, a perfect example of the strong country women Vergato was known for.

Barbieri thanked him and turned next to his star witness, Carlo Dalmonte, who sat not alongside the mayor but at a distance, by himself. Dalmonte was avoiding Bettini because the two had long been feuding and neither would speak to the other, a situation that had made the administration of the town's medical business more than a little awkward.

The country doctor had been eagerly looking forward to this day. For years he had done everything he could to call attention to the scandal of the foundling home, but he had always been treated as if he were an ignoramus, a country bumpkin. Now he had a platform that the hospital authorities and the Bologna elite could not ignore.

Straining to show that he was the equal of his big-city colleagues, Dalmonte adopted a formal, almost antiquated, speaking style. It was the case, he said, that the previous spring the Bologna foundling home had given Amalia Bagnacavalli a baby girl who bore the family name of Olivelli and the first name of Paolina, little Paola. He knew this because just a few days after Amalia received the girl, she came to his house with the little creature and showed him the booklet that the foundling home had given her. When he first laid eyes on the baby, he estimated from her size and development that she was about a month old. He immediately saw that the baby was blind, that in the place of each of her pupils were scars, which he believed were the result of syphilitic infection. He also noted that the baby was emaciated and that she had an initial syphiloma on her lower lip. When he scolded Amalia, telling her that she shouldn't have taken such a baby, she blurted out that she hadn't wanted to but that the doctor there had refused to give her any other.

Dalmonte then hesitated a moment, his air of confident authority temporarily failing him. Now that he thought about it, he said, he could not recall exactly whether he had seen the baby once or twice. If he had seen her twice, he quickly added, it would have been on the second visit that he had detected the telltale chancre on the baby's lip.

This second visit, he said, would have been six or seven days after the first. As soon as he saw the baby's syphiloma, he not only told Amalia that the baby had syphilis but predicted that she herself would contract the disease. Indeed, he recollected — he was clearly enjoying his moment in the limelight — Amalia came back to his house three or four weeks later and had him look at her breasts, and on her left nipple he found a syphiloma identical to the one that the foundling had had on her lip.

The doctor had told the story to this point with little prompting, but now Barbieri interrupted to ask if he could tell the court what, from the perspective of a man of medicine, had happened to Amalia since those days in the spring.

Just a few weeks after the syphiloma first appeared on her breast, Dalmonte recalled, the first signs of the infectious phase of the disease appeared in the form of a rash on her nipple. This, he said, disappeared thanks to treatment with mercury. But then pustules erupted on her genitalia and in her throat. And in September or October — he could not, he said, at the moment remember which — Amalia had brought in her own daughter, who, as he recalled, was about three years old. He saw clear signs that the girl was suffering from the syphilis given to her by her mother, and, sadly, she died not long after that.

How, asked Barbieri, would he describe Amalia's health today?

Currently, responded Dalmonte, Amalia was under active medical treatment. But despite this therapy, she still showed the symptoms of the disease, with pustules on her lips that were typical of syphilis. And then there was her husband, Luigi, whose first signs of syphilis had appeared not long ago.

Just one last question, said Barbieri. At the time he saw the syphilitic sore on the foundling's lip, had he seen any sign that Amalia then had syphilis?

No, replied the doctor. She showed no sign of the disease then.

Dalmonte was excused. Barbieri felt good about the doctor's testimony, which was central to his case, although he could not deny that it contained some embarrassing weaknesses. The fact that Dalmonte couldn't remember if he had seen the foundling once or twice was certainly no help to their cause, and his recollection of the age of Amalia's daughter as three when she was a little over one gave the other side a further opening to challenge his memory and his judgment. But Dalmonte had been the doctor on the scene when the foundling, and later Amalia, had shown their first signs of syphilis. And unlike the doctors from the foundling home, who would surely also testify, he had no ax to grind — or, thought Barbieri, who had learned about Dalmonte's decade-long tirades against the foundling home, at least he could be presented to the court that way.

Barbieri next called to the stand, one after the other, four of Amalia's friends and neighbors, two men and two women. They all testified that they had known Amalia for many years, that she had always been the picture of health and the soul of virtue, and they recounted the story of her returning home that day in March with a sickly foundling and the tragedy that followed. None used the word "syphilis" to describe the baby's disease. Each testified instead that little Paola had "the plague," a term used by people throughout Italy in preference to the medical label, with its uncomfortable connotations.

Rosa Magelli, Barbieri's final witness that first day, was from the neighboring community of Grizzana, but she was not a friend of Amalia's. Barbieri had called her to the stand for another reason.

Six or seven years earlier, the thirty-three-year-old woman testified, she had gone to the Bologna foundling home and been given a baby named Tommaso. When, the baby got sick a few weeks later, she had taken him to the town doctor, who told her to take Tommaso back to the foundling home because he had "the plague."

She herself, she continued, came down with the disease a month later, and subsequently her small children had taken ill as well.

Barbieri thanked the woman, and as she left the courtroom, the judge announced a recess. When the court returned to session the following Thursday morning, Barbieri had only two witnesses left to call. The first was forty-year-old Maddalena Cappelli, from Vergato, who told the court that she was the sister-in-law of Rosa Magelli, the previous witness. She had something else in common with Rosa, for three years earlier she had taken a three-week-old boy from the Bologna foundling home. She returned him a month later when, she reported, he showed signs of having "the plague." Soon thereafter she too saw the telltale sore appear on her breast.

Barbieri's final witness was Ettore Soldati, the thirty-four-year-old town secretary of Vergato. Soldati testified that Amalia had gone to the town office for a certificate of good moral character in early March so that she could get a baby from the foundling home.

Eager to raise one of his key allegations, even though his witness was hardly in a position to provide any useful evidence, Barbieri asked if he knew whether the baby Amalia was given had first received a proper medical examination at the foundling home. Before the perplexed Soldati could reply, Barbieri asked whether he knew if such examinations had been given in the many other cases in which Vergato women had taken in babies from the foundling home and then contracted the terrible disease.

No, the secretary replied. But, catching the drift of the lawyer's question, he added that what he could say was that he had received a large number of complaints about foundlings being sent to Vergato with syphilis. These babies had not only infected their wet nurses but, with tragic frequency, the women's families as well.

At this, Odoardo Ferrari, the hospital board's counsel, rose for cross-examination. He had just one question, he said. If this problem was so well known in Vergato, why did so many women keep going to the foundling home to get babies to nurse?

Soldati put some distance between himself and the peasants of his town. It was his conviction, he said, that the women who nursed the foundlings saw it simply as a *mercimonio,* a kind of illicit trade. He couldn't count the times, he said, that he had tried to convince the town officials to refuse to certify the women for such service. Indeed, he had denounced the wet nurse business as a kind of white slave trade. If word of the spread of disease had failed to move many of the wet nurses, it simply showed that all they cared about was getting their payments.

It was now Ferrari's turn to call witnesses for the hospital board. He began with Ermanno Pinzani, the medical director of the foundling home. Following the home's strict procedures, he said, he had examined Paola Olivelli before giving her to Amalia on March 24 and had found her free of any sign of syphilis. Two and a half weeks later, when Amalia returned Paola, the baby had a tiny, hard, ulcerated papule around her backside and some tiny ulcerated sores in her mouth. They had immediately examined Amalia's nipples but found no sign of any disease at the time.

Next to testify was Carlo Massarenti, the seventy-five-year-old director of the maternity hospital. The previous December 27, he said, they had admitted a young unmarried woman who, like most of the women who came there, refused to give her name. She was examined and found to be healthy. Five days later she gave birth to Paola.

Ferrari concluded by calling on the other two foundling home doctors. Emanuele Bruers, called first, claimed that Paola's only health problem when she was given to Amalia was the result of the gonorrheal eye infection that had left her blind. Giovanni Berti then testified that when Amalia brought the baby back, it was he who had charge of her, for he ran the wing reserved for suspected syphilitic children. He could assure the court, he said, that when the baby died a month later, she showed no sign of ever having had the disease. She had died of a simple lung infection.

With this, the testimony phase of the trial closed, and the judge ordered the court recessed until Dr. Ravaglia was ready to submit his report.

CHAPTER 7

Disputing the Doctor

O N WEDNESDAY, DECEMBER 10, Count Isolani called the biweekly meeting of the Bologna hospital board to order in its customary meeting room, an ornate hall with high ceilings and a massive wooden table. He updated his colleagues on the Bagnacavalli trial and told them of his recent conversation with the chair of their legal affairs committee, who warned that a decision against them would be disastrous. Isolani and his colleagues were convinced that neither the board nor the doctors bore any responsibility for the peasant women who got syphilis from the foundlings. They were doing everything possible — or so they kept telling one another — to prevent such contagion. Babies were given to wet nurses only after a rigorous physical examination. If some of the women did contract syphilis, this was inevitable because some babies showed the first signs of the disease only when they were a few months old. And when a wet nurse was afflicted by syphilis, the count insisted, the hospital board had always acted generously in paying for her treatment.

The more Barbieri thought about the case, the more nervous he became. Although he had initially been pleased that the judges approved his request for an outside medical expert, he now realized that he may have made a mistake. It was not, as he should have known, the kind of case designed to inspire sympathy in Bologna's medical establishment. An illiterate peasant woman was complaining about a number of well-known doctors, arguing that they should be held financially responsible for the harm they did to the people they treated. To make matters worse, the case relied on a mountain doctor's charge that his colleagues in the city were incompetent.

The months of waiting came to an end when, on March 2, 1891, Dr. Ravaglia submitted his lengthy report to the court. Handwritten copies were soon made, and one was sent to Count Isolani's lawyers, another to Barbieri.

Ravaglia had taken his task seriously. Not only had he carefully studied all of the courtroom testimony, he had also examined all the records dealing with Paola Olivelli's birth and short stay at the Bologna maternity hospital, as well as those documenting her months at the foundling home and the certificates prepared by Dr. Dalmonte and the Bologna syphilis clinic. Nor had he stopped there. He had personally interviewed many of those involved in the case, including the two women who had nursed Paola in the foundling home before Amalia took her. He had even interviewed and physically examined both Amalia and Luigi.

Paola had been born, Ravaglia reported, at full term, a robust six and a half pounds, showing no signs of abnormality. The name of her mother, nineteen years old and unmarried, was nowhere recorded in the maternity hospital records.

At 2 P.M. on New Year's Day, 1890, a nurse carried Paola from the maternity hospital to the foundling home. She brought with her the required health certificate, which was designed to report any sign of syphilis in the mother or the baby. Such signs were far from rare in a maternity hospital where, in recent years, more than one in eight of the women giving birth had shown evidence of the infection. But the sheet that the nurse brought with her that day pronounced both Paola and her mother to be free of the disease.

Within a few days, the baby developed a fever and soon showed signs of pleurisy, an inflammation of the membranes that surround the lungs. Before it had run its course, the disease left Paola with a twisted spine. In her early days at the foundling home, Ravaglia noted, Paola suffered another setback when the corneas in both of her eyes began to swell, and she soon lost her sight.

On the day about three months later that Amalia had returned Paola, Dr. Bruers had examined the baby and found sores extending from her backside to her navel. He had also examined Amalia quickly and as a result had some suspicion that Amalia herself might have had syphilis and given it to the baby, for Amalia's voice was hoarse, and the glands on both sides of her neck were swollen.

As a precautionary matter, Bruers reported, he had sent Paola to Ward B, which was reserved for babies suspected of having syphilis. There Dr. Berti, in charge of the ward, began bathing the baby's rash in a glycerin-starch solution, and within a few days it disappeared.

Babies on Ward B were not permitted to be nursed by healthy wet nurses. Ideally, they were given to women who already had syphilis, for they could not be infected again. The foundling home was not alone in this practice. Alfred Fournier was always on the lookout in France for syphilitic women who had recovered their health and could nurse. For those wealthy couples who had a syphilitic baby, such women were, he gushed, "rare pearls."[1]

Given the difficulty of finding such women, the great majority of the babies sent to Bologna's syphilis ward had to make do with cow's milk. This is what Paola was given, with predictable results. She began to have diarrhea, which by the second week of May got worse. In her fragile condition she then got pneumonia. On May 13, barely a month after Amalia had brought her back to the foundling home, Paola died.

All this, Ravaglia reported, was clear, but important questions remained. Most crucially, did Paola in fact ever have syphilis?

The next passage of the report lifted Barbieri's spirits and his hopes. The medical examiner said that he could not agree with Dr.

Bruers in his suspicion that Amalia had been previously infected with the disease. First of all, his colleague Dr. Pinzani had examined Amalia when she first came to take a child to nurse and found her to be in excellent health. Second, the chancre that later appeared on Amalia's nipple bore all the signs of the kind of syphilitic sore that erupts at the site of the first infection: typically, the genitals of men and women who contracted it through intercourse and on the nipple of women who contracted it from nursing.

The medical school professor was now ready to respond to the questions posed by the court.

The first was the easiest. Was it possible for an infant afflicted with syphilis to transmit the disease to her wet nurse? Of this, medical science had no doubt. Typically, he informed the court, transmission occurred when the baby had a bleeding syphilitic sore on her lips and the wet nurse had some kind of crack in the skin around her nipple. Given the nature of nursing, such cuts and abrasions were common on a woman's breast, providing an ideal environment for the disease to spread from baby to wet nurse.

If the answer to the first question was straightforward, the answer to the second — whether it was the foundling who had given Amalia syphilis — was not. If Paola had an active case of syphilis when she was given to Amalia, there was no question, in his view, that Amalia could have contracted it from her. But did Paola actually ever have the disease?

Dr. Dalmonte had based his claim on three observations: (1) the baby's emaciated appearance and the scarred growths on her corneas, which he interpreted as signs of congenital syphilis; (2) the syphilitic nature of the rash on her body; and (3) what Dalmonte had called the "initial syphiloma" on her lower lip.

To this point in his reading, Barbieri was unsure where Ravaglia was headed. But his direction became clear as, to Barbieri's dismay, he proceeded to attack Dalmonte's diagnoses one after the other.

First of all, he said, having new growths on both corneas was not common among babies born with syphilis, who tended to develop them only later in childhood (for those who survived that long). It was much more likely, he argued, that they were the result of some other cause, such as gonorrhea, which Paola could have contracted while passing through her mother's birth canal.

The baby's scrawny appearance, Ravaglia argued, was generally a sign of syphilis only insofar as syphilitic babies were frequently underweight at birth, yet Paola was not. Her emaciation, he charged, was more likely the product of poor feeding, and here he blamed Amalia, citing her admission that in her desperation to get the baby to eat something, she had fed Paola chestnut pancakes and bread soup with oil.

Ravaglia then turned to the medical evidence from the maternity hospital, which, he argued, gave no support to a diagnosis of congenital syphilis. He placed special weight on the fact that upon birth, the placenta had been examined and found to be entirely normal. Typically, he said, when a baby was born syphilitic, telltale deformities appeared there. To this evidence from the maternity hospital he added the report from Dr. Berti's autopsy of Paola, which had found no sign of the disease.

What, he asked, should they make of the other observations on which Dalmonte's case for Paola's syphilis was based? Certainly the kind of bleeding rash that Dalmonte had described, and its location, might argue for syphilis. But, Ravaglia hastily added, Dr. Berti reported that the rash had gone away with the application of a glycerin-starch solution and had not reappeared anywhere else on the child's body. These were certainly not the signs of a syphilitic rash, which would not normally fade so quickly; even if it had, it would soon have reappeared elsewhere.

The final element of Dalmonte's case for the baby's syphilis, wrote Ravaglia, was his claim to have found an "initial syphiloma" on her lower lip. But how much weight could be placed on this observation? Dalmonte had not mentioned any such growth in his original report of the examination but only in the oral testimony he gave the court on December 11, 1890, eight months later. Perhaps, Ravaglia added, the doctor confused his examination of Paola with his later examination of Amalia's daughter, Adele, whom he would later report had just such a growth.

Not only was the observation of the sore on Paola's lower lip dubious, Ravaglia continued, but Dalmonte's description of it was a medical impossibility. Adele could and doubtless did have an initial syphiloma on her lip, for such a growth by its nature comes at the point of initial transmission of the disease, and Adele contracted it at her mother's breast. But an infant born with syphilis first presented the secondary symptoms of the disease, not the initial sore.

Where, then, asked Ravaglia, did this leave the argument that Paola Olivelli actually had congenital syphilis? Truth be told, he wrote, the main evidence in its favor was Amalia's developing an initial syphilitic sore shortly after nursing the baby, with the initial sore erupting on her breast, exactly where it would be expected to appear in the case of transmission from a syphilitic infant.

Yet, Ravaglia argued, another possibility still had to be considered. It was not unusual for peasant women who took in foundlings to help one another when they were sick, or had to go off for a day, or when their milk began to dry up. Who was to say, asked Ravaglia, that this had not happened in Amalia's case? Perhaps she had helped out a friend and nursed another baby, a baby who had syphilis and who infected her.

This brought the medical professor to his final bit of evidence. In the several weeks that Paola had spent in the foundling home before she was given to Amalia, only two women had nursed her. If Paola had been suffering from syphilis, surely these women would have been at high risk. Indeed, Ravaglia reported, one of the women had reported suffering from cracked, bleeding nipples at the very time that she had been nursing the baby. Surely, had Paola been syphilitic, she would have infected her. This in turn would have produced an epidemic of syphilis among the other babies at the foundling home, for between them, the two women had nursed sixty foundlings in their months in service there. Yet the records revealed that none had contracted the disease.

Weighing all the evidence, Ravaglia thought it likely that Paola never had syphilis and so could not have been the source of Amalia's infection. Amalia, he concluded, had most likely been infected by some other baby.

Ravaglia had now addressed all of the questions the judges had put to him, but he could not resist adding something else, eager as he was to come to his colleagues' defense. In her almost three months at the foundling home before she was placed with Amalia, the doctor observed, Paola never exhibited any sign of syphilis. Even if it turned out that she was born with the disease, he argued, the foundling home doctors could have had no way to detect it.

For Barbieri, Ravaglia's report to the Tribunal was a terrible blow. If he had not seen the case as the way to make a name for himself or if he had been less self-confident by nature, he might have easily given up. After all, what chance did he have? In the best of circumstances it wouldn't be easy to get the court to find the foundling home doctors — well-respected men of the city's professional elite — guilty of malfeasance. For the court to find Count Isolani and his aristocratic hospital board negligent was no easier. Now that the judges' own expert adviser, appointed at Barbieri's request, had found no medical grounds for Amalia's complaint, the situation seemed hopeless.

But Barbieri plunged ahead. To have any chance of winning, he knew he had to discredit Ravaglia's opinion, and this, he thought, could be done only by convincing the court to appoint a new medical consultant. Because the court customarily used a single outside expert for such cases, he had to persuade the judges that Ravaglia's report was unacceptable.

On April 20, Barbieri filed just such a motion, calling for the appointment of a new consultant. When, not surprisingly, Isolani's lawyer objected, the judges decided that the request be argued before them as part of their consideration of the larger case. As a result, a critical section of the brief that Barbieri prepared for the court focused on Ravaglia.

Barbieri worked for many weeks on the brief. If he succeeded in winning the case, he would be seen as a lawyer to be reckoned with, a young man of talent who — despite his middling rural origins and his father's unsavory reputation — deserved a place among the city's elite. To make sure that the brief would have the desired effect, he took his text to the publisher Azzoguidi, whose office was in the same building as his, and arranged to have it printed as a rather impressive-looking booklet. Although having briefs published in this way was not required by the court, it was a common tactic for ambitious lawyers. On July 3, Barbieri submitted his brief to the Tribunal.

The court limited the amount of time that the lawyer could present his arguments orally, for so much rode on the persuasiveness of the written brief. He began by telling the story of what had happened, or at least his version of it. He then lost no time in launching an attack on Ravaglia's report. The doctor, he charged, had failed to directly address the questions the court had asked him and instead chose to invade the territory that was rightly reserved to the judges. Medical experts were expected to provide technical details that could help judges decide cases. They were not to substitute their own judgment for the judges'. It was up to the judges alone to determine whether Amalia had contracted syphilis from the foundling. In offering his opinion that no clear basis existed for deciding whether Paola had infected Amalia, Ravaglia had overstepped his authority and so produced a report that, Barbieri argued, the judges could not accept.

If the doctor had done what he was supposed to do, Barbieri insisted, he would have looked at the facts, which could hardly have been clearer. A healthy peasant woman was given a sickly baby who showed several of the signs typical of congenital syphilis. A town doctor diagnosed the baby's syphilis, and then, a few weeks later, the woman found an initial syphilitic chancre on her nipple. From such facts, science had no difficulty in deducing a relation of cause and effect.

Yet all this, argued Barbieri, Professor Ravaglia failed to do, choosing instead to weigh the merits of the case, thereby exceeding his mandate and failing in the agreement he entered into with the court. The professor had, in short, forgotten his role as a medical examiner and tried instead to don the robe of a judge.

Having done his best to discredit Ravaglia, Amalia's lawyer then took aim at the hospital's testimony. Going over the list of the hospital's witnesses, Barbieri observed that they had one thing in common: all were hospital employees. It was only natural, he pointed out, for them to defend what they had done. But, at the same time, it was the judges' duty not to accept their account at face value.

Before looking at the contradictions and holes in their testimony, Barbieri told the judges, a basic matter of law had to be made clear. The question was whether the hospital board could be held responsible for damage caused by the doctors who worked for it. Here there could be no doubt. If its doctors — employees of the foundling home — had not used the proper precautions in giving babies to women to nurse, the ultimate responsibility lay with the institution itself and so with its governing board. This was becoming a well-established principle of law in the new, enlightened Italian state.

Barbieri then reviewed the evidence, highlighting Dr. Dalmonte's testimony to the court. Confronted with such massive and clear evidence, how, asked Barbieri rhetorically, had the hospital officials responded? They had engaged in a titanic effort to muddy the waters, to confuse the picture. Indeed, their testimony, he argued, was a mass of obvious contradictions. Dr. Pinzani testified, he said, that shortly after entering the foundling home the baby developed "purulent conjunctivitis." Dr. Bruers described this as "gonorrheal conjunctivitis which had infiltrated her corneas and made her blind." Could this, he asked, be the same baby who was certified as being in good health and so given to a woman of the countryside? It seemed, Barbieri charged, that the foundling home was so negligent that the certificates of good health the doctors issued for its babies might more aptly be called "passports for the free passage of disease."

In the face of the evidence showing how they had infected Amalia, the men had shamelessly tried to raise doubts about her morals in an effort to protect themselves. And to give some kind of plausibility to their accusation, they had, incredibly, denied that the foundling Paola Olivelli ever had syphilis.

In making such wild accusations and in denying the obvious, Barbieri argued, the hospital lawyers had succeeded only in showing the weakness of their case.

The evidence that Amalia was in perfect health before her first visit to the foundling home was overwhelming, and the evidence that Paola had syphilis at the time that Amalia returned her was just as strong, Barbieri insisted. Dr. Dalmonte examined the baby on April 10 and found clear signs of syphilis, including a syphilitic sore on her lower lip. And when Amalia brought Paola back to the foundling home, Dr. Bruers examined the child and found an ulcerated rash of hard pustules around her backside and bleeding sores under her tongue, which led him to send the baby to the ward for suspected syphilitics.

In planning his attack, Barbieri made the most of a tactical mistake he was convinced that his high-priced legal adversaries had made in arguing that Paola had not had syphilis. The fact was, he told the court, that just two or three weeks after returning Paola, Amalia's first sign of syphilis appeared. And where, he asked, was it found? On her breast. Amid all the differences of opinion among the world's syphilis experts, Barbieri told the court, there was one matter about which there was total unanimity: such a sore was the unmistakable sign of a woman who had contracted syphilis by breastfeeding an infected baby. There could be no other explanation.

Pushing his advantage, Barbieri ridiculed the hospital's fallback position, the argument that if Amalia had gotten syphilis from nursing an infant, it must have been from nursing someone other than Paola. Where, he asked, was this mystery baby? Had anyone seen it? Such a baby, Barbieri told the judges, was but a phantom shamelessly conjured up by the hospital to mislead the court.

He then took aim at another pillar of the hospital's case, Dr. Berti's claim that his postmortem examination revealed no sign that Paola ever had syphilis. No other witness could corroborate this account, Barbieri reminded the judges. What weight, he asked, could be placed on such unsubstantiated testimony, made not by an impartial medical expert but by a man desperately trying to defend himself?

And what of the other evidence used to support the hospital's claim that Paola never had syphilis? Professor Ravaglia had made much of the fact that neither of the women who nursed the baby in the foundling home, nor any of the sixty other infants in their care, had contracted the disease. Yet even if this were true, Barbieri argued, it only meant that Paola had not, at that time, reached the state of infection that would put her wet nurses at risk.

Barbieri came to the crux of his argument. Given, he said, the overwhelming evidence that Amalia had contracted syphilis from the foundling she was given, it remained only to determine whether the foundling home personnel, in giving the baby to Amalia, had committed any of those acts of negligence or incompetence that, according to the law, would make the institution responsible for the harm done to her.

This point, too, should be clear, Barbieri argued. The court had only to ask how a baby who, in her nearly three months in the foundling home, had suffered such a series of devastating diseases and who, when she left the foundling home, was so clearly sickly, could have been judged healthy enough to meet the institution's requirement for placing her with a wet nurse.

There was already ample evidence, the lawyer concluded, for the court to rule in Amalia's favor. But should the judges believe that more information was needed before they made their final decision, they should, he advised, appoint a new medical examiner, one who would lay out the true facts for them.

CHAPTER 8

The Parade of
the Syphilitic Peasants

❋

T HE SUMMER OF 1891 was a time of ferment in Italy. The
economic crisis that had begun several years earlier continued, fueling the growth of what was still a disorganized
and chaotic popular movement that mixed socialism of different stripes with anarchism, various sorts of homegrown anti-
clericalism, and antimonarchism. Prime Minister Francesco Crispi,
a Sicilian with an authoritarian streak, had been trying to hold the
country together through the previous years with mixed results.
Once a revolutionary protégé of Garibaldi's and a leader of Sicily's
revolt against the Bourbon king of Naples, he was now comfortable with the Italian monarchy and showed a disturbing penchant
for saber-rattling and hypernationalism. Indeed, by the late 1880s,
Crispi seemed positively paranoid in his tendency to see French
plans for an invasion of Italy where none existed. Warning the
skeptical leaders of Italy's allies, Germany and Austria, that a papal-
French conspiracy to overthrow the Italian government was under
way, he recklessly ratcheted up Italy's military budget. The unpopu-
lar taxes that resulted and the exasperation of the Italian monarchy
— fearful that Crispi's ravings would lead to war — finally led to his

fall early in 1891. Yet by summer it was clear that the government that had replaced his would not last long, and it seemed that there was no one who could take Crispi's place.

The leaders of Italy's most deeply rooted institution, the Roman Catholic Church, followed these developments nervously. They became convinced that they would need to take dramatic steps to stop the inroads that the burgeoning socialist movement was making. Two months before Barbieri's argument before the Bologna Tribunal, the octogenarian Pope Leo XIII launched the church's counteroffensive, pronouncing the historic *Rerum novarum.* This encyclical, which denounced capitalism as heartless while warning the peasants and workers of the evils of socialism, marked the beginning of the church's attempts to come to terms with the social and economic problems of the modern world. For its part, the left tried to rise to the challenge. On August 2, at a workers' congress in Milan, Augusto Turati, Italy's foremost socialist, introduced a motion calling for the founding of the country's first socialist party.

Barbieri, who followed these matters closely in the press, had barely gotten a chance to read about what was going on in Milan when the good news reached him from the Bologna court. Ruling on August 4, the Tribunal announced its determination that Professor Ravaglia had indeed gone beyond his proper role by offering his opinion on a matter that was not his to decide. The judges accepted Barbieri's argument. They agreed to appoint a new medical expert, Professor Francesco Roncati, and announced that they would delay the proceedings until his report could be considered.

Roncati was a name well known to Barbieri, for he was one of Bologna's most prominent medical men. Yet in some ways he seemed a peculiar choice. Far from being an expert on syphilis — or for that matter on obstetrics or pediatrics — Roncati was one of Italy's first psychiatrists, a man best known for having founded, and long directed, Bologna's insane asylum.

If Barbieri was pleased by the Tribunal's ruling, Count Isolani was outraged and immediately told his lawyer to appeal it. Surely, the count thought, there was no need for yet another outside medical opinion, and in any case it was outrageous that the court had ordered the hospital to pay for it. If the judges thought that Dr. Ravaglia had gone beyond his authority, so be it. But why, he asked, should this require a new medical investigation? The court could simply ignore those parts of the report they found objectionable and use the rest, which responded to their questions.

The effect of Isolani's appeal was to suspend the case pending a ruling by the Bologna appeals court, a process that would take many months. But, as it turned out, the pause in the trial offered the count little respite from his syphilitic wet nurse woes. As news of the Bagnacavalli case filtered through the countryside, new complaints began to pour in.

Typical was one from Camugnano, a town near Vergato. The authorities were first notified of the case when Dr. Zanini, the town doctor, wrote to the Bologna provincial medical director. In April 1891 a Camugnano woman had been given a two-week-old foundling who, a month later, developed a suspicious rash. The doctor told the woman, Lucia Mancini, to return the child immediately and watch for any sores on her breast.

When Lucia brought the baby in, the foundling home doctors said that her doctor had made a mistake, the infant was healthy. Despite their reassurances, Lucia refused to take the baby back with her. A few weeks later, she noticed a syphilitic sore on her breast. Around the same time, although she was never told about it, the baby she had returned developed a full-fledged case of syphilis and died.

Lucia's own nineteen-month-old baby soon showed the first signs of the disease, so Zanini sent both Lucia and her child to the Bologna syphilis clinic. In late November he wrote to the foundling home director, recounting these events and noting that Lucia had five other children and the family was desperately poor.

Isolani, when informed of this latest case, launched an internal investigation. Dr. Pinzani reported that the infant given to Lucia Mancini had indeed died of syphilis, and, given the timing and nature of the woman's infection, it was very likely that she had contracted the disease from the baby. In response, Isolani authorized payments for Lucia's trips to the syphilis clinic and for her stays there. These costs soon grew when, in addition to Lucia and her baby daughter, her husband and their eight-year-old daughter developed the first signs of syphilis and were admitted to the Bologna clinic in January 1892. By the end of April, Isolani had approved payments of 454 lire, some for train travel, but most paid directly to the syphilis clinic.

In mid-May, while Isolani was awaiting the court's decision on his appeal in the Bagnacavalli case, Pinzani notified him that he had just received a letter from the mayor of Camugnano that threatened to sue the hospital board if it did not help Lucia's devastated family. Rather than reply to the mayor, Isolani decided to stall, partly in the hope that a favorable decision by the court in the Bagnacavalli case would soon strengthen his hand in dealing with the other women. The mayor waited six months while Lucia's family sunk ever deeper into misery. At last he sent Isolani a new letter that ended with a threat: unless the count took immediate steps to compensate the family, they would be forced to take legal action.

Given the Bagnacavalli case, Isolani could ill afford another lawsuit from a devastated peasant family. A few days after receiving the mayor's letter, he finally sent a reply. The foundling home, he explained, gave wet nurses only those babies who had every appearance of good health. It was unreasonable for the mayor to hold the home responsible for illnesses that the children later developed, nor was it fair to blame the home if some women contracted syphilis as a result. Yet, although it bore no legal or moral responsibility, he added, the board, acting out of a sense of compassion, always did what it could to help women in such situations get the medical treatment they needed.

Isolani's letter did not mention that the health ministry directive of 1887 required foundling homes to pay for medical treatment in these cases. He simply concluded by asking the mayor to send the woman's husband to Bologna so that proper compensation could be discussed. On Saturday, December 31, the man took the four-hour train ride to Bologna and made his way through the market to the hospital board headquarters to meet the count, who made him a proposal. The board would pay him 300 lire, plus the cost of his train trip that day, if he and his wife would sign a statement saying that they would never again ask the hospital for a lira and swear that they would never take any legal action against it.

A few days later, Lucia and her husband walked the several miles to the office of the nearest notary, who had on his desk a document prepared by Isolani's lawyer. For 300 lire, they renounced any further rights for compensation from the foundling home. Neither of the peasants signed the document, for both were illiterate.

By this time, the court proceedings in Amalia's case were finally back on track. After months of waiting, the Court of Appeals announced that it would hold a hearing on Isolani's appeal on May 17, 1892. Representing Isolani and the hospital board was the board's lawyer, Odoardo Ferrari, and his colleague, forty-nine-year-old Pietro Baldini, who had been hired by Isolani to strengthen his legal team. Baldini's clout was not based simply on his forensic skills. He was also well connected politically, having just completed eight years representing Bologna in parliament and having long been a member of both Bologna's city and provincial councils.[1] With his thick Bolognese accent and rapid-fire, nervous gesticulations, Baldini would present the case, with Ferrari beside him.

The judges called the hearing to order and asked the hospital's lawyers to present their case. Baldini got up and began his remarks, which lasted several hours, by arguing that no further medical opinion was needed. Dr. Ravaglia, the court-appointed expert, had already meticulously combed through the evidence and offered exactly the kind of objective appraisal the court required.

But Isolani and his lawyers not only wanted the judges to overrule the decision to order a new medical opinion. They wanted the appeals court to throw out the case altogether.

The problem that the hospital's lawyers faced from the beginning was that there was no doubt but that Amalia had contracted syphilis and, given the nature of her initial symptom, on her breast, little doubt how she had gotten it. They could adduce all the evidence they liked from the various foundling home doctors to cast doubt on whether Paola's physical ills derived from syphilis, but all ran into the problem that they could not credibly deny that Amalia had contracted syphilis from nursing a baby and that the timing of her infection coincided perfectly with her nursing of the foundling.

If Baldini and his colleagues sought nonetheless to make the contrary argument, insisting that Amalia was not infected by Paola, they did so with little confidence. Their private correspondence with Isolani makes it clear that they thought that Paola had infected Amalia. If they, nonetheless, kept pushing this, the weakest part of their case, it was partly because the foundling home doctors had dug in their heels, believing that their professional reputations were at stake. And there was another consideration. The court's own medical consultant, Ravaglia — surprisingly, from the hospital lawyers' perspective — had himself introduced doubt whether Amalia had been infected by Paola.

Baldini found himself in an awkward position. Unable to deny that Amalia had contracted syphilis from a baby, and unable to adduce any evidence of a different source than Paola, he was reduced to arguing that it was not his responsibility to prove the existence of such an alternative source but rather up to Amalia as the plaintiff to prove that there was none.

The weakest link in Amalia's chain of evidence, Baldini believed, was her main witness, Dr. Dalmonte, and he did his best to undercut his testimony.

How could the court, he asked, put any faith in the claims of a doctor who could not even remember if he had examined little Paola once or twice? How could the judges believe, from a man whose memory of the visit was so hazy, his recollection of finding a syphiloma on the child's lower lip when in Amalia's testimony she never said anything about such a growth? And how much faith could be put in the medical competence of a doctor who looked at a three-month-old child and thought that she was but one month old?

Once the judges realized that Dalmonte's testimony was based on vague, confused recollections, Baldini told them, they would see that the evidence showed clearly that Amalia's illness was not caused by the foundling because Paola never had syphilis. And this, the lawyer pointed out, was not simply his own view but also that of the medical expert appointed by the Tribunal.

Baldini knew that he could win his case in either of two ways. The first was through the arguments he had just made, introducing a reasonable doubt that Paola had ever had syphilis. Luckily, he knew that even if he were unsuccessful on this point, he had a second and much stronger line of defense.

Amalia's case was based on her claim that the foundling home doctors, in giving her Paola, violated the institution's rules and were guilty of imprudence or incompetence. This in turn, said Baldini, was based on two allegations: first, that the baby was sick and the rules did not permit foundlings to be given to outside wet nurses if they demonstrated any sign of illness; and second, that the baby had previously shown symptoms that should have led the doctors to suspect she was syphilitic.

Yet both of these arguments, Baldini maintained, were groundless. If the foundling home kept babies with common illnesses until they were well, it was not because of any rule that was aimed at protecting wet nurses but simply as a matter of good practice to safeguard the babies' health. In any case, he argued, the illnesses that Paola had suffered from — which had led to her blindness and deformed her spine — had run their course by the time she was given to Amalia.

As for the allegation that the foundling home doctors had ignored the signs of Paola's syphilis, no evidence supported such a claim. The accusation rested on Dr. Dalmonte's testimony of the signs he said he saw when he examined the infant, but this was only after the baby had left the foundling home. Even assuming that he had found signs of syphilitic infection, this offered no evidence to support the claim that such signs had appeared earlier.

Given the clear lack of such evidence, Baldini concluded, the appeals court should simply dismiss the case. But if the judges believed this to be premature, he added, they should at least direct the Tribunal to decide the case without recourse to any additional medical opinion.

A month later, in June 1892, the five justices of the appeals court called in the attorneys from both sides and read their decision. Baldini was to be disappointed. There was no basis for throwing the suit out, they decided. Although they agreed with the hospital's lawyer that Ravaglia's inappropriate opinion on how the court should rule did not invalidate the rest of his medical report, they found that the doctor had failed to offer them the basis for answering one of the principal questions: had Amalia contracted syphilis from the foundling? The Tribunal, the court ruled, was within its rights to seek a second expert to help it answer this question.

Barbieri was relieved, but now he was forced to wait for the new medical opinion. If it was no better than Ravaglia's, it was hard to see how Amalia could win.

CHAPTER 9

The Psychiatrist's Attack

C OUNT ISOLANI WAS FAR from pleased when he got word of the appeals court decision, and his mood was not helped by the opening of another front in his foundling home battles. This time the source of his travails was not a lowly peasant but the prefect himself.

Although not elected, the prefect was the most powerful government official in Bologna. The arm of the central government at the provincial level, he had authority over the national police and other national agencies and the responsibility for ensuring that the laws were being followed. By contrast, the mayor played a much more modest role. A policy of constantly moving prefects from one province to another ensured that they would not develop close ties with local interests and would be loyal to no one but the minister of internal affairs in Rome.

Bologna's prefect, it happened, died in office a month before the appeals court decision. Before a successor could be appointed, yet another mayor wrote to complain about the foundling home, oblivious that the man he addressed had died. On May 19, 1892, the acting prefect forwarded the complaint to the director of the foundling home and observed in his cover note that such cases were occurring with remarkable frequency. To this he added his skepticism that the foundling home was following the national guidelines that had been sent to it five years earlier, aimed to prevent such contagion.

The story was familiar: Adele Ghermandi of the mountain community of Savigno had gone to the Bologna foundling home in March of that year to get an infant to nurse. Within two months the baby developed terrible sores and Adele returned her, but the poor woman discovered that she already had the telltale chancre on her nipple. On the instruction of the town doctor, she checked into Bologna's syphilis clinic on May 15.

Isolani replied to the acting prefect's letter immediately, carefully listing all the precautions his staff had adopted. They had instituted a new policy — one effect of the Bagnacavalli case — keeping all the abandoned babies until they were at least sixteen days old to be sure they did not show signs of syphilis. Midwives bringing babies to the foundling home were required to fill out a form reporting any sign of the disease in the baby's mother. When the wet nurses were given an infant, they were carefully instructed to be on the lookout for any sores on the baby's skin and to return the child at their first appearance. In the case of the baby given to Adele Ghermandi, he asserted, they had followed every one of these measures.

The acting prefect sent a long, angry reply. The answers to his questions, he protested, were grossly inadequate, and the procedures employed in the foundling home were clearly deficient. What, he asked, was the point of the new requirement that babies remain in the foundling home for sixteen days? It was well known that many of the babies born with syphilis showed signs of the disease only weeks later. Likewise, he attacked the foundling home's requirement that the midwives certify whether they had found any sign of syphilis in the baby's mother. The first article of the 1887 Health Ministry directive, the acting prefect wrote, could not be clearer. Women abandoning babies had to provide a certificate from a medical doctor to this effect, not from an illiterate woman wholly unqualified to make such a diagnosis.

At the meeting called for June 11 to deal with these accusations,

Isolani and his fellow board members reacted indignantly. Despite what the acting prefect insinuated, said one member, the 1887 directive was not in the form of a law, and so they were under no legal obligation to follow it. Clearly, said another, the prefect's office had little understanding of the challenges they faced.

Isolani and his board members thought that Bologna's prefects, men of privileged backgrounds from other parts of the country who had little experience with rural life, had a hopelessly naïve view of the peasant world, which was implicit in their apparent belief that the foundling home was always to blame when wet nurses contracted syphilis. The wet nurses viewed the foundlings, said one board member, simply as a source of money. It was just as likely, he added, that it was these women who were infecting healthy foundlings as the other way around.

By the time Isolani wrote up the board's reply, Bologna had a new prefect, Alessandro Amour. A sixty-one-year-old law graduate from Turin, he was almost a caricature of the peripatetic high civil servant, having served as *questore* — provincial chief of police — for almost every major city in the country, from Turin, Milan, and Florence down to Naples and Messina. He then began to climb the ladder as a prefect, moving to increasingly important centers.

Barely two weeks into his new position, Amour received the long, combative letter from Isolani. Incensed by what he saw as the count's aristocratic insolence, he sent a scathing reply. The ministerial circular of 1887 was not simply a list of government suggestions, he informed the count, but an order that had to be obeyed. The midwives were not to be allowed to bring in babies unless they had a certificate from a doctor who had examined the baby's mother. The wet nurses, for their part, had to take the foundlings in for a medical exam every two weeks, at least for the first few months of the baby's life, when syphilis was most likely to appear. To that end, he was sending instructions to all the mayors of the province ordering the town doctors to ensure that this was done.

This unpleasant exchange with the prefect left the count in a disagreeable mood. But his spirits got a boost when, a week later, the hospital's lawyer, Ferrari, shared news of a recent conversation. He had run into Dr. Roncati, and the subject of the report he was preparing for the Tribunal in the Bagnacavalli case came up. The doctor had hinted strongly that the count would be pleased by his findings, which, he said, he planned to send the court shortly.

This news was a great relief to the count. He couldn't see how, with this second expert opinion exonerating the hospital, the court could possibly find in favor of the peasant woman. The hospital board would have the unanimous support of the court's own medical experts and be represented by one of Bologna's top lawyers. On the other side, all the count could see was an inept country doctor and an inexperienced, overreaching attorney.

The count of course knew Francesco Roncati, who had served a number of terms as dean of the University of Bologna's medical school, and he had always assumed that Roncati would side with the hospital. But he did have at least one small nagging worry: although Roncati was a pillar of the establishment, he took great pride in his reputation for incorruptibility and saw himself as a selfless protector of society's unfortunates. Yet while it was true that Roncati had devoted much of his career to caring for the poor, he was certainly not inclined to romanticize peasant life. In this, he shared the count's sentiments: those well placed in society had a responsibility to the less fortunate.

Born in 1832 in the Duchy of Modena, only thirty miles from Bologna but outside the Papal States, Roncati had attended a Jesuit school before studying medicine in Modena. His degree barely in hand, he attracted the attention of the duke of Modena, Francis V, and the duke himself paid for his further studies in Vienna.

By the time Roncati returned home, much had changed. There was no more Duchy of Modena, Italy was unified, and his patron lived in exile. Looking for a larger stage on which to launch his medical career, he cast his eye on Bologna, newly freed from papal rule. In 1867, hoping to bring Europe's most advanced theories for treating mental health to the new Italian state, Roncati asked the authorities to give him a building where he could create a modern institution for the mentally ill. His timing was perfect. The city found itself with extra real estate on its hands, thanks to the new state's seizure of much church property. He was given a large complex of buildings that had, until recently, been a convent. Two decades later, after teaching general medicine in Bologna for many years, Roncati was awarded the university's first chair in psychiatry.

The doctor got up each day at six and spent the morning receiving patients at home. He then took the horse-pulled tram to the university, where, at 3 P.M., he gave his daily lecture. Students never forgot Roncati, the great man famous for his scathing irony and stinging satire, never at a loss to give his opinion about what was wrong with the world, ever eager to puncture people's illusions. He gestured dramatically while lecturing, his strong opinions made all the more memorable by his practice of emphasizing the phrases he thought important by pronouncing them with exquisite deliberation. After his lecture, Roncati got back on the tram to go to the insane asylum, where he worked until evening.

Roncati's views of the Bagnacavalli case were colored by his strong opinions about life among the peasants in Bologna's mountains, people he felt he knew well as a result of his long experience in the asylum. The previous year he had written down these views in an attempt to explain the causes of insanity. Why, he asked, was the insane asylum overflowing with men and women from the peasant class? The answer, he was convinced, lay in the degraded conditions in which they lived. And of all the peasants, he thought, those in the mountains had it worst. Condemned to inactivity in the winter when they were snowed in, confined to a squalid hovel for a home, lacking any defense against the cold, with no savings to protect them, reduced to eating polenta and chestnuts and drinking only water, wracked by worry over the uncertainty of the future and the welfare of their families, Roncati wrote, it was all too easy for them to fall prey to melancholy and mental illness.

These miserable conditions, he thought, also explained the success of the rural socialist leagues, even though socialist theories, planted in the poor peasants' heads, were leading them astray. Science, he told his students, taught that people were not all created equal. Just as some were born beautiful and others plain, some were blessed with intelligence and others were condemned to stupidity. Recent attempts to introduce universal male suffrage in Italy, he taught, betrayed a fundamental ignorance of the human condition. As he put it, the opinion of one intelligent, well-informed man of good character was worth more than that of a million imbeciles.

This was the man of science whose opinion of Amalia's case would weigh heavily in her trial before the Tribunal.

On August 4, Roncati submitted his findings to the court. He had carefully reviewed all of the evidence, he told the judges, although, unlike Ravaglia, he had not interviewed Amalia or any of the doctors or nurses, and he had not performed any medical examinations of his own. The matter, he concluded, was clear. The court should reject the ill-informed opinion of the country doctor, Dalmonte. His testimony had been an appalling amalgam of contradiction, medical ignorance, and uncertain recollection. The foundling home doctors had no reason to believe that the baby they gave to Amalia Bagnacavalli suffered from syphilis. Paola had been born at a normal weight, and her early illnesses — the gonorrheal conjunctivitis and the lung infection — had had nothing to do with syphilis. Even when she was returned to the foundling home, the evidence showed that she did not have the disease, since the rash she had disappeared with the application of a simple solution, and the autopsy showed no sign of syphilis in her internal organs.

True, Roncati stated, the Vergato doctor spoke of a syphiloma on the baby's lip and the appearance of a similar syphilitic sore on Amalia's breast three or four weeks later, but this made no sense. An initial syphilitic chancre on a woman's breast would look nothing like a secondary syphilitic sore that a syphilitic baby would have on its lip. Moreover, in his initial medical report, Dalmonte made no mention of the baby's having such a sore nor had Amalia said anything about it in her own testimony.

Roncati would certainly not deny that the appearance of an initial syphiloma on Amalia's nipple three weeks after she took the baby back to the foundling home corresponded well enough with the expected incubation period for the disease. But this could only be used as evidence that she had contracted syphilis from Paola if the baby herself had the disease, which clearly, Roncati concluded, she had not.

CHAPTER 10

The Miserly Syphilologist

BARBIERI, IT SEEMED, had no case left. He had from the beginning cast it as a struggle of modern, enlightened, scientific understandings against the old, traditional, retrograde ways of doing things. But as his exemplar of modern science, he had only a country doctor whose vague recollections and questionable understanding of syphilis had become something of an embarrassment. Worse, against him stood the entire medical establishment of Bologna. All had lined up behind the foundling home doctors, leaving Barbieri with nothing but his own righteous anger and his long-suffering client.

But Barbieri did not lack courage, nor was he one to back down from a fight, even when the stakes were high and the odds against him. This was clear from the strange case that had landed him as a defendant a few years earlier in the same court in which Amalia's case was being heard.

It had begun one day in 1887, back when he had little business and was spending much of his time in the newspaper office of *La Patria.* An irate young lawyer, Giuseppe Barbanti, rushed into the office, where he found Barbieri talking with his friends. Barbanti was enraged by an article in the newspaper that day which, in its polemics against the local socialists, had made an unflattering reference to him that he was convinced had been written or, at least, inspired by Barbieri.

Thirty-four years old — nine years older than Barbieri — Barbanti had cast his lot with the socialists after earlier flirting with anarchism. When he was twenty-three, he had met Bakunin, who had come to Bologna to foment an insurrection against the new Italian state. When the police arrested seventy-nine of the conspirators, Barbanti, despite his youth, acted as the lawyer for all of them, making a name for himself by winning their freedom. Later that year he tried to convince Giuseppe Garibaldi, the icon of Italian unification, to help organize a military expedition on behalf of the Serbs, who were rising up against Turkish rule, and he himself went with two dozen other Italian volunteers to the Balkans to fight on their behalf, returning to write a memoir of his adventures.

Seeing himself as second only to Andrea Costa among Bologna's socialists, Barbanti would not tolerate an offense to his honor from the group behind *La Patria*, still less from a man like Barbieri, who cast himself as a champion of the downtrodden and avatar of the new elite, a man who was known to be the son of a dishonored notary from the mountains. In front of Barbieri's friends, Barbanti told the lawyer what he thought of him in terms so strong that Barbieri found himself left with little choice. He challenged Barbanti to a duel, a challenge Barbanti quickly accepted.

Dueling had become something of a mania among Italy's political class after Italian unification, and the Barbieri-Barbanti duel was typical in having its origins in newspaper polemics. Countless newspapers had sprung up with the freedom of the press brought by the end of the old regimes. With little money for reporters, they devoted much of their space and practically all of their energy to arguments with their rivals.

Barbieri had some reason to be concerned when he returned home and told Bianca, whom he had married just a year earlier, what had happened. After all, Barbanti was not only several years older and more experienced but had fought — albeit briefly — in a war. Barbieri himself had little experience with duels and knew of many people like him who had been maimed for life or even killed on the field of honor.

The duel was to be fought by sword, and a suitable location was found on the grounds of an estate just outside the city.

Late in the morning of July 8, the two men arrived at the appointed place, each bringing two seconds. They drew lots, and one of Barbieri's seconds, Francesco Ballarini — who owned the newspaper whose article had caused the conflict — was selected to direct the duel. The sun was already brutally hot, so he chose a spot in the shade of a tree and told the men where to stand.

At Ballarini's signal, the duel began. After they warily circled each other, Barbieri made his move, his sword cutting into Barbanti's right hand. Seeing blood drawn, Ballarini shouted, "Halt," but while Barbieri began to lower his sword, Barbanti continued to advance. Barbieri saw the blade arc through the air as he swung his head to the right, trying, too late, to avoid its path. He felt the steel slice through his left cheek.

Alarmed, Ballarini shouted, "This is a duel, not an assassination!" Belatedly, Barbanti lowered his sword.

Word of the duel quickly reached Bologna's prosecuting magistrate, who launched an investigation. The duel became the talk of Bologna, and over the following year, newspapers from Rome to Turin chronicled the controversy with a series of breathless accounts. Although duels were common, they were illegal, and the wounding and death of prominent citizens had become a public scandal. Hearing the rumors of the incident, the magistrate decided not only to charge both lawyers with dueling but to bring an additional accusation as well. It was this charge that had Italy's newspapers abuzz. Barbanti, the prosecutor held, had not in fact been engaged in a duel when he had wounded Barbieri because, according to the rules, dueling combatants must stop as soon as the director calls "Halt." Barbanti, he charged, was guilty of criminal assault.

Barbieri's friends and political allies soon began a whispering campaign against Barbanti, painting a picture of his dishonorable behavior. On July 27, Barbanti replied with an indignant letter to

Bologna's major daily newspaper. Those who were spreading such rumors, he wrote, were either liars or fools. Although he claimed that Barbieri himself would support his account of the duel, in his own letter two days later Barbieri was evasive, saying that, given his aroused emotional state at the time, he could not say with certainty what had happened.

When the trial began almost two years later, on March 29, 1889, a large crowd pushed into the courtroom. It was the trial of the year, with the mayor and other members of Bologna's elite called as character witnesses and competing accounts of the duel given by the two lawyers' seconds.

In a dramatic flourish avidly reported by the journalists present, the judges arranged for a special jury to advise them whether Barbanti had in fact violated the rules. Composed of six nationally known dueling experts, the panel, in a kind of trial within the trial, deliberated separately. Among its members was Felice Cavallotti, head of the extreme left in parliament. Cavallotti did not lack for experience. He would die nine years later, at fifty-five, fighting his thirty-third duel.

Yes, the men found, Barbanti had continued his attack after the duel's director had shouted "Halt," a potentially serious offense. But he had done so in the heat of emotion and had stopped when Ballarini had physically stepped between the duelists with his own sword held up, something they criticized Ballarini for not doing sooner. Given these facts, they concluded, Barbanti could not be accused of acting dishonorably.

The next day newspapers throughout the country reported the judges' decision, with one Bologna weekly publishing a special supplement about the trial. Barbanti was found not guilty of willful assault, but both lawyers were deemed guilty of illegally engaging in a duel. The court tried to make an example of them by sentencing each to several months' banishment from Bologna, but the following year, just a few months before the illiterate wet nurse came to see Barbieri, the Bologna Court of Appeals reduced his sentence to a token fine of 20 lire and Barbanti's to 50 lire.

The duel had briefly made Barbieri quite a public figure in Bologna, and he was eager to nurture this reputation as a man to be reckoned with. He was not going to back down in the face of his setback in Amalia's case, not when he still had the chance to show that he was not just any lawyer who would run at the first sign of difficulty.

In the aftermath of the Roncati report, Barbieri realized that he had only one hope, meager as it was. He would have to find a medical expert to testify on Amalia's behalf whose credentials exceeded those of the court's two experts. But where could he find such a person, someone not only of national stature but also willing to call into question the professional judgment of his colleagues? And even if he could find such a doctor, how could he pay him? Amalia, of course, was penniless.

If Bologna had a nationally renowned expert on syphilis who could make the court's medical advisers look unqualified by comparison, it was clearly Pietro Gamberini — the first man Barbieri thought of. When Amalia had first gone to the Bologna syphilis clinic, Gamberini was then director. In fact, not only had he directed the clinic for thirty years, but he had taught dermatology and syphilology (then considered part of the same specialty) at the University of Bologna's medical school. Nor was his reputation merely local. He was the editor of the major journal of syphilis studies in Italy, and each year he published a ream of new articles on the subject in Italy's top medical journals.

Gamberini would be an ideal champion of their cause, but, as Barbieri discovered, there was no chance he would ever testify on Amalia's behalf. Few doctors were more part of Bologna's medical establishment than Gamberini. For him to call into question the judgment and credibility of his two medical school colleagues — Ravaglia and, especially, Dean Roncati — was unthinkable. To do so in a case that would establish the ability of a peasant woman to publicly hold the city's most respected doctors responsible for her ill health was to ask too much of him.

Gamberini's personality also gave Barbieri little reason for optimism. The syphilologist was well known in Bologna as a miser. His students delighted in spotting him furtively carrying his tattered clothes to one of the used clothes vendors whose booths lined Bologna's *piazze* so that he could sell the garments he could no longer wear for a few coins. Although his expertise was generally recognized among his colleagues, his unusual theory of the origin of syphilis had given him a bit of a reputation as a crank. Most experts traced the disease to the New World, brought back to Europe by Columbus's crew on their return voyage in the early 1490s. But Gamberini was convinced that syphilis had existed in Spain before then. It was, he believed, a plague then known only among the Jews, who had brought it with them from Palestine centuries earlier. The massive outbreak of syphilis in Europe in the mid-1490s, then, was not explained by the coincidence of Columbus's return but by the expulsion of the Jews from Spain in 1492. It was these wandering Jews, Gamberini argued, who spread their disease to the Christian population of Europe.[1]

Just when Barbieri's task of finding a syphilis expert seemed most hopeless, he got a break. Gamberini was getting on in years. In fact, two days before Amalia's first visit to his clinic he had celebrated his seventy-fifth birthday. Suffering from cataracts that had practically robbed him of his sight, he offered his medical students an unending source of side-splitting stories. They told of how, on his hospital rounds, he pronounced one outrageous misdiagnosis after another as a result of his unwillingness to admit that he could barely see. With great difficulty (and not a little arm-twisting), the hospital and medical school authorities finally convinced him that he should step down and let someone younger take up his burdens. The following year he grudgingly left the clinic and the university where he had spent most of his adult life.

If Gamberini was a product of the old world — a graduate of a Catholic seminary under the rule of the Papal States — his replacement, Domenico Majocchi, was very much a product of the new. While Gamberini was from Bologna and part of the city's old guard, Majocchi was from Rome, where he had studied medicine and begun his specialty in syphilis. When only thirty years old, he won the chair in dermo-syphilology at the University of Padua. His national reputation grew in the following decade as he published a slew of scholarly studies. He was named to take Gamberini's place at the University of Bologna in 1891.

Majocchi had been in Bologna for just a year when Barbieri went to see him at the hospital. The newcomer did not yet feel entirely comfortable amid all the signs of his predecessor, from the walls of his medical books — as many in French and German as Italian — to the heavy, dark furniture. The young lawyer did his best to explain Amalia's case in the few minutes that Majocchi was willing to give him. Barbieri was not sure what to expect, and were it not for his determination — his detractors would call it his unwholesome ambition — he might well not have put himself in this position at all. How likely was it that the new medical professor would want to take up a cause in which he was being asked to invest a good deal of time and his professional reputation without much chance of payment and with only one thing of which he could be sure: if he accepted Barbieri's offer, he would make his acceptance into Bologna's medical world a hundred times more difficult.

But the more Majocchi heard, the more intrigued he became. Although he and the young lawyer had very different personalities, they had both come of age in the heady years when the new Italian nation was taking form and the old regime of popes, dukes, and foreign rulers demolished. They were both convinced that a new, younger generation committed to introducing modern, scientific methods was destined to replace the old generation, bound as it was to the traditional ways. Furthermore, in his first year at the Bologna clinic, Majocchi had come across an appalling number of cases of peasant women from the mountains who had contracted syphilis from babies from the foundling home and who had then infected others in their family. This was a scandal about which, he thought, someone needed to do something.

Barbieri, fearing that the doctor would simply turn him down, produced a sheaf of papers for him to read. They included copies of the medical certificates prepared by Dr. Dalmonte and by the doctor who had examined Amalia at the syphilis clinic in which they were sitting. Also included was a copy of the autopsy report on Paola submitted by Dr. Berti, copies of all the medical testimony gathered in the earlier stage of the trial, and the reports submitted by the two court-appointed doctors.

Amid all the hubbub of the clinic, with dozens of men and women undergoing sickening mercury treatment and the constant battle to detect the signs of syphilis in women desperate to hide their sores to avoid confinement, Majocchi could not read through the imposing pile and decided to take it all home. Over the next several days he read through it all and, after carefully weighing the implications of championing Amalia's cause, he sent Barbieri a message. He would take the case.

CHAPTER 11

A New Champion

W HEN BARBIERI received a draft of Majocchi's report a
few weeks later, he felt hopeful for the first time in a
long while and, with renewed energy, prepared his argument for the Tribunal. On April 18, 1893, three years after Amalia
returned Paola to the foundling home, the chief judge called the
full court into session to hear final arguments. Barbieri would
go first.

It was the moment Barbieri had long been waiting for. He had
mulled over how he could best make his case and decided that an
appeal to the emotions was as important as an appeal to the law. As
he rose to address the black-robed judges in front of him, he began
on an emotional note.

The case before them, he said, was but one of many such tragic
cases that had plagued the women of Bologna's hinterland. These
poor peasants, lured by the prospect of making the paltry sum of
nine lire a month, were being ruined, infected with a terrible disease whose name itself inspired dread.

Barbieri then briefly recounted Amalia's story: how she was given
the sickly baby, how she took her to the local doctor, and how
Dalmonte told her the baby had syphilis and ordered her to return it.

But for Amalia, he told the judges, it was too late. She was already infected, and soon the first signs of the tragic disease would appear, heralding the onset of a malady that would rob her of her health and leave her without any hope of cure. As if this were not enough, she would soon endure the horror of infecting not only her husband but her little daughter as well.

Barbieri reviewed the testimony from the earlier stage of the trial, beginning with Dalmonte's account of his examination of Paola and his discovery of the first signs of syphilis in Amalia.

He then turned to the testimony of the foundling home doctors, who insisted that they had acted responsibly and followed all the prescribed procedures. Barbieri again went on the attack. The Court of Appeals, he reminded the judges, had, in upholding their decision to seek a second outside medical opinion, observed that the foundling home doctors' testimony could not be taken at face value. The court had to consider the possibility that, as defendants in the trial, the doctors were crafting a story that wove fact and fiction, a story aimed at telling not what actually happened but what they wished had happened.

The problem that Barbieri faced in this line of argument was that it highlighted the importance of Roncati's report. By claiming that the court could not rely on testimony from partisans in the case but needed to rely on expert, objective medical testimony, he seemed to be placing great weight on the opinions of the two doctors appointed by the court for just this purpose. Yet both had sided with the hospital. In his earlier court appearance he had attacked the first medical report, presented by Dr. Ravaglia. He had then urged the court to appoint a second medical examiner. But that report, by Dr. Roncati, had been even more hostile to Amalia's cause. This left Barbieri with only one way of winning the case. He would have to discredit Roncati, one of the giants of Bologna's medical establishment.

If Professor Ravaglia had erred in offering too many doubts, Barbieri began, and in offering judgments about matters that were not his to decide, Professor Roncati had erred in not sufficiently taking into account the evidence that was supposed to serve as the basis for his expert judgment. Instead of performing his court-ordered task of providing an objective examination of the evidence, Barbieri charged, Roncati had simply accepted the foundling home doctors' testimony at face value. Indeed, what Roncati provided was not a scientific examination but a misguided attempt at defending his colleagues. The illustrious "phrenologist" — as Barbieri called him — would, he hoped, forgive him for saying so, but his report was wholly at odds with the most basic principles of dermo-syphilology.

A simple glance at Roncati's report, said the lawyer, revealed his methods. Dr. Dalmonte had testified that he found a syphilitic sore on Paola's lip when he examined her. In the face of this simple, categorical evidence, Roncati had summarily dismissed its existence. He simply asserted: "We must hold firm in our judgment that such a syphiloma never existed on the baby's lips." Unable to deny the existence of the chancre on Amalia's nipple, he had followed Dr. Bruers's insinuations in suggesting that it must have had some other cause. And, after admitting that the kind of ulcerated rash that Paola had on her body was a common sign of syphilis, he had hastened to deny the possibility that it was syphilitic, citing the foundling home doctors' claim that it had healed rapidly through simple treatment.

Professor Roncati, Barbieri charged, clearly had one goal and one goal only: to defend the foundling home and, especially, his colleagues, even at the risk of contradicting himself.

But beyond these problems, the lawyer said, lay another. While he was an eminent expert on nervous and mental disorders, Roncati was much less familiar with the medical questions at issue in this case. Clearly, when the judges were looking for an expert, the first place they must have thought to look was to the holder of the professorship in dermo-syphilology at the university. It was no doubt only because, at the time, that chair was vacant, after the retirement of its holder, that a less satisfactory solution had to be found.

When he had read Roncati's report, said Barbieri, and seen just how deficient it was, he realized that he had only one choice. In this, he said, he was propelled not only by a desire to see justice done and out of a sense of duty, but by the pity he felt for a family whose health had been destroyed, whose loved ones had taken ill and died. He turned to Professor Domenico Majocchi, who now occupied the university's chair of syphilology and was the new director of the syphilis clinic, to clear away all the confusion.

Unable to call Majocchi to the stand since no witnesses could be summoned at this stage of the trial, Barbieri introduced the doctor's testimony through his own concluding argument.

Majocchi's report, Barbieri noted, first addressed the question of whether Paola had syphilis. After examining all of the evidence, he reported, there was no doubt that the foundling did have the disease. This was most obvious, the doctor claimed, in the kind of mucus coming out of her nose and mouth and also, later, in the sore on her lip and the distinctive rash around her backside. These latter two symptoms were unquestionably manifestations of the second stage of syphilis, when it was most contagious.

But even before the most obvious signs appeared, Majocchi argued, Paola's loss of sight should have led to the suspicion that she suffered from the disease. The description of the symptoms, he observed, did not accord with those associated with gonorrheal conjunctivitis, in which one usually saw signs of inflammation. But, even more important, the foundling home doctors had neglected to use the latest medical knowledge. In 1879, Albert Neisser had identified the spirochete that caused gonorrhea. It was now, Majocchi argued, the mark of good medical practice to use a microscope to determine if it were present when gonorrhea was suspected.

In the absence of a proper microscopic investigation, Majocchi argued, he found no reason not to see Paola's eye disease as a product of congenital syphilis, which, he said, often produced such symptoms. In any case, lacking any proof that the disorder was produced by gonorrhea, the doctors could not exclude congenital syphilis as a cause.

In their defense, Majocchi noted, the foundling home doctors made much of the fact that neither of the two women who nursed Paola in her first months in the foundling home had contracted syphilis. But, he pointed out, it was only when the baby developed the full infectious secondary stage of the disease, especially with the appearance of the syphilitic sores on her lips and on her tongue, that she would be at high risk of infecting the woman at whose breast she nursed. Paola was born with syphilis, but its first symptoms appeared in her eyes and in her nose, whose products were much less contagious. Bologna's professor of syphilology was convinced that Paola suffered from congenital syphilis and that there were abundant reasons for the foundling home doctors to suspect that this was the case even before she was sent out to nurse.

When Barbieri completed his reading of Majocchi's testimony, he felt that Amalia had a chance, that he had a chance. In what was left of his remarks, he pressed home his advantage, trying to dismantle the hospital's defense.

That Amalia had contracted syphilis from the foundling there could be no doubt, Barbieri argued. All that was left for his adversaries to argue was that the hospital should bear no legal responsibility. Toward this end, they had claimed that proper procedures were in place to prevent the spread of syphilis to the wet nurses. They had argued that it was inevitable that despite these measures, some women would still contract syphilis from the babies they were given, and that for this the law could not hold them responsible. But, Barbieri argued, these proper procedures were clearly not followed in Amalia's case.

The hospital also argued, Barbieri noted, that nothing in its contract with the wet nurses gave the women any legal right to claim damages for contracting syphilis. The contract, according to the hospital, stipulated only what work was required of the women and what the hospital was willing to pay them for it. It made no guarantee that they would be unharmed and promised them nothing if they were injured.

Here Barbieri was on familiar ground, for in his treatise on proper modern government he had denounced just such arguments as unbefitting an enlightened society. Both heart and mind rebelled against this line of defense, he told the judges. Legally speaking, the question boiled down to whether an employer was obligated to watch out for the worker's safety. Did employers have the duty to do everything possible to guard against dangers to their employees? Yes, he insisted, they did.

Barbieri called on the judges to declare the foundling home and the hospital board responsible for the actions of its employees and for the material and moral damage suffered by Amalia Bagnacavalli as a result of the baby that she was given to nurse. They should, he urged, order the hospital board, in the person of its president, Count Francesco Isolani, to compensate her for all the damages she had suffered. Finally, Barbieri pleaded, they should make the hospital board pay for all of Amalia's legal expenses.

The young lawyer, after two days on his feet, was finished. Although exhilarated by his marathon argument, he knew that he was fighting against much stronger forces. The judges might have found his arguments reasonable, but they had yet to hear from the other side, and the other side would be represented by one of Bologna's foremost citizens.

Domenico Majocchi's testimony, introduced at the last minute by Barbieri, came as a shock to Count Isolani and his lawyers. Until then, in almost three years, not a single medical expert had supported Amalia's claim. The lone medical witness that Barbieri had been able to produce, Dr. Dalmonte, offered an easy target for the count's lawyers, backed as they were by the testimony of the several foundling home doctors as well as by both of the court-appointed experts.

Pietro Baldini, the count's lead lawyer in the courtroom drama, lost no time in launching a counteroffensive, preparing himself by finding out what he could about the new director of the syphilis clinic. He soon learned that he would have a ready ally in Pietro Gamberini, for the former director deeply resented the man who had replaced him. That the new professor would attack the hospital board and ridicule Gamberini's old colleague, Francesco Roncati, further fueled his anger.

On April 28, little more than a week after Barbieri had introduced Majocchi's testimony, Gamberini's attack appeared in the form of a short booklet, "The opinion of Pietro Gamberini, formerly professor of Dermopathology and of the Syphilis Clinic of the University of Bologna, in the case of Bagnacavalli v. the Hospitals."

It took the form of a letter to the hospital lawyer. Whether Gamberini himself paid for its publication or whether the hospital board offered to cover the expense is unclear. Although Gamberini was famously stingy, he might well have indulged himself in order to try to tarnish his successor's reputation. It maddened him that the younger man was now trumpeting his more modern scientific approach.

"Bowing to your most courteous invitation to concern myself with the examination of the two eminent reports regarding the Bagnacavalli case, the one by Professor Majocchi, and the other by Professor Roncati," Gamberini began, "I offer the following reflections."

In telegraphic style, he rattled off all the deficiencies he found in Majocchi's analysis. The baby's eye infection, he began, did not, despite Majocchi's claim to the contrary, show the signs of being caused by syphilis. The autopsy clearly showed that the baby died from a pulmonary infection, with no sign of syphilis in her internal organs. It was claimed that the pustules around the baby's mouth and backside were evidence of syphilis, but how then could they have gone away after the simple application of a solution? Professor Majocchi had made no mention of the classic signs of syphilis on the body of a baby, a series of enlarged lymph notes, symptoms which, if they had appeared, could not have escaped the attention of the foundling home doctors. Concerning the initial syphilitic chancre on Bagnacavalli's breast a few weeks after she returned the foundling, Gamberini asked, was it so difficult to believe that she had contracted this from nursing some baby other than the foundling?

In short, Bologna's former syphilis clinic director concluded, he fully supported Professor Roncati's findings. The baby had shown no sign that could have properly led the foundling home doctors to suspect that she had syphilis.

Although Baldini was able to introduce the doctor's tirade as evidence, submitting it as a supplemental document to the court, the audience that Gamberini himself seemed most interested in was not the judges but rather his hospital and university colleagues, who had forced him out. For them Gamberini's message was clear: Bologna's new chief syphilologist did not measure up to his predecessor.

If Gamberini was angered by his successor's meddling in the case, Francesco Roncati was livid. In all of his decades of practice and teaching and running a large hospital, he had never had his competence called into question in such a way. Because Barbieri had arranged to have Majocchi's testimony published, Roncati soon had a copy in his hands. He did not need the hospital's lawyer to convince him to write a reply for the court and have it published. No one could stop him from defending his good name. A month after Gamberini sent in his defense of Roncati, the insane asylum director handed the lawyer his own detailed rebuttal.

It was with a sense of deep displeasure, Roncati began, that he had read Majocchi's opinion. He realized that this report had no official standing in the court proceeding, but given Majocchi's great authority and that its conclusions so directly contradicted his own, he thought it his duty to reply.

For reasons he could not fathom, Roncati wrote, his colleague was so eager to defend the work of Dr. Dalmonte that he was willing to ignore all the deficiencies in the mountain doctor's testimony. Similarly, he had ignored or inexplicably misinterpreted all of the clear medical evidence from the foundling home showing that the baby never had syphilis.

In his first paragraphs, Roncati, with evident difficulty, adopted a respectful if formal tone. Yet he could not control his anger for long, and by the letter's end he unleashed a withering attack on his new colleague. Professor Majocchi, he charged, had used a series of sophisms, unsupported allegations, dubious facts, and fallacious premises in order to speciously sustain a wholly arbitrary thesis.

Baldini now had what he thought he most needed: a point-by-point refutation of Majocchi's attack. The redoubtable Dr. Roncati had demonstrated the weaknesses in Majocchi's argument, and Majocchi's predecessor, a giant in his field, had himself gone on record as dismissing Majocchi's claims. The hospital's lawyer now faced the final stage of the trial with great confidence. He prepared his own concluding argument for the court, knowing that the judges would issue their final decision soon afterward.

CHAPTER 12

Conflicting Opinions

O N JUNE 12, 1893, ALMOST two months after Barbieri presented Majocchi's accusations of medical malfeasance to
the Tribunal, the judges assembled to hear the hospital's
defense.

It was an unsettling time for the men of Bologna's professional
classes. The economy had still not rebounded from the agricultural
crisis, helping to fuel a growing socialist movement. Especially
alarming to them was that just as the socialists were making sharp
inroads, the state itself seemed hopelessly inept.

For their part the socialists, long riven by internal conflicts, had
recently shown signs of coming together. The previous year, on the
four hundredth anniversary of the sailing of Columbus from the
port of Genoa, they gathered in that city and — after a walkout on
the first day of the meeting by the anarchist wing — founded the
national Party of Italian Workers, which would soon become the
Italian Socialist Party.

Although the organized workers' movement, with its rapidly
spreading network of local urban trade unions and rural peasant
leagues, was concentrated in the northern half of Italy, the biggest
news that year came from an area long thought to be farthest removed from modern political movements. Just two weeks before

the Tribunal met, hundreds of delegates gathered in Palermo to establish a Sicilian Peasants' League. Calling for an end to the semi-feudal rule of the large landowners, the meeting followed the massacre of a dozen peasants outside Palermo who, on January 20, had been fired on while demonstrating for land to farm. Newspapers throughout the country were filled with fierce polemics about the role of the carabinieri in this bloody confrontation.

With the socialists organizing in both north and south, the Italian government itself seemed paralyzed. The prime minister, Giovanni Giolitti, of the moderate left, was barely able to hold on to power, the victim of a huge banking scandal. In January, the heads of several of the country's major banks had been arrested on charges of corruption. The popular anger grew when, later that month, the papers reported the assassination of the vice president of the Bank of Sicily shortly after he had denounced the bank's director for corruption.

Yet the disorders spreading through the country played into Baldini's hands. The judges, men of the propertied classes, were jittery. The times seemed to call less for a sense of noblesse oblige than for a circling of the wagons, a protection of the proper lines of authority. At least this is what the count's lawyer hoped as he rose to dispute the claims of the syphilitic wet nurse.

Amalia Bagnacavalli, Baldini began, had clearly failed to prove her case either through her own witnesses or through Dr. Ravaglia's report. Yet the judges had, in their wisdom, decided to get a second expert opinion to be absolutely sure that justice was done. The man they had called on, the illustrious Professor Roncati, was a sage choice. It was, in fact, difficult to judge which was greater, Baldini said, Roncati's vast scientific authority or his legendary integrity. After carefully examining all the evidence, he found, beyond any doubt, that Paola Olivelli had never had syphilis and so could never have given it to her wet nurse.

In desperation, the unfortunate woman's lawyer had cast about to find some way to save his doomed case. In Professor Majocchi, Baldini acknowledged, Barbieri had finally found someone willing to dispute Professor Roncati's findings. But who knew, he asked, how many other experts he had approached before finding one to accommodate him? Yet he might have saved himself the effort. It was not, Baldini argued, by unofficial opinions such as this, prepared as a result of the request of one of the parties in dispute, that one could seriously undermine the authoritative findings of a court-ordered investigation. Unlike Majocchi, Roncati had acted on behalf of the court, his only aim being to establish the truth and see that justice was served.

Having done his best to show that Amalia had not gotten syphilis from the foundling, yet aware that this was not the strongest part of his case, the hospital's lawyer moved to his second line of defense.

What if, for the sake of argument, he asked, the evidence had shown that Paola did in fact suffer from syphilis and had given her terrible disease to Amalia? Even in this case, the lawyer insisted, Amalia's claim would have no legal basis, for her injury would not have come through the fault or negligence of the hospital board or the foundling home doctors.

The board had seen to it that the foundling home was governed by an appropriate set of rules: babies who, following careful medical examination, showed no sign of having syphilis were given to women to nurse in the institution and then to outside wet nurses. Where there was any reason to suspect that a newborn might have syphilis, the baby was either given to a syphilitic woman to nurse or was put on artificial feeding. Through these regulations, Baldini argued, the board balanced two crucial needs: ensuring that wet nurses were not unduly exposed to the danger of contagion, and providing the abandoned babies with the kind of feeding that nature demanded and which for the newborns was the very source of life. Indeed, almost identical regulations were in place in foundling homes throughout the country.

Certainly, the hospital's lawyer said, even with these and similar precautionary measures, it was impossible to prevent all cases of infection, for in some cases the first signs of syphilis did not appear until many months after birth. To eliminate any danger for the wet nurse would mean depriving even those foundlings who had shown no sign of the disease of the milk they needed. To take such a heartless measure would, Baldini argued, be tantamount to condemning the vast majority of them to a certain death.

Baldini then moved confidently to what he knew was his strongest argument. Consider, he said, the implications of the contrasting testimony of Drs. Roncati and Majocchi. If we were simply to view these as the respectable opinions of two prominent men of science, we would have to conclude that in examining the facts before them, the foundling home doctors could have themselves reached different conclusions, each perfectly respectable. To attribute legal guilt to a doctor for his diagnosis, when the question before him was a matter of conflicting interpretation in the profession, would, the lawyer argued, be outrageous.

Here Baldini cited a series of court rulings to the effect that a doctor could not be held responsible for any error unless it could be shown that it resulted from his negligence, ignorance, or gross incompetence.

How, the lawyer asked, could anyone seriously claim that the foundling home doctors were guilty of negligence or even imprudence? Had not a man as learned, as respected, of such great integrity as Professor Roncati asserted, in his meticulous investigation, that the doctors had followed all necessary caution in this case? And if they were so fooled by the signs of syphilis that Paola showed before being given to Amalia — something, Baldini quickly added, that Professor Roncati had clearly excluded — how could one say that such a mistake was the effect of inexcusable ignorance, when one of the most illustrious men who honor their profession would have fallen into the same error?

The other side, Baldini told the judges, claimed that when an employer hired someone to do dangerous work, he must assume responsibility for the worker's safety. But in fact, said the lawyer, this legal obligation consisted only of the employer's obligation to ensure that conditions were as safe as they reasonably could be. Once he had done this, he could not be held responsible for any injuries that his workers suffered.

True, Baldini admitted, both modern science and modern legislation had moved in recent years toward offering workers greater protection. But if they already enjoyed the kind of expansive protection that the other side claimed, he asked, why was there so much controversy in parliament over new laws that the radical left was proposing to protect workers even more? If such protections already existed, why would the workers' movement be agitating for such legislation today?

Finally, said the lawyer, came the question of the payments that the hospital board had made in the past to women who had gotten syphilis from the babies. It was true that in those cases where wet nurses had contracted syphilis, the hospital had offered to pay for their treatment. But this could hardly be used to show that the hospital recognized a responsibility to compensate such women for their damages. Rather, such payments were required under the ministry circular of 1887 with the sole intention of protecting the public from the spread of syphilis.

In concluding, Baldini reminded the court that in a civil action such as the one before them, it was up to the accuser to prove her allegations, not up to the defense to disprove them. Yet, he asserted, the other side's version of the case had clearly been shown to be erroneous, the fault that they asserted had been shown never to have occurred, and the obligation that they claimed the hospital bore to Amalia had been shown to derive neither from the law nor from the contract under which she was hired.

Not only should the hospital board be found not guilty of the charges against it, urged Baldini, but the court should order the hospital's accuser to pay all of the legal expenses that her groundless suit had cost them.

Barbieri could sense that the case was not going well. His strategy had depended on Majocchi's having the last word, and when he introduced the doctor's report in his own concluding argument, he was confident that he had outwitted the opposition. But when he learned that Roncati had prepared a lengthy reply, a point-by-point refutation of Majocchi's critique, and that Majocchi's predecessor's rebuttal of the report was also being read into the record, he again grew nervous.

What could he do? It was the privilege of the defense to have the last word at trial, so he had to listen to Baldini as he triumphantly cited Roncati's rebuttal of Majocchi's attack. But he had to do something. A few days earlier he had received a copy of Roncati's text and given it to Majocchi. It took none of his powers of persuasion to get the new professor to prepare a reply.

Barely had Baldini finished his concluding argument when Barbieri sent the court what he termed an "addendum" to his own closing argument. Although he would not be able to present his rebuttal orally in court, he submitted it in writing, hoping to get around the requirement that the defense be heard last. He could hardly have been more aggressive, given the niceties required by court etiquette.

He had already offered his conclusions, he wrote the judges, when he had received an extraordinary document. It was a copy of the extrajudicial correspondence of the court's medical examiner for the case, Professor Roncati, regarding the opinion offered by Professor Majocchi. It was difficult to say, Barbieri wrote, which was greater, the inappropriateness of Roncati's combative tone or the impropriety of a man appointed by the court to abandon his impartial role and reveal himself so clearly to be the paladin of one of the parties in the case.

As for the scientific substance of Roncati's claims, wrote Barbieri, there could be no better response than from Professor Majocchi himself. Barbieri then inserted Majocchi's reply, which was in fact considerably longer than his initial report.

Majocchi began by saying that he could not begin to describe the unpleasant effect created by his reading of Roncati's reply. Given the acrimonious tone that the doctor had used and his failure to observe the most minimal respect toward his person, he added, he found it difficult to respond dispassionately, but he would do his best to treat the matter in the objective manner that science required.

This dispassionate approach, Majocchi argued, had marked his original opinion. He had reviewed the evidence, the fact that Paola Olivelli clearly suffered from congenital syphilis, that she developed the highly contagious secondary form of the disease, and that Amalia Bagnacavalli, shortly after nursing the baby, developed an initial chancre on her nipple, and he had demonstrated the causal relationship between the two. He had detailed all of this, he insisted, without any personal attack on his esteemed colleagues. Contrast this, said Majocchi, with Professor Roncati, who had launched an aggressive personal attack against him, full of expressions that had no place in a discussion of scientific questions.

His only desire, Majocchi insisted, was to bring the truth to light. The insinuation that his opinion was affected by a personal desire to support the wet nurse's argument was absurd. The hospital board well knew that if he were the sort of man whose conscience would allow him to adopt any argument he found convenient, he would have supported the hospital board, to which he was bound by daily professional bonds, rather than the illiterate wet nurse whom he had never even met.

Majocchi then went through all the details in Roncati's critique, displaying his own medical erudition. In each case he explained why the director was mistaken. Paola's blindness was indeed of a sort that syphilis could cause. That the two foundling home wet nurses did not contract syphilis from Paola meant only that she was not yet highly contagious when she was in the foundling home. The autopsy performed by Dr. Berti without microscopic investigation could easily miss the signs of syphilis. The disappearance of the ulcerated rash around Paola's mouth and backside on the application of a simple solution once she was back at the foundling home meant nothing. It was common knowledge among the experts that such sores could disappear quickly through the use of a common treatment. But this did nothing to affect the underlying infection, which then inevitably appeared elsewhere.

He could only conclude his reply to Professor Roncati, wrote Majocchi, by reiterating his earlier findings. The foundling Paola Olivelli had shown clear signs of having syphilis before she was given to Amalia, and she should have been sent to the ward for those babies suspected of having the disease. Of the fact that she then gave the disease to Amalia, there was no doubt.

Barbieri added a final plea of his own. The hospital, he declared, was so desperate, so lacking in evidence to support its case, that it was reduced to submitting the passionate and, at this late date in the proceedings, extrajudicial, opinion of a psychiatrist. Professor Roncati was undoubtedly a prominent man, a talented physician, the lawyer acknowledged. But in dealing with syphilis, he had neither the training nor the experience to give him any claim to expertise. Between the two men, the court could have no doubt of whose judgment it should trust.

Barbieri thought he might improve his chances by presenting the case as one that had implications that went well beyond the fate of an obscure peasant woman, so he built up to his concluding appeal by telling the judges that the seemingly small case offered them the chance to play a historic role. The Bologna foundling home, he charged, was responsible for sowing disease and disaster throughout the countryside. Now was the time for the court to put an end to this terrible plague. It was the judges' duty to see that the men responsible for ruining so many lives be, at last, held accountable for what they had done.

Barbieri was finished. He had done the best he could.

CHAPTER 13

The Tribunal Decides

THE JUDGES OF THE Tribunal reached their decision on Thursday, July 20, but kept it secret until they could prepare their written opinion, which they read in court on Tuesday, August 8.

Amalia took her seat in the courtroom. The previous three years had been a nightmare for her. Since her daughter's death she had twice gotten pregnant. The first time led to the birth of a son, Domenico, whom she had watched anxiously for signs of syphilis. They were not long in coming, and in September 1891 Domenico died, not yet two months old. The second time came a year later, and the baby, whom they named Giuseppe, was born a month early in the middle of the night. But he never took a breath. Stillborn, he was Amalia's third child to fall victim to her disease.

Nothing could bring Adele, Domenico, or Giuseppe back to life. But finally, Amalia hoped, the foundling home doctors would have to pay for what they had done to her. It was only three months after Giuseppe's stillbirth that the judges announced their ruling.

"Amalia Bagnacavalli," the decision began, "a young and robust peasant woman of Oreglia, in Vergato, was given a baby named Paola Olivelli to nurse by the foundling home in this city on March 24, 1890." Following a recitation of the facts of the case and of the previous court proceedings, the judges explained their view of the matter.

"Both the gravity of the case before us and the difficulty of determining the truth are exceptional, for what is at issue is whether it was through the fault of the doctors working for a respectable hospital of this city, which has served the public good in so many ways, that a poor, young woman lost the flower of her health, and was wounded in that holiest of affections, that of a mother, with the loss of her child, taken from her by a cruel disease."

The basic facts before them seemed clear enough, the judges said. It was true, they noted, that in their testimony Dr. Pinzani and Dr. Bruers had both suggested that Amalia might have suffered from syphilis previously. But Dr. Ravaglia determined that she developed the first signs of syphilis only after returning the foundling. On this decisive point — who had infected whom — the judges cited the "illustrious syphilologist," Professor Majocchi, as having offered the best response that science could give.

Before reviewing his analysis, the judges paused to justify their reliance on his opinion, an opinion whose legal standing Count Isolani's lawyer had fought so hard to dispute. It was true, the judges observed, that Majocchi did not have the standing of a court-appointed expert. But judges, they insisted, were entirely free to determine which evidence they found most convincing, whatever its source.

It was a basic principle of logic, they asserted, that if Amalia contracted syphilis from nursing an infant, as shown by the appearance of an initial chancre on her breast, and she got it after nursing the foundling, the foundling must have already had syphilis. The only exception would be if it had been shown that Amalia had then been nursing some other child who had syphilis. But, the judges stated, the defense had not provided the slightest evidence of the existence of any such baby.

There remained the question, they continued, of whether Paola had suffered from syphilis from birth or whether she somehow contracted the disease later. This question was of the utmost importance because if she contracted the disease only shortly before she was given to Amalia, the earlier signs of ill health could not have been symptoms of syphilis, and the foundling home doctors would be blameless.

But here, the judges ruled, it was ironically the hospital's own evidence that showed that Paola was born with the disease. If she were not born with it, she could only have contracted it from one of her wet nurses in the foundling home. Hospital records showed that up to the time that she was given to Amalia, she was nursed by two women. Yet Dr. Ravaglia had carefully examined both of them in February 1891, a year after they had nursed Paola, and found them both to be free of the disease. It therefore followed that if Paola suffered from syphilis, she must have been born with it. She could have gotten it nowhere else.

In an aside, one that would enrage Dr. Ravaglia and Dr. Roncati, the judges expressed their dim view of the quality of the two court-ordered medical investigations. Both doctors, according to the judges, had committed the error of failing to view the various symptoms shown by the baby, and by her wet nurse, in their totality. They failed to place the sequence of symptoms, as they appeared first in Paola and then in Amalia, in a broader picture that would make clear the causal link of the one to the other. And so these two men of science, the judges concluded, ignored one of the principal canons of logic governing medical science. Had they only used a different method in their inquiry, namely the truly rational one used by Majocchi, they would have had to recognize that Paola was born syphilitic and had given the French disease to Bagnacavalli.

The Bolognese judges' reference to syphilis as the "French" disease followed a curious practice that was as old as the malady itself. People everywhere believed that the disease's origins lay elsewhere. Equated with moral depravity, syphilis had from its earliest days been blamed on others. The British called it "the French pox"; in France it was called "the German plague"; the Florentines had, in previous centuries, called it "the Neapolitan disease"; and the Japanese called it "the Chinese" or "Portuguese disease." The name "syphilis" was itself an Italian innovation. In 1530, a doctor from Padua published a Latin poem in which he linked the disease to a shepherd named Sifilo, who, in ancient mythology, had offended Apollo and was punished by being given terrible sores all over his skin. It was from that time that the name "syphilis" began to be used.[1]

Amalia found the proceedings impossible to follow. They were conducted in Italian, a language she did not speak and barely understood, so different was it from her Bolognese dialect. But even had she spoken Italian she would still have had trouble, for the arcane, legal language of the court came from another world. The only way she could tell how the case was going was to look at her lawyer. From his expression now she had reason to think they had a chance.

Barbieri was excited, but he knew that the judges still had to rule on the crucial point. The hospital lawyers' argument had two main pillars. While the judges had just demolished one of them, they only now began to reveal their views of the other, the claim that even if Amalia had been infected by Paola, the foundling home doctors could not be blamed.

It soon became uncomfortably clear to Barbieri that although the judges found Professors Ravaglia and Roncati's opinions deficient on the first point, they gave them more credence on the second.

Certainly, the judges ruled, the baby showed signs of having syphilis. Among these were the appearance of the moist pustules in her mouth and around her backside, which, especially in conjunction with a runny nose and her severe emaciation, were clear indications of the disease. But when did these signs first appear? The evidence demonstrated, the judges said, that they appeared after March 24, 1890 — after Paola left the foundling home.

The judges reviewed the evidence as they saw it. The baby had been born at term, at normal birth weight, and arrived at the foundling home with a certificate from the maternity hospital saying that both she and her mother showed no sign of syphilis. After five or six days at the foundling home, she ran a fever from a case of pleurisy, which left her with a deviated spinal column. Her emaciation also dated from her time in the foundling home, but there too the doctors had good reason to believe that it was a result of the pleurisy. True enough, the baby also suffered from an infection of her eyes that left her blind, but as Professor Majocchi himself observed, this was not necessarily a sign of syphilis unless it had come together with the other symptoms of the disease. Here it was also worth observing, said the judges, that, by the time she was given to Amalia, Paola had lived for 87 days, and syphilis specialists agreed that three months is the period in which babies with congenital syphilis most often showed the first clear signs of the disease. Certainly, as Professor Roncati himself admitted, cases were known of children showing the first signs much later, sometimes only at puberty, but the foundling home doctors could hardly be accused of that degree of negligence or professional ignorance that would rise to the level of legal guilt for having relied on the likelihood that Paola did not have syphilis. Indeed, the three-month rule of thumb was so well recognized that the Austrian government had made it a policy that in all of the foundling homes in the empire, babies suspected of having syphilis could be given out to wet nurses if, after three months, they developed no clear signs of the disease.

It was in the very nature of medicine, the judges argued, to have many different opinions and competing hypotheses. It would be barbarous, not to say a blow against science, they concluded, to take a respectable opinion on which a doctor based his diagnosis and treatment and then, when that diagnosis was proved wrong, hold him legally at fault for the damages that followed.

In the current controversy, the judges ruled, the lively polemics between Professor Roncati and Professor Majocchi showed just how impossible it would be to hold the foundling home doctors guilty of negligence or of actionable ignorance. Accordingly, they found the hospital board not guilty. The charges were dismissed.

Now Amalia was left with nothing, her hopes, encouraged by her legal champion, extinguished. Barbieri himself, although always inclined to put the best face on things, was, for the moment at least, at a loss.

At the offices of the hospital board, however, the mood was bright. Count Isolani's relief on hearing the Tribunal's decision was all the greater because of the stack of similar complaints that had been piling up. The reports of peasant women who were blaming the foundling home for their syphilis seemed never-ending, and the Bagnacavalli case, he was convinced, had emboldened not only these poor unfortunates but a whole assortment of rural mayors, town doctors, and, what was worse, lawyers, whose threatening letters littered his desk. Now, vindicated by the Tribunal, he thought he was again in a position to fend them off.

Many of these cases involved women who had gotten syphilis years earlier but, hearing about Amalia's suit, had thought that they too should get some kind of compensation from the foundling home. Such was the story of Rosa Magelli, the woman who had testified at Amalia's trial and who had contracted syphilis from a foundling in 1884. Learning of the suit, Rosa had returned to the syphilis clinic, this time with both of her infected children, and asked that the foundling home pay for their care. Although advised by his lawyers that the 1887 ministry directive required the hospital to pay for such treatment, Count Isolani was now eager to do something about this drain on his budget. On August 17, 1893, just a week after learning of his victory over Amalia, he informed Rosa that the hospital would give her one final payment of 300 lire, but only if she signed away her right to ask the hospital for anything ever again.

At the same time, the count took care of another lingering case, one that involved a woman who had been forced to serve as a wet nurse at the foundling home.

In 1888, Stella Fiorini, a young unwed woman from the country-side who had been working as a servant in Bologna, found herself pregnant. Her circumstances were typical of the unwed women driven by desperation to the maternity hospital. Living as a servant in the city was a common stage of life for girls from poor rural families, and they all too often were preyed on by their employers. But whether taken advantage of by an employer or seduced by an importuning lover, these young women faced losing their jobs as soon as their pregnancy became known. For such women, the maternity hospital offered some sanctuary, and with it the hope of one day being able to resume their former lives.

When she could hide her bulging belly no longer, Stella went the few blocks to Bologna's maternity hospital, where she spent the final weeks of her pregnancy. After her baby's birth, the hospital sent her to the foundling home to serve as an internal wet nurse. Her first syphilitic sore appeared a few weeks later.

Count Isolani saw Stella's case as another example of the hemorrhaging of hospital resources that it was his job to stop. Her treatments had done no apparent good. In fact, they seemed to make her symptoms worse. He told Stella that he would see that she got one final payment of 280 lire if she would renounce all further claims against the hospital. On August 29, the servant signed a legal document to this effect. She was paid 100 lire on the spot, with the remaining 180 lire to appear in installments of 15 lire each month for the next year.

Isolani seemed to believe that the hospital board was now in the clear, but his lawyer, Odoardo Ferrari, was much less sure. The hospital had won its case against Amalia, but the count's behavior had him worried. On September 1, Ferrari sent a warning.

They were fortunate, he wrote to the count, that the Tribunal had accepted their argument that the hospital board was not responsible for Amalia Bagnacavalli's infection. But, he reminded him, the court had shown great deference to Professor Majocchi and embraced his opinion that the baby had indeed been the source of Amalia's syphilis. It was well to recall that Majocchi had also accused the foundling home of unnecessarily putting rural women at risk by failing to use the latest scientific advances to identify the early signs of syphilis in the infants. It would be prudent, he advised, not to wait for any more such cases before introducing new procedures to lessen the danger of contagion.

A day later, the count received yet another warning from the lawyer, saying that he should not assume that because they had won their case, the court's decision had somehow been inevitable. The victory had been based on the Tribunal's ruling that an employer was not responsible for the harm done to an employee in the course of performing her duty. But times were changing, Ferrari said, and other courts had recently been taking a different view. Increasingly, a new theory was gaining ground, holding employers responsible for their employees' injuries.

To protect them from judges who might adopt this new legal philosophy, the lawyer recommended that the hospital revise the booklet each wet nurse received when she took a foundling. He proposed adding a disclaimer: "If the foundling is given to a wet nurse and accepted by her with the appearance of good health, and the wet nurse subsequently develops syphilis from nursing the infant, the foundling home will incur no civil responsibility."

Ferrari added that it would also be a good idea to make the woman sign a form when she took the child, stating that she agreed to these terms.

Yet new cases kept cropping up. One of the more memorable ones came about shortly after the lawyer made his recommendations, when the doctor of the remote mountain town of Castiglione wrote to the foundling home about an epidemic of syphilis there, all caused by the arrival of a single foundling. The report was so serious that the foundling home director asked Dr. Berti to undertake the arduous winter trip to Castiglione to investigate. In early December, the doctor returned with a dismal story to tell.

In March, one of Bologna's midwives had brought a baby girl to the foundling home, along with a certificate stating that the baby's mother was free of syphilis. The baby was premature; she weighed only four and a half pounds and seemed weak, her skin cold. Although over the next days she suffered from various ills, none was deemed symptomatic of syphilis and, because she began to grow and show signs of improvement, on May 12 she was given to Annunziata Biacchesi to take home.

Annunziata had already given birth to seven children of her own. One had died in infancy, and another four died of diphtheria or scarlet fever. Only her two most recent children, both girls, survived. Amid her various childbirths, she had also nursed four babies from Bologna's foundling home.

Within a few weeks, this fifth foundling took ill. She lost her voice, her nose kept running, and she nursed poorly. Afraid that she was not getting any nourishment, Annunziata alternated frustrating attempts at nursing her with trying to squirt milk directly into her mouth and, when that did not work, giving her the milk in a spoon or on her finger. Because Annunziata still worked in the fields, she occasionally left the baby with her sister-in-law. Six months pregnant with her first child, this sister-in-law, Gelsomina, did her best to comfort the child, even giving the foundling her milkless breast to suckle in the hopes of calming her.

Annunziata eventually took the child to the town doctor. He said that although he was not sure, the baby might have syphilis, and she should come see him again at the sign of any new symptom. But before she could return, the baby died. When the doctor came to examine the infant's body, Annunziata showed him a sore that had just appeared on her left nipple. Two months later, she began to suffer from the full-blown symptoms of the disease.

Shortly after Annunziata noticed her sore, her sister-in-law was terrified to find that she too had such a chancre. Both women soon suffered from genital and cervical sores and huge sores in their mouths. Before long, Annunziata's two daughters showed the first signs of the disease as well. This pattern was reported in a large number of other cases, where syphilitic mothers transmitted their disease not only to their nursing infants but also to somewhat older children. For the youngest, it seems most likely that infection came through nursing, but for children of ages three, four, or five, the matter is far from clear. Could they still have been placed occasionally at their mother's breast, or was there some other means of infection? Doctors at the time attributed such transmission to other kinds of bodily contact between mother and child, yet its exact nature remains something of a medical mystery.

When Annunziata noticed her first sore, her husband was off working in Tuscany, following the common practice in Bologna's mountains of seasonal migration in search of work. When he came home, she was too embarrassed to tell him that she had the plague, and so that first night he "used" her, as Dr. Berti put it in his report, oblivious to any danger. His brother similarly "used" Gelsomina, and, not surprisingly, both men soon developed the disease themselves.

In short, Berti concluded, from the one syphilitic foundling, six members of the wet nurse's family had ended up getting the disease. He had left them with the ingredients for mercury skin rubs, as well as mercury pills, but unfortunately, he reported, the two children refused to take the pills and the parents were able to apply the noxious ointment to the children's bodies only with great difficulty.

Reading this report upset the count. His only consolation was that no lawyer had gotten wind of it, at least not yet.

CHAPTER 14

Amalia's Appeal

WHILE COUNT ISOLANI was doing his best, with his lawyer's help, to unburden the hospital of the accumulated claims made by the syphilitic women, he was not especially worried about the reappearance of Amalia's case. But Amalia's lawyer was not yet willing to concede defeat, and two weeks after the Tribunal read its decision, he sent in his appeal to Bologna's higher court.

Amalia herself knew nothing of the Court of Appeals and could not image how her case, which had already lasted so long and had been so solemnly decided in court, could still offer her any hope. Barbieri did his best to explain that she had a right to appeal, and he tried to lift her spirits by saying that she still had a chance to get justice.

After the court's decision, another man might have sought to limit his losses and drop the case or try to cut a deal with the foundling home out of court. Neither solution appealed to Barbieri. Count Isolani felt vindicated by the Tribunal's ruling and, offended by Amalia's presumption in bringing him to court, was not likely to want to reward her now. Barbieri also knew that there would be little in it for him even if the count were willing to give something to

Amalia. He would certainly not want to encourage the lawyer responsible for causing him so much aggravation, and if, having won at the Tribunal, the count were to pay him anything at all, Barbieri knew that it would be pathetically little.

But there was another reason that Barbieri did not give up. Through the newspaper coverage of the trial, along with the distribution of his briefs in published form and the comments in Bologna's small community of lawyers, he had already attracted a certain amount of attention. Both his oratorical powers and his legal skills had already become better known, all in a context that cast him as a defender of the poor and downtrodden, a champion of modern science and enlightened government. Taking the suit to the higher level promised him even greater visibility. Proud of the closing arguments to the Tribunal, which he had recently published, he looked forward to being able to wax even more eloquently in his argument to the appeals court, an argument whose publication would advance his reputation even further.

Barbieri spent a great deal of time over the next three months preparing his brief. Following appeals court procedures, he had to submit it in writing, and when he took it to the court in late November, already printed by Azzoguidi, it was seventy-five pages long.

He did his best to cast the case as the story of a poor but virtuous young woman who was victimized by a powerful exploiter. A country woman of spotless reputation, the pride of her family, he wrote, was poisoned by one of the most hideous evils to plague humanity, all as the result of the foundling home's negligence. Yet, tragically, the Tribunal had failed to see that justice be served. In absolving others of responsibility for her misfortune, Barbieri argued, the Tribunal had in effect decided that Amalia alone should pay for what had been done to her.

Barbieri's strategy, since he could not call any witnesses, was to convince the appeals court judges that the Tribunal had misinterpreted both the evidence and the law. The judges had erred in finding that the foundling home doctors had followed their own rules. The regulations, Barbieri argued, required that before an infant could be given out, the doctors must perform a detailed physical examination. Yet, he insisted, the judges would look in vain in the trial transcript for any good evidence that such an examination had actually been performed. True, Dr. Pinzani had testified that he himself had examined the baby, but in his testimony he said absolutely nothing about just what this consisted of and had given no evidence to support his claim. This was not a case, Barbieri argued, that hinged on mere disagreements among conflicting medical opinions, as the Tribunal ruled. It was a case about the failure to follow the most basic rules of prudence and diligence that governed the work of all physicians.

Having skewered the foundling home doctors, Barbieri turned to the hospital board itself. The Tribunal, he told the appeals court judges, had failed to rule on the board's own fault, its own negligence. The hospital had argued that Amalia's case was unusual and that if the foundling home were required to keep babies on artificial feeding until even the most remote possibility of syphilis was past, the result would be a slaughter of little innocents. But just how unusual was Amalia's story? Barbieri asked. In fact, he told the judges, her case was simply one in a long series.

The foundling home, he noted, had produced 116 receipts for its payments to women whom it had infected over the past decade, and this was only a small glimpse of the enormity of the damage the home had wrought. Many, many young women whose lives had been ruined were too ashamed of the disease to make themselves known, so there was no way of knowing the true extent of the scourge. The hospital board looked out only for the interests of the foundling home while ignoring the equally — indeed, more important — problem of the health of the young wet nurses. It was a basic principle of humanity, and of justice, argued the lawyer, that faced with the danger of infecting a healthy woman, it was better to run the risk that a foundling placed on artificial feeding might not survive.

Nothing better demonstrated the hospital's negligence, Barbieri maintained, than its not having bothered to get a modern microscope. It took this case, with the alarm raised by Professor Majocchi, to prompt the hospital to finally acquire the necessary equipment the previous summer.

The foundling home's greatest enemy was syphilis, the lawyer asserted, and it should certainly be expected to take every possible means to prevent its spread. Yet it had not taken the most elementary precaution of all, for it had never bothered to hire a syphilis expert to examine the babies before they were sent out to nurse. The hospital board had left matters in the hands of such doctors as Pinzani and Bruers, reputable physicians to be sure, but so lacking in expertise on syphilis that, as shown in this case, they could not recognize its most obvious warning signs.

In the face of this inexplicable indifference, Barbieri asked, could the court fail to hear the cry of a poor mother who had relied on assurances that no child showing even a single sign of the disease would be given out to nurse? Could the court fail to be moved by the woman's naïve belief in assurances that the baby she was given had undergone a rigorous and complete medical examination? Could the court ignore the cry of such a woman who, because she was foolish enough to trust the hospital to follow its own rules, had been robbed of her health, seen her children die painful deaths, and watched her husband be ravaged by the disease?

If, he argued, from the very first of these cases, instead of contenting itself with the shameful gesture of giving such women a few lire, the hospital board had given the foundling home a laboratory for microscopic analysis, hired a syphilis expert, and been quicker to send children showing suspicious signs to the ward for artificial feeding, just think of how much human suffering could have been avoided.

With this, Barbieri was finished. To learn whether his arguments had made an impression on the appeals court he was going to have to wait quite a while, for the chief judge, apparently in no hurry to conclude the case, gave Isolani's lawyer four months to prepare his response.

Now that Amalia's appeal was under way, the count's earlier optimism had begun to fade. At a board meeting on Wednesday, January 10, 1894, he told his colleagues that they needed to introduce new measures. In the secrecy of the boardroom he could admit what his lawyers were busily denying in court. The Bagnacavalli case demonstrated that they were giving foundlings to wet nurses without observing all the necessary precautions. He had spoken again with Dr. Pinzani and urged the doctors to observe greater care in the future.

The board had a medical advisory committee, which had recently sent in its own advice. Because the first symptom of congenital syphilis often appeared several weeks after birth, they told the count, the only way to stop infecting the rural women was to keep the babies in the foundling home for at least their first three months. Although this would not eliminate the problem entirely, it would drastically reduce the number of cases.

All this would make sense, the count told the board, if they had a way of keeping alive the large number of babies who would have to remain in the foundling home if such a rule were in place. But the unfortunate fact was that they did not.

As these discussions were going on, the hospital board's lawyers submitted their final brief to the Bologna appeals court. While in their private advice to the board they were urging that dramatic action be taken to stop infecting so many rural women, in court they continued to deny that hospital procedures had been deficient in any way.

Two days after receiving the brief, the judges called a public session in order to hear from the defendants. It was Tuesday, March 20. Pietro Baldini urged the judges to reaffirm the Tribunal's ruling that neither the hospital nor the foundling home doctors bore any legal responsibility for Amalia's plight.

Not content merely to have the lower court decision upheld,

Baldini called on the appeals court judges to overturn the portion of the Tribunal findings that had gone against the hospital. The Tribunal, he reminded them, had ruled that Paola had syphilis when she was given to Amalia and had subsequently infected her. This, he argued, could not be sustained. It was up to the accuser to prove that Paola had had syphilis, not up to the hospital to prove that she had not. The testimony had been contradictory, with Dr. Dalmonte claiming that the baby was syphilitic and the foundling home doctors claiming that she wasn't. All rested on the expert opinion of the outside medical consultants. Both of the experts appointed by the court, Baldini pointed out, had cast strong doubt on Amalia's claim, and only Amalia's own expert had argued in its favor. In ruling for Amalia on this point, Baldini insisted, the members of the Tribunal had committed an egregious error, for in effect they had dismissed the two expert opinions that they themselves had commissioned in favor of an opinion that had no legal standing at all.

On the other hand, the lawyer said, the Tribunal had wisely ruled that even if Amalia had been infected by the foundling, the hospital could not be held legally responsible. By its very nature, the nursing of foundlings, even with all possible precautions, presented the risk of contagion. Baldini then repeated his earlier arguments about how the foundling home had careful procedures to ensure that the babies given to wet nurses showed no sign of syphilis, and he again cited the testimony of the two court-appointed experts to the effect that the foundling home doctors had no way of knowing or even suspecting that Paola had the disease.

A week later, the five judges met to discuss the appeal. Although the case had gone on for almost four years and had by now generated a massive file, they came to a decision surprisingly quickly. Over the next two weeks they prepared their lengthy written text and informed the parties that on April 24 they should appear in court to hear it read.

Barbieri sat anxiously on one side of the courtroom with his client, while Baldini and his colleague Ferrari sat on the other. Again the judges sat at a table in front of the courtroom.

The case before them, they explained, consisted of not one but two appeals. The hospital, for its part, had appealed the Tribunal's finding that Amalia Bagnacavalli was infected with syphilis by her contact with the foundling Paola Olivelli. Amalia had appealed the Tribunal's ruling that the hospital was not responsible for the harm done to her. As a result, said the judges, they had in effect been required to retry the entire case. They turned first to the hospital's appeal, considering the question of how Amalia got syphilis.

It is not clear how much hope the count and his lawyers held out for this appeal. The question was of no legal consequence, the appeal made more to satisfy the foundling home doctors than to serve their own cause. It is likely that Baldini, savvy attorney that he was, was not surprised by the result. But he was certainly taken aback by the ferocity with which the judges proceeded to rebut his arguments. The judges were clearly incensed by Baldini's suggestion that they were somehow bound to accept the conclusions offered by their court-appointed advisers. Baldini's argument that the court had an obligation to cede to the authority of such experts, the judges ruled, had absolutely no validity. His view, if adopted, would lead the judges to become the servants of the men they appointed to serve them. In arranging for outside experts, they proclaimed, the court did nothing to limit its authority to decide for itself which arguments were most persuasive.

With this point cleared away, the judges turned to their own examination of the medical evidence. All the experts agreed that a syphilitic infant could transmit her disease to the woman who nursed her. The evidence was also clear, and admitted by virtually all witnesses in a position to know, that within weeks of nursing Paola, Amalia had developed an initial syphilitic chancre. Such a sore could only appear in a woman who had not previously had syphilis. Against this, the hospital had been reduced to arguing that Amalia might have contracted the disease from some other source. But, the judges ruled, they could give such a supposition no weight, for there was no evidence to support it.

The fact that Amalia contracted syphilis through nursing in the spring of 1890 was absolutely clear, the judges ruled. By contrast, the question of whether Paola had had syphilis had been hotly disputed. Yet when the evidence was examined properly, the judges concluded, Professor Majocchi had clearly offered the most convincing account.

Barbieri heard the judges' reasoning with rising excitement. He allowed himself to hope that this day would be different from the one in the lower court several months earlier. But he could scarcely fail to recall that at a comparable point in the reading of the Tribunal's decision, the judges had been just as favorable to his side. The crucial test would come when the appeals court judges turned to the question of whether the hospital should be found legally responsible for what had happened to Amalia.

This court, they announced, could not agree with the way that the Tribunal had viewed the case. The regulations governing the foundling home held that those babies who, following careful examination, showed no grounds for suspicion that they had syphilis were to be given to healthy wet nurses. Those babies showing any sign of the disease were either to be given to a syphilitic wet nurse or placed on artificial feeding. If Paola had shown any suspicious sign, it had been the foundling home doctors' responsibility not to place her with Amalia.

Yet the evidence clearly showed, said the judges, that by the time they gave Paola to Amalia, the baby had already exhibited a variety of symptoms that suggested that she might have the disease. True, the sores on her lip and around her backside had not yet appeared, but she had already suffered from the eye infection that left her blind and the emaciation that was so marked that Amalia at first did not want to take her. In the face of these symptoms, ruled the judges, and especially considering the girl's unknown origins, it had been the doctors' obligation to place her under close observation and certainly not allow her to leave the foundling home until at least the full three months had passed, when the first signs of syphilis ordinarily appeared.

The hospital had claimed that even if there had been some negligence on the part of the foundling home doctors, the hospital itself bore no legal responsibility. Baldini had argued that an employer who hired professional experts could not be held responsible for any damage they did in the course of their specialized work. But this argument, ruled the judges, was groundless, for it rested on a distinction among kinds of employees that was nowhere to be found in the text of the law. Neither doctors nor their employers enjoyed any special legal status.

The Tribunal's decision was in error, the appeals court judges declared. Count Isolani and the hospital board were legally responsible for the material and moral damages done to the woman from Vergato. Pending a later hearing at which the exact amount of these damages could be determined, the hospital board was to pay Amalia 15 lire each month. Furthermore, the court ruled, the hospital board was to pay all of the legal expenses she had incurred in bringing her suit.

Barbieri was elated. Finally he would be taken seriously as a lawyer to be reckoned with in Bologna. For all those who thought him crazy for devoting so many hundreds of hours to this case, he now felt vindicated. He had proven them all wrong. We can only imagine Amalia's reaction. After years of suffering, she had finally won. But it was in the nature of peasants from the mountains to be suspicious of such victories, not to allow themselves too much hope, not to get carried away with dreams of a better future. Amalia had plenty of reason to celebrate but also the good sense not to allow her hopes to get the better of her.

CHAPTER 15

The Loan

O N TUESDAY, MAY 1, Count Isolani found a copy of the appeals court decision on his desk. He wrote two notes in the margins of the front page for his attorney, Odoardo Ferrari. The first asked him to consult with Pietro Baldini and then to give his opinion on whether they should appeal to the Supreme Court. The second asked if he thought that they should fire the foundling home doctors. This, Isolani believed, might lessen the risk that the Bagnacavalli case would be followed by a series of similar suits.

Ferrari met with Baldini and reported back to the count. They said nothing about letting the doctors go, but both strongly favored an appeal. At stake, they argued, was a principle that had dire consequences not only for the Bologna hospitals but for the employers of doctors throughout the country, at all levels. If those who employed such men of medicine were now held responsible for any harm they did to their patients, the impact would be enormous. Not only would city hospitals be held to account for the doctors who worked there, but even small towns would be responsible for what their doctors did. A hospital board, or a town government, could not oversee a doctor's work with his patients and second-guess his judgment. It was outrageous, Ferrari wrote, for the court to hold them responsible for their doctors' mistakes.

The same day that the count received the appeals court decision, Amalia and her husband, Luigi, took the train to Bologna for an appointment that must have filled them with foreboding. Since they had filed their suit against the Bologna hospital, Count Isolani and the board had refused to pay for the expensive treatment that they were getting, partly at the syphilis clinic in Bologna but mostly at home. The cost of the trips and of the mercury and iodine had already amounted to hundreds of lire. And then there was the terrifying problem of their legal expenses. Barbieri had told them from the beginning not to worry, that the hospital board would, in the end, pay for everything. But it had been years now, and while they had only the vaguest notion of what the sums involved, they knew that Barbieri was spending freely in preparing the case. There was also the question of Dr. Majocchi. Without him, they would have had no chance at all, but exactly how he would be paid was not clear. Barbieri did his best to reassure them. The doctor, too, he said, would be taken care of by the hospital after they won.

When, the previous year, the Tribunal had ruled against them, Barbieri had to make the difficult decision of whether to abandon the case or to forge ahead with an appeal. He had explained to Amalia that, if they dropped the suit, she would get nothing and he would not be able to help her pay her medical bills. If they appealed, he told her, he was confident they could win, and then the hospital would both pay her bills and compensate her for all the damage it had done. But the costs of the case had grown to the point, he said, that they could only continue their battle if they could find someone to help them pay their debts.

Fortunately, the lawyer told Amalia, he knew a man who could be helpful, a man who came from her hometown, from Vergato, who now had a modest hotel in the city. Barbieri had told the man, Nono Veggetti, how certain he was that Amalia would win her suit and how with victory would come a large sum of money from which she could easily repay the loan. Although he ordinarily would not lend money to someone as poor as Amalia, said Barbieri, Veggetti was willing to make an exception in her case.

Amalia was undoubtedly ill at ease about all this, but her lawyer assured her that he would take care of everything.

Having gotten Amalia's agreement, the lawyer had arranged for the Vergato notary who had drafted his original agreement with Amalia to draft a new contract. This one gave Veggetti the authority to act as Amalia's legal representative, loaning her money and dealing with her creditors. It was only after he had arranged for the loan that Barbieri sent in his appeal of the Tribunal's decision.

Now, in the wake of their appeals court victory, Amalia wanted to know when she would get her money from the hospital. The lawyer explained that it might still take some time. While in the interim the hospital would pay her 15 lire each month, she would, unfortunately, have to come up with more money. The problem, he said, was that they would have new expenses in preparing for the hearing that would determine how much money she would get. There was also the problem of the additional expenses they would face if the hospital appealed to the Supreme Court.

They had little choice, he told her, but to get more money from her patron, Signor Veggetti. This was why she and Luigi found themselves on the train to Bologna on May 1. With the stakes getting higher, Barbieri was no longer comfortable placing his affairs in the hands of the notary in the mountains. In all future dealings with Amalia, he would work only with his close business associate, Alberto Pallotti, a notary whose office was in the same palazzo as his.

Amalia's ability to focus on these financial matters, never very great, was now further undermined because she was again pregnant. It was hard to concentrate on anything other than her own physical travails and those of her family. She worried that this pregnancy would end no better than her last one.

Barbieri found himself in a difficult situation of his own. Over the course of the appeal his expenses kept growing, yet compensation still seemed to be far off. Until the appeals court ruling, not even Veggetti had been willing to lend them much. Now, with the victory in hand, Barbieri lost no time telling the hotel owner of Amalia's victory and persuading him to provide a larger loan. For Barbieri this was crucial, because the longer the case went on, the more creditors he accumulated. If he gave up now, neither he nor Amalia would receive anything. Getting a loan for Amalia meant getting money to keep his creditors at bay.

At Pallotti's office, Amalia and Luigi were joined by Veggetti, and the notary proceeded to read the long, complex document that he had drawn up according to Barbieri's instructions. Relations between notaries and lawyers were not always so harmonious. The lawyer's greater prestige was a sore point, in part because a notary was required to take only two years of studies in the law faculty, but lawyers had to complete the full course. When some notaries of the time, in an effort to improve their status, suggested that the government require a law degree for them as well, they were accused of overreaching. As one member of parliament put it, a notary "must know little, but know it well."[1] What was crucial was that the documents they prepared cover every eventuality and leave no room for later disagreement. Barbieri had full confidence in Pallotti and used his services whenever possible.

The document that the notary drafted recorded Veggetti's loan to Amalia and Luigi of 5,000 lire, a huge amount of money. Even if Amalia and Luigi were healthy, they could each not hope to earn more than about one lire per day for farm labor, and such labor was seasonal at best. In exchange for the loan, they promised to give him one-third of all the money that they would ultimately receive from the hospital. Should they not receive anything, or should they get less than 15,000 lire, they would still owe Veggetti the full amount they had borrowed. In the meantime, the contract required them to pay him 7 percent a year in interest, plus the tax levied by the government on the 5,000 lire, each of these to be paid for the full year in advance.

Given Amalia's lack of experience in either business or law — the contract read — and given the complete faith she placed in Nono

Veggetti, she named him her special representative, legally able to act in her place in using the money he had just loaned her to pay her various bills. The contract specified that on the day the agreement was signed, Veggetti would take 2,500 lire of the loan to pay off as many of these debts as he could, including the money owed Azzoguidi, who had printed Barbieri's various briefs.

Only one item was specifically excluded. Amalia's lawyer's fees were not covered in this agreement. Here the notary's language — suggested by Barbieri himself — stood out from the bureaucratic style that marked the rest of the document: Amalia's lawyer, it read, who first and foremost among all men deserved compensation — the man who had not only argued her cause with the greatest ability and diligence but who had demonstrated selflessness so complete that no praise could do justice to it — had insisted that he be given nothing. He asked that proper payment be postponed to that time when the competent judicial authorities, in their final decision, fixed the amount that the opposing party would pay him for his efforts.

Amalia felt sick. She was at sea in this world where people could talk of thousands of lire as if it were nothing and wholly baffled by the legal document, in a language she did not know and which in any case she could not read. But even if Dr. Dalmonte had read the document, he would have been terrified by the amount of money she was borrowing. Even the chief physician of Bologna's foundling home was paid only 1,000 lire per year. Barbieri's assurance that she should not worry, that they would get that much money and more from the hospital, might have eased her mind a bit. But only a bit.

A week later, on May 8, Amalia and Luigi had to make yet another trip into the city, this time to return to the Bologna syphilis clinic. But unlike their previous visits, when the assistant doctors had given them their mercury treatments, this time they were seen by the chief doctor, Domenico Majocchi himself. It was a visit that Barbieri had arranged.

Majocchi gave each one a careful examination and wrote up his report in the form of a letter that Barbieri would submit to the court as part of his brief justifying the amount of damages to be awarded. It was now four years since Amalia and Luigi had contracted syphilis. At this point, wrote Majocchi, their health was quite good. They had passed through the virulent, infectious stage of the disease and were now in what doctors considered the third phase. The major symptom of the disease was the pain they felt in their bones, but it was not debilitating. Majocchi himself took some credit for their surviving the secondary stage so well, praising them for how carefully they had undertaken the noxious treatments given by the clinic.

Barbieri had asked Majocchi to describe for the court what Amalia and Luigi could look forward to as the third phase of the disease ran its course. The doctor offered a list of potential effects, noting that cases varied and that it was impossible to predict exactly what would happen to them.

They were likely, he reported, to develop lesions in their subcutaneous connective tissue, and these would ulcerate and radiate throughout their bodies. Lesions were also apt to develop in their muscle tissue, further weakening them. The disease was especially likely to affect their bones, permanently deforming them. That this was already under way in the case of Amalia and Luigi was clear from the pains they both complained of.

But the ravages of syphilis in its third phase did not stop there. The internal organs were also often affected, especially the liver and kidneys, both of which could become impaired. Most serious of all, as the syphilis developed it was likely to affect their nervous systems, both their brains and their spinal cords. Common symptoms included a loss of motor ability and, ultimately, an assortment of psychiatric disorders, which, in the worst cases, could drive the sufferer to madness before ending in death. Finally, the doctor observed, both Amalia and Luigi might well suffer further genital disorders, with lesions developing in Luigi's testicles and Amalia's ovaries.

Majocchi concluded by insisting that Amalia and Luigi begin a course of iodine mercury treatments, aimed at preventing, or at least limiting, the effects of the third stage.

Across town their lawyer was putting the final touches on a formal request to the president of the Tribunal of Bologna. He had spent a great deal of time enumerating all the expenses he had incurred in preparing Amalia's case, as well as listing all the time he had spent in preparing its various phases. What he delivered to the court later that day was a request for the huge sum of 10,008 lire. The lengthy list contained ninety-three separate entries, next to which were two columns of numbers. The first recorded Barbieri's expenses and the second the value of his time. Listed in chronological order, it began with the entry "Long initial informational session," referring to the first day that Amalia had come to see him and for which he requested 30 lire. The second item requested 50 lire for his time and 7 lire in expenses for his preparation of the brief on Amalia's behalf to enable her to be granted free legal aid. The list went on and on, from his initial meetings with Dr. Dalmonte (10 lire for his time) through his many meetings with Dr. Majocchi (280 lire). It left out nothing, including as its final entry his costs in preparing the list itself (7.2 lire in filing expenses and 5 lire for his time). In all, he requested 2,267 lire for his expenses and an additional 7,741 lire for all his time.

Moving with unaccustomed speed, the president of the Tribunal of Bologna quickly approved the lawyer's request and, noting the recent decision in Amalia's favor, ordered her, within twenty days, to pay Barbieri the full amount he had requested. Barbieri of course had no notion of trying to get the money directly from Amalia, who clearly could never hope to pay it herself. His goal was to have the court approve the full amount of what he believed was due him so that it could become part of the damages that the hospital board would be ordered to pay.

If neither Barbieri nor the court felt the need to bother Amalia about the claims he was making against her, it was just as well. With the ink barely dry on the court's order that she pay Barbieri his huge claim, she went into labor. Her newest baby came into the world just like the last, lifeless, unable to draw a breath.

CHAPTER 16

The Counteroffensive

WHILE BARBIERI WAS PREPARING for the Tribunal's hearing to fix the damages, the hospital was busy launching a counteroffensive with help from colleagues throughout the country. Even before Isolani's lawyers could file their appeal to the Supreme Court, Italy's medical circles were buzzing with news of the case.

Barely had the decision appeared when one of Italy's medical journals published a long, bitter reply to the court by Dr. Ermanno Pinzani.

He had recently read the sentence pronounced by the Court of Appeals of Bologna, Pinzani wrote, and was shocked to find the court repeatedly accuse the doctors of the foundling home and maternity hospital of *negligence* and *imprudence* — he emphasized each of these terms. He had refrained from responding until the final decision so he would not appear to be trying to improperly influence the judges' work, but now he was obliged to set the record straight.

The court, Pinzani complained, had accepted Barbieri's outrageous charge that the doctors had given the foundling to Amalia without first carefully examining the baby. But, he wrote, he had testified under oath that he had himself examined the baby that day. If he hadn't specified that such an exam entailed looking inside the baby's mouth, at her backside, and the like, it was simply because he had not thought it necessary to go into such obvious detail.

Pinzani denied that Paola had shown any sign of syphilis before he gave her to Amalia. In page after page of heated defense, he considered each of Majocchi's arguments and tried to rebut them. Paola's eye infection showed all the signs of being caused by maternal gonorrhea, so doing a microscopic analysis of the pus would have been a "pure scientific luxury," even if they had had a microscope. Majocchi's argument that the baby's emaciation was so severe when she was seen by Dr. Dalmonte that it could not have been the result of her time in Vergato only showed how little he knew about pediatrics. In fact, lacking proper feeding, a baby could become emaciated in but a few days.

Even if Majocchi were correct and Paola did have syphilis, Pinzani argued, the doctors did nothing wrong. While he and his colleagues were of course saddened by what had happened to Amalia, they rejected the notion that they were in any way to blame. They had performed all of the required examinations and never encountered any sign of syphilis in Paola.

To further buttress his argument, Pinzani offered evidence from Italy's largest foundling home, in Milan, to show that what happened to Amalia was far from unusual, indeed, that it was the inevitable result of efforts to keep foundlings alive. From 1855 to 1864, he recounted, 371 wet nurses had contracted syphilis from Milan's foundlings. And more recent figures showed the same pattern: in 1889, 37 wet nurses there had gotten syphilis, and another 29 in 1890. Similarly, in Turin's smaller foundling home, in the five years from 1886 to 1890, the institution had admitted to infecting 31 of its wet nurses with syphilis.

Pinzani concluded on a melancholy note: Certainly, humanity weeps at the thought of this misfortune, which strikes down these poor women and, often enough, their whole families. But, he argued, an effective remedy had yet to be found.

Protests against the court's decision were not limited to the men whose reputations were directly at stake. In a June 1894 article in another medical journal, one of Pinzani's Bologna colleagues, Temistocle Santopadre, offered his own denunciation of the court's decision.

Against all of the scientific evidence, he argued, the judges of Bologna's appeals court had systematically distorted the facts. Rejecting Dr. Ravaglia's penetrating analysis and Dr. Roncati's equally thorough, unassailable logic, they had instead embraced the bizarre opinion offered by Dr. Majocchi. He called on Italy's medical practitioners to raise their combined voice in protest, a protest aimed at overturning the deplorable ruling. The stakes were high. Not only would the decision, if allowed to stand, undermine the work of all doctors and endanger hospital administrations everywhere, it also threatened to deal a death blow to Italy's foundling homes. It would offer them an impossible choice: either to close their doors or to consign countless babies to artificial feeding. After the court's ruling, he asked, what foundling home director would be willing to risk sending one of these unhappy babies to a woman to nurse?

Santopadre made an unlikely leader for this crusade. Not only was he unknown to his colleagues nationally, but his reputation in Bologna itself was none too sterling. He regularly placed advertisements in Bologna's main daily newspaper, soliciting patients for his venereal disease dispensary in the middle of the city. His ads were nestled among those of several others who promised cures for syphilis, differing from them only in trumpeting his use of a new cure for the disease that used a recent invention: electrical current. Other ads, run by would-be healers lacking Santopadre's medical credentials, offered even more certain results for a more modest investment. "Radical antivenereal cure," read one in the Bologna paper at the time. "Antisyphilitic syrup for secret illnesses and for cases of syphilis resistant to all other cures. 5 lire."

Dr. Santopadre, as one of the more respectable healers, was, in effect, in direct competition for patients with the Bologna syphilis clinic, and he was not displeased to have this chance to publicly question the judgment of Domenico Majocchi, its director.

Meanwhile, Count Isolani and the board's lawyers were fighting the Bagnacavalli case on two different fronts. They had filed their appeal with Italy's Supreme Court and were preparing new briefs, but the Bologna Tribunal refused to delay its own proceedings in determining damages. The judges called in both parties for an initial hearing on May 31.

That Barbieri played for higher stakes than did any of the lawyers that the hospital had dealt with previously became clear when he announced his demands. He asked the court to order the hospital to pay 4,311 lire for Amalia's legal expenses and demanded the enormous sum of 45,000 lire in damages.

Although Barbieri asked the judges to award the damages immediately, the hospital lawyers objected. When the hearings continued in October 1894, the presiding judge called in Barbieri and his counterpart, Ferrari, and told them that it would be better for everyone if they could come to an out-of-court agreement on the sum of money to be paid. But this proved impossible. Count Isolani thought he had a good chance of winning the case on appeal and was worried about the impact the decision would have on future cases of syphilitic wet nurses. Yet he was known for his prudence, and had Barbieri been willing to accept a much lower figure, more in keeping with what the hospital had paid other such women, he might well have considered a settlement. But by this point Barbieri was hoping for — and, given the years and the effort he had put into the case, depending on — getting a large amount of money from the hospital.

In early February 1895, Barbieri and the hospital's lawyer, Pietro Baldini, again faced off in the Tribunal. Baldini had come prepared to show why the amount of money that Amalia's attorney had proposed was unreasonable, indeed outrageous, and he proceeded, item by item, through the bases of her request to dispute each in turn, from the cost of medical treatment for syphilis to the expense for the better foods prescribed by the doctors.

Baldini then turned to the damages that Amalia claimed for the suffering caused by the death of her children: Adele Elisa, born in 1889; Domenico, born in 1891; and Giuseppe, born in 1893.

While the hospital was willing to admit, he said, that the death of the first child — if it could be shown that she died of syphilis — could be considered in the calculation of moral damages, the deaths of the other two could not. Her second and third children, he pointed out, were conceived when Amalia was suffering from a virulent form of the disease and when she had already initiated legal action against the hospital board. Two people, and two alone, Baldini argued, were responsible for these children's deaths: Amalia Bagnacavalli and her husband. They had refused to heed their doctors' warnings and shown no compunction about giving life to poor souls whose blood would harbor the fatal stigmata of the disease. If instead of crying about their unbearable pain at the death of their children, argued Baldini, they had shown any real concern for the short, tortured lives these children would have, they would have exercised some self-control and not have had them in the first place.

Amalia was also demanding damages for what had happened to her husband, on the grounds that he contracted syphilis only because she had gotten it from an infected foundling. But the court, Baldini insisted, could not grant any payment, either for material or moral damages, on such grounds. If Luigi Migliorini contracted syphilis, it was certainly not the fault of the foundling home. He alone was responsible, for he knew that his wife had syphilis and he was told by the doctors that it was dangerous to have relations with her. If in his folly he paid them no heed, he and his wife could not now blame the foundling home for the wholly predictable result.

It was also the court's duty, Baldini told the judges, to reject Amalia's claim that she receive additional damages for the harm that the disease was likely to inflict on her in the future. All of the medical testimony provided by her lawyer on this count was, said the lawyer, irrelevant. It was a well-known principle of law, he insisted, that damages could not be presumed but must be proven, and that compensation could be given only for those damages that had actually been suffered, not for those that might occur someday.

The hearing had barely ended, the judges' decision about the payment to Amalia still unknown, when the lawyers' attention was diverted. The Supreme Court had decided to hold its own hearings on the hospital's appeal and sent word to Baldini and Barbieri to come immediately to Rome. If the hospital succeeded there, all the months of haggling in Bologna over the amount of money Amalia was to be paid would turn out to have been a waste of time.

CHAPTER 17

Mixed News from
the Supreme Court

❧

TAKING THE TRAIN from Bologna south to Rome, Augusto Barbieri glanced out at snowbound Vergato. At this level of appeal, there was no point taking Amalia with him. He doubted that the judges of that august body would be influenced by the sight of the long-suffering woman, and Amalia would be completely lost in the capital. Moreover, she was already so heavily in debt that she could scarcely have faced the additional expense.

Rome was in rapid transformation. Only a quarter century earlier, Italian troops had cannoned their way through its walls and seized the city from Pope Pius IX. Now Pope Leo XIII, following his predecessor's example, proclaimed himself a prisoner of the Vatican and refused to venture outside. Church officials were irate, having lost their rule over the Eternal City after a millennium of control, and they excommunicated the Italian king and his ministers. But although the clerics and their allies were unhappy, many others were now enjoying Rome's status as capital of the new Italian state. Building projects were everywhere, and the jobs offered by the construction and rapid expansion of government ministries, many housed in palazzi taken from the church, served as a magnet for migration. Yet native Romans had mixed feelings as well, complaining about the soaring costs of housing and the hordes of foreigners — the non-Romans — who now lived among them.

All this was familiar to Baldini, who had, until recently, often come down to Rome to attend sessions of parliament. Barbieri was much less familiar with the city, its grandeur, and its hubbub. He would in any case have little chance to gaze at the monuments or wander along the banks of the Tiber, for he soon had to make his way to Palazzo Altieri, the home of the Supreme Court. The vast baroque structure — built by Cardinal Altieri in the mid-seventeenth century and completed through the patronage of his nephew, Emilio Altieri, who became Pope Clement X in 1669 — made Bologna's imposing courthouse look puny by comparison. So immense was the building that the adjectives commonly used to describe it — "vast," "enormous" — scarcely did justice to its scale. At the time of its construction, Romans grumbled that if the aristocracy's self-aggrandizing drive for ever-larger palaces was not stopped, the whole city would before long be covered by one massive building. Nor was it simply the size of the Altieri palace that impressed; its hundreds of rooms were decorated with sumptuous furnishings, famous frescoes, and precious paintings from the seventeenth century.

The judges of Italy's Supreme Court, comfortably ensconced in the palace, had already read the accumulated file, and at the brief open session they called to order on Friday, February 22, 1895, they gave each side only a short time to state its case. Baldini spoke first, beginning with a capsule history, giving particular emphasis to the Tribunal's initial finding in the hospital's favor. According to the rules governing the Italian judiciary, matters of fact could only be determined at the lower levels of the court, so Baldini had to persuade the judges that the appeals court had made an error either in procedure or in the proper interpretation of the law.

Baldini based his argument on two points. First, he told the judges, even if the foundling had infected Amalia with syphilis, the appeals court had been mistaken to rule that it was the foundling home doctors' fault. If the doctors had made a mistake in interpreting the child's symptoms, such an error, he argued, clearly fell under the rubric of those professional mistakes that were not legally actionable. How could the judges hold the foundling home doctors responsible for an error of judgment so great as to be legally actionable when, at the same time, the court recognized that other prominent doctors would have made the same error?

Baldini then turned to his other major argument. If the doctors who worked for the foundling home were found guilty of negligence or major error in the conduct of their duties, they might themselves be held liable, but the hospital administration could not be. The hospital had hired qualified experts to perform the work, and it was not the hospital's fault if they made mistakes, as the administration had no way of overseeing each of the thousands of medical decisions.

Baldini concluded by calling on the court to overturn the appeals court decision and to make Amalia pay for all of the hospital's legal expenses.

Barbieri then rose and urged the high court to uphold the decision, praising not only the wisdom but also the sense of compassion of the judges who had ruled on behalf of the stricken peasant woman. The record, he said simply, spoke for itself.

The court adjourned. Three weeks later, on March 15, they called the lawyers back for their decision.

As the facts of the case were to be taken as given, the judges explained, the decision before them turned on a single issue: Was the foundling home doctors' mistake in judging Paola Olivelli to be free from syphilis and so giving her to Amalia Bagnacavalli legally actionable? Certainly, the judges held, if the doctors acted negligently, this would be the case. But the hospital had argued that the doctors' error, if there was one, was entirely innocent.

For the appeals court to rule as it did, Italy's highest court found, it had the obligation to provide clear reasons for rejecting the hospital's most compelling argument. This, in the Supreme Court's view, was the claim that since other prominent physicians — such as Roncati and Ravaglia — would have made the same mistake, the action of the foundling home doctors was within the bounds of responsible professional judgment.

The court pronounced that the Bologna appeals court had offered insufficient grounds to justify its decision against the hospital. Its finding for the wet nurse could therefore not stand.

Amalia's victory was overturned. Baldini felt vindicated, while Barbieri was unnerved. But more was yet to come.

In cases of this sort, the Supreme Court had two options. The judges could simply reverse the appeals court ruling and end the case there. Amalia's suit would then be over. But they could instead decide to send it back to the appeals court for a new hearing and so give Amalia one last chance. Much to Barbieri's relief — and Baldini's chagrin — the Supreme Court chose this second path. Yet Barbieri's relief was tempered by the realization that he would not face the judges who had already shown themselves sympathetic to Amalia's cause but an entirely new court. According to Italian judicial procedures, when an appeals court decision was overthrown, it could not be sent back to the same court to be tried again. The Supreme Court sent the case to the appeals court of Ancona, a city on the Adriatic coast of central Italy, several hours by train from Bologna. Barbieri was going to have to try his luck with a court in a city he had never before set foot in.

The obscure case of the syphilitic wet nurse had by now attracted national attention, not only in the medical world, but in the legal community as well. Lower court judges around the country were beginning to cite it, and lawyers were emboldened to sue on behalf of women who had suffered fates similar to Amalia's.

Emblematic was a case in Genoa. A young woman who was nursing a foundling went to her rural town doctor, who told her she had a syphilitic sore on her breast. On his instructions she returned the baby, but the foundling home doctor insisted that the baby was healthy and sent it to a second wet nurse, Domenica Righetti. Before long, Domenica contracted syphilis from the foundling and died, leaving her husband to care for their ten children. The Genoa hospital board — echoing the argument used by the board in Bologna — defended itself by arguing that it could not be blamed for its doctors' diagnostic errors. But the court, citing the Bagnacavalli case, ruled in the family's favor and ordered the hospital to pay damages of 12,000 lire.[1]

From the viewpoint of many in the legal community, these were dangerous developments. At the same time the Genoa decision was announced, a blistering attack on the Bologna appeals court verdict appeared in a national law journal. The author savaged the judges: "Reading this decision produced the deepest repugnance. I immediately recognized the gravity and the inadmissibility of the practical results of the legal principle that it proclaimed, if this became accepted into Italian jurisprudence." If the decision were allowed to stand, the legal expert argued, hospitals would risk their patrimonies every time one of their doctors treated a patient.[2]

Back in Bologna, in the wake of the Supreme Court's reversal, Barbieri was worried. Having no experience with the Ancona appeals court judges, he had no sense of how they would view the case. His prospects, he knew, were not helped by the skepticism that the Supreme Court had clearly expressed about the grounds for the earlier decision in Amalia's favor.

By this point, what most concerned Barbieri were the ruinous financial consequences if he were to lose the case. He did not look forward to dealing with Nono Veggetti if they lost in Ancona, having assured him that Amalia would be receiving a large sum of money from the hospital. And over the many months since Amalia took her latest loan, Barbieri's own expenses had continued to mount, what with his travels to Rome and the time he spent preparing for the Tribunal hearings to fix the damages.

If Barbieri was feeling nervous, Count Isolani was feeling besieged. Haunted by the specter of a parade of sickly peasants blaming the hospital for infecting them with syphilis, he was impatient with the foundling home's failure to stop the spread of the disease. The year before, he had ordered yet another inquiry into the possibility of introducing more modern methods of artificial feeding as a way of minimizing the risk of infecting wet nurses.

The count viewed Dr. Berti as his main expert on artificial feeding. As the doctor in charge of the syphilis ward, Berti had for years despaired over the horrific death rate of the babies there and was constantly looking for a better way to keep them alive.

In the mid-1880s, he had performed an experiment of his own. He procured a milk cow for the foundling home, then took four healthy newborns and placed two with women to nurse in the foundling home and two to be fed with cow's milk. The first two were given nurses who were far from ideal. One had milk described by Berti as of "mediocre" quality, the other not only had "old" milk — having given birth ten months earlier — but was nursing two other babies at the same time. Yet the first two babies flourished, while the babies who were fed cow's milk rapidly lost weight, and Berti, fearing for their lives, had felt compelled to end the experiment and give them back to a woman to nurse.

Foundling homes had for centuries been the major centers for experimenting with the artificial feeding of newborns, especially those babies suspected of having syphilis. They faced strong opposition to the practice, not only because consigning a baby to animal milk was widely regarded as a death sentence, but also because of popular beliefs that those babies who did survive acquired the traits of the animal whose milk had nourished them. A baby nursed by a goat would end up acting and looking like a goat.

Various animals were tried in the hopes of finding the one best suited to nourish the syphilitic newborns. For a time, in Turin, goats were the animal of choice, and the babies suckled directly from their teats. Trying to make the most of it, the doctors bathed the goats' skin in a mercury solution so that the babies would get some mercury with their milk. These attempts had to be abandoned when the goats reacted so violently to the mercury that they would no longer eat.[3]

In May 1894, having just returned from an international medical congress in Rome, Berti prepared a report for the hospital board. If the Bologna foundling home held on to all the babies whose health was in question for three months, about forty infants would normally remain there. This, he said, would require keeping three cows in a special stall on the foundling home grounds. It would also mean adding ten women to bottle-feed these babies. Building the stall and keeping the cows would be an expensive task, but, he advised, it would cost relatively little to keep the ten additional women. They could be forcibly recruited from the unwed mothers who gave birth at the maternity hospital. Hospital rules required all of these women to move into the foundling home after birth and spend at least two months nursing the infants. But some avoided this unpleasant duty by claiming that they had inadequate milk. It was just such women, Berti suggested, who could now be put to work bottle-feeding the babies.

The board received Berti's report shortly after learning of their defeat at the Bologna appeals court, a blow that had led the count and the board to ever more frenetic activity to limit their future liability. Within days of the ruling, Isolani received the board's approval for a new set of regulations for the foundling home designed to prevent the spread of syphilis to wet nurses.

The doctors were now to divide the babies into various categories. Only those with absolutely no suggestion of the possibility of syphilis and a medical certificate stating that their mothers showed no sign of the disease were to be given to external wet nurses in the first month. The rest fell into two groups. Those who showed any sign of syphilis — prematurity, low weight, a constantly runny nose, or an eye infection involving pus — were to be placed on artificial feeding. Babies who appeared healthy but who lacked a doctor's certification of their mother's health were to be given to wet nurses at the foundling home for three months. And here something new was introduced. These wet nurses were to wear protective rubber covers over their nipples; a small opening allowed the milk to trickle out.

The count, a cautious man, was beginning to allow himself the luxury of believing that they had finally found a solution to their problem. But his confidence did not last long. In August, just three months after the new procedures were introduced, he heard about a new case that provoked his anger.

Gelsomina Venturi, a woman from a mountain hamlet, had come to the foundling home on March 10 and taken a one-month-old baby home to nurse. Before long, she discovered a troubling sore on her nipple and took the baby with her to the town doctor. Indeed, she had contracted syphilis from the infant, a fact that not even the foundling home doctors denied. What especially enraged the count when he read the report was that before being given to the wet nurse, the baby had had an eye infection that oozed pus, a symptom that seemed to him to come right from the Bagnacavalli case.

Isolani wrote a scathing letter to the foundling home doctors, berating them for their continued failure to exercise the necessary caution. He said that he found it particularly upsetting to learn of their behavior when they were in the midst of a nasty suit brought about by a case of just this kind.

Two days later, the count had a long reply on his desk from Dr. Pinzani, who was also losing patience, for he was under attack from all sides.

He failed to understand what Isolani meant, wrote the doctor, in accusing them of failing to observe the proper procedures. The baby in question had been brought in by a wet nurse who declared the mother to be free of syphilis. It was true that the baby had developed an acute infection in both eyes, but the staff had used their new microscope to examine the pus and determined that it was gonorrheal in origin, not syphilitic. In any case, all this happened before the most recent rules were introduced, so they were then operating under the 1892 regulations, which specified that such babies were to be kept only one month. When at that time, having recovered fully from his eye infection, the baby appeared to be healthy, the doctors gave him to the wet nurse. In short, they had done absolutely nothing wrong.

Pinzani added that he had been no less affected than the count or the board by the Bagnacavalli case. Not only did the foundling home have much at risk financially but, he pointed out, his own reputation was at stake. People failed to realize that since he had become medical director in 1888, the spread of syphilis to wet nurses had become less frequent. He attached a table to his letter, listing the names of twenty-three women who had contracted syphilis from Bologna foundlings in the half-dozen years of his tenure. The doctor went on to compare this with the situation at other foundling homes, which, he argued, was often worse.

Looking at the list, Isolani noted that the doctor had placed a blue cross by the side of eleven names. These, he realized, were the women whom the hospital's lawyers had been able to convince over the past decade to sign notarized statements renouncing any further claims against the hospital in return for the payment of a few hundred lire. Should Amalia win her case, and especially if she got an amount of money anything like what her lawyer was demanding, the count feared that this practice would become a thing of the past. Only the most ill-advised and credulous peasant would ever again sign away her rights for a paltry sum.

Convinced that the solution lay in modern methods of artificial feeding, the count was impatient with the slow pace of change. He proposed building stalls at the foundling home and buying cows, but was taken aback when he learned how expensive such an operation would be. New, hygienic stalls would cost 5,000 lire and four cows would cost another 2,000 lire. In addition, there were the salaries of a stable boy and people to milk the cows, as well as the cost of ten kilograms a day of straw for each cow, gas to boil the milk, and keeping ten women in the foundling home to feed the babies. It would all amount to over 11,000 lire each year.

The count decided instead to begin on a more modest scale. They would fix up the existing stall at the foundling home — it had not been used in many years — buy just one cow, and use only two women to feed the babies.

Meanwhile, the women locked up in the foundling home began to revolt. Ever since the rubber nipple covers had been introduced they had complained about them and, the doctors soon realized, only used them when they thought one of the doctors was looking. It was a constant struggle to get them to use the protectors even though it was for their own good.

The problem was that, while a good idea in theory, the thick rubber devices left much to be desired in practice, and the babies struggled to affix their mouths to the women's breasts. Constantly frustrated, the infants could not extract more than a trickle of milk. The women, for their part, not only felt pity for the struggling babies, who seemed to be shriveling before their eyes, but felt increasingly uncomfortable with their own milk-laden breasts. Some of the women, hoping to make money by nursing babies after their discharge from the foundling home, were also worried that if they kept using the rubber protectors, their own milk would dry up.

In mid-December, the women announced that they would never again use the protectors. "They now refuse openly, expressing their repugnance to the medical director," Isolani read in a report sent from the foundling home.

The revolt threatened all of the count's careful regulations to prevent the spread of syphilis, for he also knew that with the modest scale of cow milk production, the board had said there was no way they could nurse the dozens of babies now being kept in the foundling home for the first few months of their lives. If a solution were not found soon, few of these babies would survive.

The good news from the Supreme Court, coming in March 1895, only weeks after the rubber nipple revolt, had finally raised the count's spirits. He once again grew confident that the Bagnacavalli suit would be defeated. But, to his irritation, the Bologna Tribunal kept demanding that he pay the court costs connected with the case. On the first anniversary of the appeals court decision, Isolani received yet another demand from the court chancellery, giving him three days to pay 1,754 lire. Isolani wrote a note on the document, telling Ferrari to inform the court that, given the recent Supreme Court ruling, any such payment was premature.

Two months later the count received another bill, which, by contrast, he hastened to pay. Totaling 2,044 lire, it had been sent by Pietro Baldini for his time preparing the Supreme Court appeal. This was in addition to the thousands of lire the hospital board had already paid him for his work on the case.

As the count waited for the Ancona appeals court to issue its decision, it seemed that he did nothing but deal with one crisis after another at the foundling home. Although the artificial feeding ward was now in place, cases of syphilitic wet nurses still kept coming to light.

The last months of 1895 found the hospital board members arguing about what they should do. Some called for placing all the babies on artificial feeding for their first three months. But the count insisted that this was not enough. He proposed placing all the babies on artificial feeding for twice as long, giving them to rural wet nurses only when they had reached six months of age.

The count's principal opponent in this battle was Domenico Peruzzi, who had recently been named director of the foundling home and maternity hospital. Peruzzi attacked the count's plan on various grounds. First of all, he said, it was wholly impractical. Babies who were fed with bottles for six months would not, after all that time, take to nursing at the breast. But there was a more important reason, he argued. Even with all of their efforts to modernize their artificial feeding system, the babies fed by bottle were dying at a horrifying rate. Of the 128 sent to the artificial feeding ward in the first ten months of the year, 95 had already died, most within two months. And those babies who survived, he said, could easily be distinguished from those of the same age who had been breastfed by their pallor, their small size, and their susceptibility to disease.

Recognizing the crisis, Peruzzi proposed a series of other changes. He proposed that no baby be given to a wet nurse before three months of age. To prevent large-scale death among the babies as a result, he called for doing everything possible to get their own mothers to nurse them in these early months. The women who gave birth at the maternity hospital should be required to spend three months in the foundling home nursing their own children. This would obligate these women to stay in the foundling home one more month than the current requirement, but the more radical change was having them nurse their own babies.

Until recent years, this had been absolutely forbidden, for the whole point of the system, ever since the Counter-Reformation in the sixteenth century, had been to separate unwed women from their babies. From this perspective, the last thing that the foundling home authorities wanted to do was to encourage these women's maternal instincts and thereby make it all the more difficult to separate mother and child.

After two stormy sessions, the hospital board agreed to try the new system. Women giving birth in the maternity hospital would be required to nurse their own babies for three months, following which, if they agreed to keep their babies, they would be paid the attractive sum of 20 lire per month for the rest of the year. All other babies would be required to remain at the foundling home for three months, being fed with bottles by women called dry nurses, each of whom would have at least four such babies to care for and would sleep next to their cribs.

A week after the count reluctantly agreed to this proposal, he received a report from Modena. Since the Bologna appeals court had ruled against him, Isolani had been curious to find out what was going on elsewhere, because it seemed unfair to him that Bologna had been singled out for legal scrutiny. Modena, not far from Bologna, was of particular interest to him, and the report from the lawyer who represented its foundling home made compelling reading.

The lawyer said that he himself had represented the Modena foundling home in three recent legal actions brought by syphilitic wet nurses. Two were still in the courts, and certainly not helped by the Bagnacavalli case. The third had resulted in a finding in the foundling home's favor. Modena's Tribunal had ruled that contracting syphilis should be considered a "professional risk" inherent in being a wet nurse and that women took this risk on themselves when they decided to do such work.

The lawyer attributed the difference between the Modena decision and the Bagnacavalli case to the fact that in Modena the entire medical community had declared that the foundling home doctors had done their best and that despite this, the spread of syphilis to wet nurses was inevitable. He contrasted this with the case in Bologna, where a prestigious doctor — Majocchi — had broken ranks with his colleagues.

In fact, the Modena lawyer said, Bologna and Modena were doing better than many other foundling homes. In Turin, he reported, 7 percent of the women taking in foundlings to nurse in recent years had been infected with syphilis, and in Milan too the rate was frighteningly high.

They were now in a dangerous situation, the lawyer warned. In the past, these cases were resolved easily, quietly, with small payments made to the poor women. Everything had been kept quiet. But now, if the Bagnacavalli precedent were allowed to stand, the court cases would surely multiply. It was only prudent for them to do what they could to limit their risk.

As in Bologna, the hospital board members in Modena had proposed making the wet nurses sign a declaration at the time they got the foundling, saying that they would not hold the foundling home responsible for any illness they contracted. But, the lawyer said, such a clause would carry no weight with the courts, for employees could not sign away their basic rights. Instead, he came up with a novel idea. The foundling home, he proposed, should pay for each wet nurse to hire a doctor of her own choice to examine the baby when she picked it up. The doctor would then sign a statement saying that he found the baby free of syphilis. Should the baby then develop the disease, the woman could not blame the foundling home. If she wanted to sue someone, she could sue her own doctor.

CHAPTER 18

A Split Decision

❖

BARBIERI KNEW THAT he had just this one last chance and, he had to admit, the odds were against him. The Bologna appeals court decision in Amalia's favor had been a shock to Italy's legal and medical establishment, and the Supreme Court judges, although circumspect in their language, seemed surprised themselves that Amalia's claim had been received so favorably.

In the months before the Ancona appeals court deliberation, Barbieri frantically tried to get a copy of the regulations governing the Bologna foundling home, for they were critical to his case that the doctors had not followed the rules. When Isolani refused to give him one, he went directly to Bologna's prefect to enlist his help. But when the prefect asked for a copy to honor Barbieri's request, Isolani again refused, saying that he could not be forced to do anything to help someone who was suing him.

In April 1896, more than a year after the Supreme Court overturned the Bologna verdict, Barbieri finally appeared before the Ancona court to make his case. A seaside city on the Adriatic, more or less equidistant from Rome and Bologna, it had been an important port, connecting the Papal States to the world of the Ottoman Turks. For Barbieri it seemed not much more than a provincial town; with thirty thousand people, it was not even a third of Bologna's size. But Barbieri was not interested in the ancient sites or the harbor. He had more pressing problems, for he still had not procured a copy of the foundling home regulations. At the courthouse, he found himself having to bluster his way through his argument, making generic references to the rules without citing any directly.

The Supreme Court, he said, had accepted the basic facts of the case as found by the Bologna court. The Supreme Court also ruled, said Barbieri, that the hospital could be held responsible if it were shown that the foundling home doctors had been negligent in not suspecting that the baby had syphilis or if they had failed to follow the proper guidelines in their examinations of the baby.

It was at this point that, desperately afraid that the case would go against him, Barbieri decided that his best chance lay in bending the evidence a bit. He needed to convince the judges that the foundling home doctors had been incompetent or negligent. To do this, he tried to leave the impression that Paola's later symptoms of the disease had appeared before the foundling home gave her to Amalia. And so, along with listing the symptoms that all agreed she did show early on, he included not only those that were in dispute, such as her emaciation, but even those that no one ever claimed had appeared before Amalia took her. Here the crucial symptoms were Paola's runny nose and, especially, the lesions in her mouth and on her backside. Presenting them as though their early occurrence had been established by the evidence, he attacked the claim that, on the day the baby was given to Amalia, Dr. Pinzani had examined her carefully.

Barbieri ridiculed the hospital's argument that if there were any fault to be assigned in the Bagnacavalli case it lay only with the doctors, not the hospital board. What, he asked, had the hospital board done about the syphilis epidemic that the foundling home had spawned in the countryside? Again, he cited all the receipts for payments to wet nurses who had contracted syphilis in a nine-year period, more than a hundred in all. But he did not mention that many of these were made out to the same women, leading the judges to believe that the board was paying off many more wet nurses than the actual number. Had the board, he asked, thought it necessary to take any action? No, he said, they had done absolutely nothing. They had even left Dr. Pinzani in charge of determining if the babies had syphilis, although he was not a syphilis expert.

Adding an emotional appeal to his legal argument, Barbieri asked the judges to think for a moment of the person the case was all about: poor, unfortunate Amalia Bagnacavalli. Here was a young woman whose life had been ruined, condemned to stand helplessly by as horrible lesions spread through her body. Here was a woman, he said, who once could look forward to being the mother of a growing family but had instead endured the heartbreaking deaths of all her children and the sad infirmity of her husband, all because of what the Bologna foundling home had done to her.

With this, Barbieri concluded.

On July 11, 1896, after hearing Baldini present the same arguments in defense of the foundling home that he had used at the previous stages of the case, the five judges met to decide what to do. While they could not hear new evidence at the appeals level, they were not limited to ruling on points of law, and they began their deliberations by deciding which version of the basic facts of the case was to be preferred.

Despite the hospital board's continued denials, the judges had no difficulty deciding that Paola had been born with syphilis and that the foundling had infected Amalia. They focused especially on the symptoms of the disease that Dr. Dalmonte had found. And they found it important that when Amalia returned the baby to the foundling home, the doctors did not argue with her when she said Paola had syphilis, and in fact they immediately placed the infant in the special syphilis ward, where she remained until her death a month later.

The judges showed no more sympathy to another of the hospital's basic arguments: that a hospital's relationship with the doctors it employed differed from other employer-employee relationships, and that as a result, the hospital bore no legal responsibility for any harm caused by the doctors' professional judgment. The civil code, the judges ruled, specified that employers were responsible for the damages done by their employees in the course of doing their duties. No exceptions for doctors were to be found in the law.

On all this the five judges agreed. But this still left ample grounds for hope on the part of Baldini and the count. In the hospital's victory at the Bologna Tribunal, the judges had ruled both against its claim that Paola had not given Amalia syphilis and its claim that hospitals could not be held responsible for their doctors' damages. The crucial question — and the one where the hospital's case was strongest — was whether the doctors had been negligent or had failed to follow good professional judgment. The Tribunal judges had found the hospital's case convincing: if even the court's two medical experts, Ravaglia and Roncati, had thought Paola showed no sign of syphilis before she was given to Amalia, how could the foundling home doctors be found negligent or incompetent in coming to the same conclusion?

Although neither Barbieri nor Baldini was privy to the judges' deliberations on that summer Saturday morning, each would have had grounds for optimism had they overheard the debate. On one side, the chief judge, Gioacchino Bonelli, argued that signs of syphilis — or in any case signs that should have led the doctors to suspect syphilis as a possibility — were clear from the first days of Paola's life. He also agreed that if Amalia had thought the baby so emaciated on the day she came to the foundling home that she did not want to take her, there must have been grounds for the doctors to suspect that the baby had the disease. The foundling home regulations, as Barbieri had argued correctly, even though he did not have a copy of them, specified that babies who showed signs leading to the suspicion of syphilis should not be given to a wet nurse. Here was clearly a case, said the chief judge, of doctors acting negligently.

But not all of his colleagues agreed. For Giovanni Gelli and Adriano Adriani, the evidence clearly favored the opposite conclusion. How could the judges claim to have greater expertise than the distinguished medical school professors consulted by the court? Gelli and Adriani thought that the chief judge was unduly swayed by subsequent developments. True, in retrospect, it was clear that Paola had syphilis and gave her disease to her wet nurse. But the foundling home doctors could be found guilty of negligence only if they had ignored the symptoms of the disease that appeared before they gave the baby to Amalia. The symptoms she did have were much more ambiguous. Ravaglia and Roncati made a convincing case that the doctors had good reason to believe that Paola's eye infection was not caused by syphilis, even if in retrospect they had turned out to be wrong. And the timing of the baby's emaciation was less clear-cut than the chief judge thought, they argued. Although Amalia had testified that she was horrified at her first sight of the baby and had attributed her feeling of dread to the baby's shriveled appearance, her reaction was just as likely to have been produced by her horror at the infant's glassy eyes.

Amalia's fate would be decided by the two remaining judges, Domenicantonio Galdi and Nicola Limoncelli. When it became clear that all five judges would never reach a consensus, the chief judge decided to call for a vote. He would need to get the support of both of his wavering colleagues if Amalia was to win her case.

The week before the judges called the lawyers back in to hear their decision was a long one for Barbieri. It was now practically six years since Amalia had first told him her sad story. He had devoted more time to this case than to any other in his life, and while he felt he had sacrificed a great deal for Amalia, he was also aware that as a result of his counsel, she now found herself at risk of being worse off. She was under a crushing debt, a debt she never would have contracted if, on that August day in 1890, he had simply sent her away.

It was a Saturday when the Ancona court released its decision. In its Sunday edition, Bologna's daily newspaper — knowing that its readers were eager to learn the latest in the long saga — reported the trial's dramatic conclusion:

Given the great interest it has generated, the wet nurse Amalia Bagnacavalli's suit against the hospitals of Bologna is by now well known to our readers. In nursing a foundling she became infected with syphilis, which she then gave to her husband and to her two little children.

With the foundling home being charged with the responsibility for the grave harm done by this contagion, the hospital board, under which the foundling home comes, disputed the basic facts of the case. And, in any event, they argued that what was involved was at most a professional error committed by the doctors, and that the hospital could not be held responsible for the doctors' honest mistakes.

The questions raised in the case were of great importance and great interest, both from the scientific point of view and for the consequences that a decision would have one way or the other. . . .

In its decision announced yesterday, the Ancona court fully reconfirmed the decision that our Court had made. It has held the hospital responsible for its doctors' work and ordered it to pay for all the material and moral harm it has done, and in addition condemned it to pay for all of the legal expenses of both sides.

Baldini, who had been in Ancona for the reading of the decision, returned to Bologna later in the week and wrote Count Isolani a short letter, informing him that the judges had ruled, three to two, against them. He included a copy of the decision, adding that in his opinion, its reasoning was even worse than that of the Bologna appeals court. After reading the letter, an angry Isolani scribbled a note to the board's legal adviser, Ferrari, asking him whether they should appeal the Ancona sentence to the Supreme Court.

CHAPTER 19

A Staggering Sum

T HE BAGNACAVALLI SUIT had already cost the hospital many thousands of lire and the amount kept growing. Baldini submitted his latest bill, covering the Ancona appeal, which included 1,140 lire in expenses and another 1,700 lire for his time. Meanwhile, the Ancona court had notified Count Isolani that the hospital owed it 2,238 lire for court expenses.

The court in Ancona had also ordered the hospital board to pay Barbieri for his legal work on behalf of Amalia in the Supreme Court and Ancona appeals, his compensation for the Bologna phase of the case to be set separately by the Bologna court. In October 1896, the count approved a payment of 3,100 lire to Barbieri. While this was only half of what they had paid their own lawyer for his work in Rome and Ancona alone, the count felt the figure was reasonable. After all, Barbieri was only thirty-four years old, and a lawyer, the count thought, who was so lacking in respectable clients that he made his living by chasing after illiterate peasants. However, Barbieri was far from satisfied. He expected to get more, much more for all the work he had put into the case and for the risk he had taken. This was to be but the first installment.

While these legal maneuverings were going on, the effects of the new nursing policy on Bologna's foundlings were becoming clear.

Over the course of 1896, 470 babies had been admitted to the foundling home. Of these, 157 had been born in the maternity hospital, with most being nursed by their mothers. By the end of the year 19 percent of them had died, a percentage not dramatically higher than the death rate of babies in the larger population. But the effects of the new policy on those who had no mother to nurse them were quite different. Of the 313 babies placed in the artificial feeding wing, 202 had already died by the end of the year. This 64 percent death rate actually underrepresented their mortality because some of those born near the end of the year might yet die before reaching their three-month anniversary. The doctors were also worried because the new policy had been put in place at the end of March, so the babies born early in the year had been initially nourished at the breast of wet nurses. Worse, they knew, was yet to come, and all because of the case brought on Amalia's behalf by the tenacious Barbieri.

Over these months, the Ancona court, which had ordered the hospital to compensate Amalia, was becoming increasingly concerned that it had received no word from Bologna that such a payment had been made. In early January 1897, the court wrote to the count, asking what he had done. Isolani responded immediately that because they had appealed the Ancona ruling to the Supreme Court, he was not planning to pay Amalia anything before hearing the court's final verdict.

The hospital board had voted unanimously to go ahead with their last chance to win the case, taking it to the Supreme Court for a second time. At the meeting in the fall when the vote was taken, one of the board members argued that their chances of victory would be increased if, rather than being represented by Baldini alone — a good lawyer, one of Bologna's best, but not well known to the judges in Rome — they found someone with more political clout to stand up for them. They approached the most politically well-connected Roman lawyer they knew, Alessandro Fortis, and asked if he would represent them. A member of parliament for sixteen years, a recent deputy minister of internal affairs, and a man who would later, albeit briefly, become prime minister of Italy, Fortis seemed well suited for the role.

After getting assurances that Baldini would do all the work, Fortis agreed to help them, and the count allowed himself new hope that his side would finally win. After all, the one other time the case had gone to the judges of the Supreme Court, they had overruled the Bologna appeals court decision and, in the count's eyes, clearly shown their lack of sympathy for the case.

On April 28, 1897, the seven judges of the Supreme Court heard oral arguments by Barbieri on Amalia's behalf and by Baldini and Fortis for the hospital. Four weeks later, on Monday, May 24, Amalia's legal odyssey reached its final day in court when the lawyers for both sides were called to Palazzo Altieri to hear the verdict. Nicola Tondi, president of the court, read the decision.

Italy's highest court, he announced, found that there were no grounds for overturning the Ancona ruling. It was not the role of the Supreme Court to determine the facts of the case but only whether any error had been made in interpreting the law. The Ancona court had determined that Paola had infected Amalia with syphilis, and that at the time that Paola was given to Amalia, the baby showed signs that she might have syphilis. The doctors had given the baby to Amalia anyway, in clear violation of the foundling home's rules. This, the Supreme Court decided, was not a case of an excusable professional error. It was a case of negligence.

Baldini had the unpleasant task of sending the count a copy of the ruling. The Supreme Court judges, he told him, had used tortured logic and, if read carefully, made an outrageous accusation. They had clearly implied that the foundling home doctors had knowingly given a baby they suspected of having syphilis to a healthy woman to nurse. If the judges really believed this, Baldini said, they should not have simply affirmed the civil suit findings. They should have ordered the arrest of the doctors and held them for criminal trial.

The hospital board lawyers had not waited for the final Supreme Court decision before moving aggressively to limit their liability in the rapidly proliferating complaints that Amalia's Ancona victory had prompted from aggrieved former wet nurses. Late 1896 and early 1897 saw the lawyers busy trying to settle these cases. The goal, as before, was to have the women sign notarized forms relinquishing any further right to take action against the hospital.

Just before the Ancona court decision, in July 1896, the hospital settled a case with Cattarina Tonelli for 500 lire, the woman having contracted syphilis the previous year from a foundling and then transmitted the disease to her husband. But now lawyers in the Bologna area were more than eager to help such women, and the price of getting them to sign was going up. In January 1897, Argia Matteuzzi and her husband received 1,500 lire in compensation for the syphilis she had contracted from a foundling three years earlier. The following month it was the turn of Maria Masi and her husband. Maria had taken in a foundling on March 24, 1890, three days before Amalia had first ventured to the foundling home, and suffered from a still-active case of syphilis as a result. She settled for 1,100 lire. Later that year the hospital drew up a settlement with Giuditta Caselli, who had gotten syphilis from nursing a baby in the foundling home, following her forced service there after her own baby was born in the maternity hospital. In September 1897, Barbieri himself warned the hospital's attorney that he would sue on the woman's behalf unless a satisfactory settlement was arranged, so Giuditta was given 1,200 lire in exchange for a pledge not to sue. But the biggest payment of all that year — indeed, the largest payment the hospital had ever made to a syphilitic wet nurse — came two months earlier. It involved another woman, Luigia Guernelli, who had gotten syphilis while forced to nurse babies in the foundling home. Citing the Bagnacavalli case, her lawyer actually did bring suit. In July 1897, Luigia agreed to withdraw her suit and pledge never again to ask for anything from the hospital board in exchange for the sizable payment of 3,500 lire.

Count Isolani felt some relief that this backlog of complaints was at last beginning to be cleared and that the hospital board's exposure to the risk of suits inspired by Amalia's was being reduced. But all this came at a cost. With the end of 1897, the count received the foundling home doctors' report on the first full year of the new nursing policy: 126 babies born in the maternity hospital had been admitted with their mothers, and of these only 13 percent had died. But of the 320 abandoned babies with no mother to feed them, fewer than a third had survived.

Throughout all the years of their ordeal, Amalia and Luigi remained in Oreglia, although as time went on their household shrank. Luigi's sister and one of his brothers had married and moved out, so Amalia and Luigi now shared their home only with Luigi's aging parents and his unmarried brother, Giuseppe. Together, they eked out what living they could from the rocky soil.

When, in early 1898, after the final Supreme Court decision, the count received the new proposed settlement from Barbieri, he was outraged. Barbieri had practically doubled his earlier request — a figure the count had already viewed as preposterous — and now demanded the staggering sum of 70,000 lire. The count consulted his lawyers. Agreeing that the amount was enormous, they advised against direct negotiation, which they thought could at best lead to a modest reduction. The only way to set the figure much lower was to go once again to court and have the matter decided there.

Barbieri knew that he would anger the count by seeking so much and thought it unlikely that he would get all that he asked, but after all the years he had spent on Amalia's case, this was the time for him finally to make good on his promises to her. No less important, now was the time to make good on his own hopes for a generous reward.

He realized, as Amalia did not, that this final phase was going to be the most delicate and he would have to be careful. Although Amalia herself could hardly have been less sophisticated in financial and legal dealings, he knew that the courts were still watching the case closely. The Ancona court was regularly peppering Count

Isolani with requests for information about Amalia's payment and what she was doing with all her money. It was only prudent, he thought, to protect himself from what he feared might be coming.

With this in mind, before sending in his ambitious request to the count, Barbieri asked Amalia to come with Luigi to see him in Bologna. When they arrived at his office on Thursday, January 6, 1898, he said he had a document that they needed to sign. He then led them one floor down to the offices of his longtime collaborator, Alberto Pallotti.

Barbieri had never fully trusted Nono Veggetti, who had loaned Amalia the money she needed for her case. All would have been simpler if he had been able to get one of his associates in Bologna to make the earlier loans, but back then no one was willing to take the risk. Now, with the actual disbursement of funds in sight, Veggetti would only get in the way.

When the lawyer entered the notary's office with Amalia and Luigi trailing behind him, Riccardo Orlandi, a friend and business associate of Barbieri's, was already there. The lawyer knew that it would not be difficult to convince Amalia and Luigi to sign the paper that was about to be put in front of them. Orlandi, he told them, was much more knowledgeable than Veggetti and much better able to help them. The hospital, he warned, was not eager to give them what they deserved, and so this last part of their battle was not going to be simple. But, he said, with Orlandi's help, all of the complicated finances and negotiations would be taken care of. They needed only to sign the agreement.

The notary read it aloud. In bureaucratic prose, it stated that Amalia, with her husband's consent, named Riccardo Orlandi as her representative and authorized him to handle all financial matters relating to her suit. It specifically assigned to him responsibility for determining how much her lawyer was to be paid for both his time and his expenses and excluded everything that Barbieri had already been paid by the hospital board from the calculation of what Amalia was to pay him.

Orlandi would loan Amalia the money to pay off her debt to

Veggetti and in so doing enable her to terminate his role as her representative. She would be charged 8 percent interest, plus the wealth tax on the funds she borrowed.

The notary called on Luigi to place his signature at the bottom of the document. If the lawyer had any qualms about what he had just done or what he was about to do, the records remaining in the archives show no sign of them.

CHAPTER 20

Amalia's Lawyer
Submits His Bill

❖

TO AMALIA IT MUST have seemed that the judges and the lawyers would never tire of all their arguing, and she must have wondered if she would ever see the riches Barbieri had promised her. The amounts of money being discussed were, Amalia knew, well beyond what any of her friends or family could ever hope to see in a lifetime. With money like that, she and Luigi could buy a good-sized farm and live comfortably, hiring day laborers to help with the heavy work of planting and harvesting.

By this time Amalia had survived the secondary stage of syphilis and no longer showed any obvious signs of the disease — no sores on her body, no patches of baldness on her scalp, no ulcerations in her mouth. But she felt tired all the time and hadn't the energy she used to have. The woman once described as a fine physical specimen now had a sickly look about her. Her skin, although no longer discolored from mercury treatments, had an unhealthy ashen tint; her formerly robust body was now emaciated.[1]

When the new century came, Amalia was just as poor as she had ever been. But the end of her legal suit, it turned out, was near. A few days into 1900, Barbieri sent word that the Tribunal would soon be announcing how much money the hospital owed her.

With payment finally in sight, Barbieri was both excited and nervous. The possibilities for a last-minute misunderstanding in his relationship with Amalia were, he realized, great. Deciding to leave nothing to chance, he again turned to Alberto Pallotti. Together they crafted what they hoped was an airtight agreement between Barbieri and the woman who had, for a decade, seen him as her selfless champion. Barbieri wanted to make sure that there was no uncertainty about how much money he was to get paid.

Having learned just after the new year that the Tribunal might issue its decision any day and worried that it might come at the beginning of the following week, Barbieri insisted on having Amalia and Luigi come in that Sunday to sign the document. As a result, on the first Sunday of the century, almost two years to the day from the last time Barbieri had asked them to come to his office, Amalia and Luigi took the train through the wintry mountains to meet him. After all the time the case had taken, it would have been hard for them to imagine why their lawyer was now in such a rush.

When Amalia and Luigi arrived, Barbieri told them that, with the Tribunal's decision coming soon, it was important that they put all of their affairs in order. Again he led them downstairs to the notary's office, and again they sat as Pallotti read another bewildering declaration.

The text recounted the story of Amalia's infection while nursing Paola, the filing of her suit against the hospital, the long and lively series of trials culminating in her victory at the Ancona court of appeals, and the order that the hospital pay her damages. Despite this July 1896 court order, the notary read, and although Amalia's weakened health had meant she often could not work and her medical expenses kept piling up, the hospital board continued to resist paying her what it owed.

Pallotti then got to the heart of the document: although Amalia had been provided with free legal aid by the courts, her valiant and zealous protector, Professor Augusto Barbieri, had, in defending her, incurred substantial travel and printing expenses, as well as expenses for his own time, and had relied on the work and the cooperation of various colleagues, who understandably were now asking to be paid.

Pallotti again, as he had two years earlier, read a phrase that, while central for Barbieri, must have meant nothing to Amalia and Luigi.

"Signor Barbieri, notwithstanding any reimbursement of expenses and other amounts due him paid directly to him by the hospital, or that would in the future be paid him in this way, has the right to the reimbursement of his expenses and to the compensation that Bagnacavalli has the most solemn duty to provide given the long and loving assistance he has offered her."

The text then turned briefly to other obligations that Amalia was to recognize. She also, the notary read, had the great fortune of obtaining the assistance of the distinguished Professor Domenico Majocchi, whose medical findings contradicting the court-ordered reports had allowed her to triumph. In addition, she had discovered in the Azzoguidi Publishing House of Bologna an establishment willing to advance her the considerable costs involved in printing her lawyer's briefs.

Pallotti then got to the central point.

Wishing to guarantee that she meet her debts to those who so valiantly cooperated in making her triumph possible, Signora Amalia Bagnacavalli, assisted and authorized by her husband, Signor Luigi Migliorini, of her own free will spontaneously recognized the following legal debts:

For attorney Augusto Barbieri: the sum of 3,000 lire in repayment of loans provided her on various occasions, at her request, to meet expenses for both medical treatment and personal needs. Plus the sum of 10,000 lire, in compensation for his zealous, intelligent assistance provided from 1890 through a long series of judicial proceedings involving the Bologna hospital board, this amount independent of any other sum that said attorney Barbieri received directly from the hospital.

In addition, 2,500 lire to Professor Domenico Majocchi, for his expenses and time spent on the various reports prepared for the court; and another 2,500 lire to the Azzoguidi Publishing House.

In recognizing these debts, Pallotti read, Amalia Bagnacavalli agreed to have these sums, totaling 18,000 lire, deducted directly from the amount the hospital paid her. In the remote event that she could reach an out-of-court settlement with the hospital, she swore that she would not agree to a sum less than this.

The notary finished reading the document and asked Amalia to make her mark. Although she could understand little of what he had said, the dizzying amounts of money he had cited and the repeated reference to all of the people to whom she owed money could not fail to make an impression on her. It would have taken someone of nerves much stronger than hers not to be frightened. But Barbieri urged her on, no doubt reminding her that the amount of money they were demanding of the hospital was much larger than what she would need to pay off these debts.

As it turned out, Barbieri need not have rushed Amalia and Luigi down to Bologna that Sunday, for it was another two months before Bologna's Tribunal announced its decision.

In compensation for the material harm done to Amalia, the court ordered the hospital to pay her 4,600 lire, plus another 6,000 lire for her legal expenses. To this was to be added interest due on both amounts calculated from the time, almost three years earlier, when the Supreme Court had rejected the hospital's appeal. The hospital was also ordered to pay all the court costs, plus 2,500 lire, to Professor Majocchi and another 1,628 lire for Amalia's other legal expenses. Finally, the hospital was to pay Amalia 30 lire per month for the rest of her life. Such a permanent pension would give her more money than she could have made by working, even if she were healthy. For a peasant from the mountains, it was a considerable income.

Although Count Isolani thought the Tribunal had been overly magnanimous, his lawyer was not displeased, reminding the count that Amalia had asked for much more. Two weeks after learning of the verdict, Isolani called a meeting of the hospital board to decide whether they should pay the required amount or appeal for a reduction to the appeals court. Ferrari told them that he was sure that Barbieri himself would appeal the Tribunal's decision.

It did not take long for Barbieri to do the calculations. The Tribunal's decision, if allowed to stand, would mean he would receive only 6,000 lire of the 10,000 lire that Amalia now owed him for his services. While Majocchi would get his entire, extremely generous fee of 2,500 lire — his assistant doctors in the syphilis clinic had a annual salary of 1,200 lire — the money for legal expenses would leave Amalia several hundred lire short in paying what she owed the publishing house. And then there were Amalia's other debts, not least the repayment of the 3,000 lire he had loaned her, as well as repayment of the original 5,000-lire loan he had arranged for her from Nono Veggetti, now owed to Riccardo Orlandi.

On April 17, Barbieri filed his appeal, renewing his request that Amalia be awarded 70,000 lire. But his bravado was now gone. Earlier he had resisted any compromise with the hospital, certain that the courts would, if not accept the full amount he proposed, at least award half of it. Now pressure from his creditors weighed on him. He was no longer quite so young and, thanks in part to his success in Amalia's suit, his services were in demand by other clients. There was little more, from a professional point of view, that he could get out of the case. His thoughts must also have turned to his own family. He had a wife and two children to support, and he wanted them to live in a manner befitting a successful member of Bologna's professional class.

Barbieri, in short, was rattled, and now did something that he had long avoided. He contacted Pietro Baldini and proposed that rather than go to the additional expense of an appeal, they reach an amicable agreement and bring the case to an end. Baldini, all too familiar with Barbieri's aggressive tactics, was skeptical. Worried that the offer was simply an opening salvo in an appeals court battle over the size of the settlement, he warned Barbieri that the hospital board would never agree to anything near the 70,000 lire he was asking. Trying to project a sense of confidence that he did not in fact feel, he told Barbieri that he was certain the appeals court would leave the much more modest Tribunal figure intact.

Although Barbieri was serious about wanting to settle on terms favorable to the hospital, he could not resist reminding Baldini that the hospital had expressed similar confidence years earlier, when the original appeal had gone to the Bologna appeals court. They both knew that the appeals court was more sympathetic to Amalia's plight than the Tribunal and that it might well substantially increase the amount she was to be paid.

If it were up to him, Barbieri told the hospital's lawyer, he would appeal the decision, and he had no doubt that his side would win. But there were other considerations. It had been ten years since the first syphilitic sore had appeared on poor Amalia's breast. It had been a decade since she had brought her suit, ten years of living in misery. She wanted to wait no more. If they could bring the case to a close while offering her a reasonable payment, she could try to live out her remaining days in some small comfort. To drag the case on further would be cruel.

On June 18, Baldini sent Count Isolani the surprising news that he and Amalia's lawyer had reached a tentative agreement on an out-of-court settlement, subject to the hospital board's approval. Baldini was pleased to report that in the end Barbieri was being accommodating. Amalia would accept the amount set by the Tribunal with only one condition. She asked that the hospital board agree to convert the 30 lire per month lifetime support into one payment. Barbieri had been very clear on this point. His client wanted all of the money right away. Baldini had consulted with a number of insurance companies to determine what the equivalent amount of principal would be. They estimated that a policy that would pay an annual premium of 360 lire would cost about 7,000 lire. Adding the court costs to the other amounts specified in the Tribunal's figure, Baldini calculated that the original decision would have cost the hospital 16,318 lire plus 30 lire per month for the rest of Amalia's life. Converting those monthly payments into a single sum of 7,000 lire produced a figure of 23,318 lire. But he had told Barbieri that they would want to subtract the 780 lire they had paid Amalia as a preliminary settlement two years earlier, and that left, in round figures, a total of 22,500 lire. Amalia's lawyer, in his new, conciliatory mood, had agreed. Isolani, surprised, scheduled a meeting of the hospital board to consider the proposal.

Meanwhile, Barbieri had his own matters to attend to. Alberto Pallotti was accustomed to transacting his business in Bologna, but Barbieri insisted that the matter he now had for him could not wait, and on Tuesday, June 26, the two men boarded a train. When they got off at the Vergato station, they had to ride on mules to get to Oreglia, not a means of travel either was accustomed to. Neither Pallotti nor Barbieri was happy about making the trip, but Amalia was over seven months pregnant and not feeling well. If they were to get her to make her mark on the agreement, they were going to have to go to her bedside.

At the last minute, Pallotti had rounded up two local people to serve as the required witnesses. One was a man who worked as a railway signalman in Vergato. So great was Pallotti's haste that he had to make do for the second with a woman. Following the required form, he asked her what her father's name was, but she could not tell him. She, too, was a foundling.

The document that Pallotti read to Amalia as she lay in her bed, Luigi at her side, attested to her acceptance of a final settlement of 22,500 lire and her pledge that she would never again request any money of the hospital. She also authorized her lawyer, Augusto Barbieri, to receive all of these funds on her behalf and to distribute them as he saw fit.

In the hospital headquarters in Bologna two days later, the full board met to discuss the proposed settlement. Isolani was pleased to see so many of them present, ten in all. He reported on the surprising offer from Amalia's lawyer, accepting the Tribunal figures with the sole proviso that Amalia's monthly support payment be converted into a single payment. He reminded them that if they declined the offer, Barbieri would continue to press Amalia's request for 70,000 lire before a court that had shown itself in the past to be all too sympathetic to her cause.

The board's vice president, Aldo Gattoni, himself a lawyer, spoke next.

None of us, he began, was pleased to be paying such a large sum. The case had been rightly decided in the first instance, when the Tribunal threw it out, but, he reminded them, they all knew what had happened in the years since then and how much it had cost them in legal fees. They were too well bred, he added, to say what they really thought of the appeals court decision or the subsequent Supreme Court ruling. Many of them undoubtedly felt, as he did, that it was beneath them to be forced to pay Amalia anything other than what their charitable impulses would have certainly inclined them to give her had she not dragged them into court. It felt as though they were somehow admitting that what had happened to her was their fault. Yet, given the situation they found themselves in, he thought the proposed settlement not inappropriate. In fact, financially it was not so bad at all.

But, he added, one thing did bother him. It concerned the woman's husband, Luigi Migliorini. He reminded his colleagues that there had earlier been some speculation that the man might take his own legal action against the hospital, based on a separate claim of being damaged by the foundling home's alleged negligence. Given this danger, said Gattoni, he would be more comfortable if the proposed settlement included a formal pledge from Migliorini that he would never take any future action against them.

The men at the table, pleased to have a lawyer on their board, murmured their assent. One of them asked the count what impact the settlement would have on the hospital's finances. Isolani replied with some satisfaction that, knowing that payment of the court-ordered damages was imminent, they had reserved 36,500 lire in the current year's budget for this purpose. Should they agree to Barbieri's settlement, they would in fact be paying Amalia 14,000 lire less than they had, in their prudence, anticipated.

It took a month to make the remaining arrangements. Barbieri got word to Amalia's husband that he would need to come to the city again to sign another important document. Leaving Amalia, now near the end of her pregnancy, Luigi boarded the train for Bologna.

Later in the day, with Luigi's notarized statement in hand, Barbieri walked the short distance to Count Isolani's office. The count, along with his lawyers, Ferrari and Baldini, and the board vice president, Gattoni, were waiting for him with their own notary. The atmosphere, although formal, must have shown signs of the relief that Isolani and his lawyers felt. Their long saga was nearing its end.

Gattoni asked to see the statement they had insisted Amalia's husband sign. Barbieri passed him the document bearing the date of July 25, 1900, that very day. In it, Luigi explicitly renounced any future claim against the foundling home or the hospital board.

Baldini took the statement from Gattoni's hands and read it himself. Isolani and Barbieri then sat at the table and signed the agreement. Amalia's lawyer left the room clutching a bank check for 22,500 lire made out in his name.

CHAPTER 21

Lives Lost and Lives Saved

O N THE AFTERNOON OF THURSDAY, August 16, 1900, Amalia went into labor. Since she had first met Augusto Barbieri and her legal travails had begun, she had been pregnant four times. Twice she had suffered the pain of giving birth to sickly babies whose suffering ended in death. Twice she had given birth to babies who were stillborn.

But this time she dared to hope that her luck might change. Although syphilis had left her weakened, she was free of the earlier symptoms that had plagued her, and Vergato's new doctor told her that having passed the infectious stage of the disease, it was possible that she could give birth to a healthy child.

Before the sun set, Amalia pushed the baby out. It was a girl and, to her great relief, very much alive. The midwife held her up for Amalia to see. The next day the parish priest baptized her with the name of Maria.

Their new, healthy baby, Amalia and Luigi hoped, was the first sign of the beginning of their new life. Barbieri had told Luigi to send word when the baby was born so that they could arrange for a final meeting in Bologna as soon as Amalia could make the trip.

On Tuesday, August 28, with Maria — not yet two weeks old — in her mother's arms, Amalia and Luigi took the train down the river valley to Bologna. By the time they reached the city, they felt a heat they never encountered in Vergato and again must have thought what a horrible place the city was. This, they hoped, would be the last time they would ever go there. With the money they would get, they would buy a farm in the mountains, no longer remaining objects of pity back home.

Waiting for them, Barbieri must have reflected on the past ten years. Neither a sentimental nor a weak man, he nonetheless must have felt some unease about this last encounter with the woman who had entrusted so much to him. Perhaps he tried to dispel the gathering cloud of guilt he felt by telling himself how lucky Amalia had been to find him in the first place. Few other lawyers would have taken her case. Who else would have rushed off to defend an illiterate peasant woman against the powerful hospital board and its formidable lawyers with the prospect of payment remote at best? And if anyone else had taken her case, none, he could be sure, would have continued to fight on even after the Tribunal ruled against them. What would she have gotten then? Nothing, or practically nothing. The other lawyers would have counted themselves lucky to settle early for a few hundred lire. None of his colleagues had ever won a legal victory like his, a case that had twice gone before Italy's highest court and that lawyers and judges from Genoa to Sicily were now citing. Others could only express their astonishment at the amount of money he had wrested from the hospital.

When Amalia and Luigi arrived with the baby, Barbieri said they needed to go downstairs to the notary's office to sign what he promised would be the last document he would ever need to prepare for them. This was one promise he would keep.

Pallotti welcomed them and then turned to the matter at hand. After some of the complicated documents they had had to deal with in the past, he assured them, this one was very simple. In fact, it really was just a way for them to recognize all of the work that had been done for them. He would simply read the document before getting Luigi's signature.

Because her lawyer had so fully and completely performed the task she had assigned him, Signora Bagnacavalli, the notary read, deemed it her duty to express her profound gratitude to him for his generosity of spirit in agreeing to take her case, that of an impoverished woman reduced to the most miserable state of indigence by the terrible illness she contracted from the infant who had been given her. She wanted to acknowledge her gratitude to him for his unshaken faith in her cause and the zeal with which he had pursued her case for ten long years and to congratulate him for arranging the final settlement with the hospital board. Because he had so fully and satisfactorily performed all the duties she had asked of him, she declared that, with the signing of this document, all of his responsibilities toward her were to be considered fully discharged.

By the time Barbieri led the couple back to his office it was getting late, and Amalia and Luigi must have been nervous about making the last train home. They had no idea what they would do if they missed it, for they had no money.

Of what exactly was said in this last conversation between the couple and their lawyer no record remains. Barbieri clearly had no interest in leaving an account, and of course neither Amalia nor Luigi — whose literacy went no further than his signature — was capable of writing one. Most likely Barbieri took advantage of their evident unease with the lateness of the hour and told them that he would explain matters quickly. They should be proud, he would have told them, for important people throughout the country were talking of the courageous Amalia Bagnacavalli and her loyal husband, Luigi. They had won an important victory, not only for themselves, but for poor people everywhere.

But, he must have then said, the victory had not come easily. They had overcome many obstacles, many setbacks, and throughout it all, no thanks to the hospital that kept fighting them, their expenses had grown. Luckily, the money they had won from the hospital board — the most money any hospital had ever paid someone like Amalia — would cover all of their debts. He likely reminded them of how much they owed Dr. Majocchi. Had the good doctor not stood up to his colleagues, they would never have won. Similarly, Barbieri himself had over the years spent a great deal of money battling their case, traveling to Rome, to Ancona, spending endless hours of his time.

Barbieri could no longer put off the news he had to give them. Unfortunately, he said, given these expenses, when all of their debts were paid, nothing was left. Indeed, the money from the hospital had not been enough to pay all of their debts. A few remained, including one to Riccardo Orlandi. He would have liked to have had better news, but he knew they would understand that they had gotten as much as they could and, after ten years, he knew how eager they were to get on with their lives. Barbieri must have in the end tried to reassure them with his pledge that he would pay off the several hundred lire of remaining debt they had from the funds that were meant for him.

How did Amalia and Luigi react to this news? Did they use the rich palette of profanity their mountain dialect provided to denounce their erstwhile defender? Did they remind him of all the assurances he had given them over the years, how many times he had told them that they should trust him completely? Were they tempted to get up and wring his neck, or did Amalia simply sit there, stunned, cry softly, and hug her uncomprehending baby? Did the dumbfounded Luigi simply stare vacantly at his hands?

Whatever transpired, the couple soon left and walked to the train station. They would never see Barbieri, or Bologna, again.

If their suit against Count Isolani, the hospital board, and the foundling home doctors had, in the end, brought Amalia and Luigi nothing, it certainly had a fateful impact on the hundreds of babies left every year at the Bologna foundling home. In 1896, frightened by the court's decision against them and the seemingly endless number of wet nurses getting syphilis, the hospital board had ordered that all babies whose mothers could not be dragooned into nursing them were to be placed on artificial feeding for the first three months of their life. In its first two years, the horrifying result of the new policy, a direct product of Amalia's suit and her lawyer's success, became clear. By the time Amalia's case finally ended in 1900, the results from the previous two years showed that, if anything, things had gotten worse. Of the over seven hundred babies left there without their mothers, only 30 percent survived long enough to ever suckle at a woman's breast. And many of those who made it that far were by then so sickly that they expired within another month or two.

The death of these hundreds of babies in the middle of Bologna, just as the city's elite was launching a major modernization and expansion campaign, did not go unnoticed. Within a year of the introduction of the new policy, provincial councilors were denouncing the carnage, and in 1900 they created a special commission to investigate, presided over by the provincial president himself. Among the commission's six members, in deference to the hospital board, was Count Isolani. Its other members included Giuseppe Barbanti, the same man whose sword had sliced through Barbieri's cheek over a decade earlier, and Bologna's preeminent man of medicine, Dr. Augusto Murri.

Although not a councilor, Murri was the most prominent critic of Isolani and the new foundling home policy, which he viewed as a blueprint for murdering large numbers of babies. Ironically, Murri would himself soon be an object of one of Italy's most famous murder investigations. In 1902 his son, Tullio, plunged a dagger thirteen times into the chest and neck of Murri's son-in-law, Count Francesco Bonmartini, in his lavish home not far from Isolani's own palace in the center of Bologna. That Murri's daughter, Linda, was alleged to have begged her brother to murder her husband and that sister and brother were rumored to have had an incestuous relationship themselves ensured that Bologna's foremost physician would for months have his portrait appear in newspapers throughout the peninsula.

But all this was in the future. After a year of deliberations, the commission on which he sat released its voluminous report.

Why, asked the commissioners, did Italy compare so poorly to other civilized countries when it came to these unfortunate children? Why did Italy have so many babies abandoned each year? Referring to the Papal States, of which Bologna had been a part until four decades earlier, they blamed the problem on the previous epoch of "theocratic domination." Farther north in Europe, under what they called the Germanic or Anglo-Saxon system, parents — both men and women — were required to take responsibility for their actions and, in the case of children born outside wedlock, to pay for the consequences of their behavior. Under the Latin system, inspired by the church, paternity searches were forbidden, and men were freed from any responsibility for fathering illegitimate children. Similarly, while the church insisted that the unwed woman's honor must be protected, enabling her to jettison the product of her illicit behavior, in northern Europe such women were expected to keep their babies.

This Protestant model was one that the commissioners thought Italy should emulate. The poor women producing Italy's abandoned babies should be paid to encourage them to keep the infants. Yet, they warned, in instituting such a system, certain cautions had to be observed. Many of the illegitimate babies, they found, were not the offspring of virginal women who had been momentarily lured into sin but the progeny of women who had a long history of wayward behavior. Indeed, a not insignificant proportion of the babies were the second or third or even fourth child of such women. The foundling home had no business helping them, the commissioners argued, for they had no honor to protect and did not merit society's largesse. The commission recommended that the centuries-old practice of offering anonymity to the mothers who abandoned their babies be ended. In the future, all such women were to be identified so that those who were found to be deserving could be separated from those who were not. The women of loose morals would be left to fend for themselves, their babies their responsibility alone.

Once these measures were taken and the flood of babies left at the foundling home was reduced, the current policy of assigning all abandoned babies to artificial feeding should, the commissioners advised, be changed. No modern society could tolerate the deaths of so many foundlings, and the only way to keep the infants alive was to allow them to nurse at a woman's breast.

As for the risk of infection of the wet nurses and so the risk of further suits, the commissioners urged that the greatest caution be exercised in identifying babies who showed the slightest sign of syphilis. Such babies should be placed in a special ward for suspected syphilitics and fed artificially. Toward this end, a physician specializing in syphilis should be employed in the foundling home.

The commissioners also backed the idea that Isolani had first heard from the lawyer he had consulted in Modena a few years earlier. They suggested that each wet nurse be required to have a doctor of her choosing examine the infant before she took him and certify that he found no sign of syphilis. The foundling home would pay the doctor for this service, after which the woman would put her signature — or mark — on a document noting that this rule had been followed.

The commission first presented its report to Bologna's provincial council at a meeting on Saturday, June 22, 1901. Count Isolani, feeling personally attacked by the criticisms of the policies he had introduced at the foundling home, gave a long history of the hospital's efforts to keep the foundlings alive while protecting the health of the wet nurses. It was only after everything they tried had failed, he told them, that they decided that they had no alternative but to place the infants on artificial feeding.

The count's argument made little impression on the socialist firebrand Giuseppe Barbanti, Isolani's fellow commissioner and Barbieri's old antagonist. The underlying problem, he argued, went far deeper. It lay in a society that was based on inequality, a society in which the masses of people were oppressed and too poor to cope with the children they produced. Of every 100 women who abandoned their babies, he claimed, 98 would have kept them if they only had the means to do so.

Although Barbanti could scarcely give a speech without first denouncing the evils of capitalism, he soon turned to the point he was most eager to make in attacking the count. "Let us ask ourselves," said the lawyer, "which is regarded as worse: having made four or five or even ten wet nurses sick with syphilis, a disease that can be treated in a few months if proper hygiene is followed, or having caused this immense massacre of foundlings?" Answering his own question, he thundered: "Better, far better, to have three or four sick women who get better than to cause seventy deaths!"

The head of the provincial council, seeing that the hour was late and the debate still heated, adjourned the session. The following Friday he gaveled them back to order, the new session beginning with a long report from Bologna's Medical Society. The Medical Society had devoted its last three meetings to the foundling crisis, during which the foundling home doctors had given their own reports. The society's members had reached a conclusion not very different from the commission's. If all proper precautions were used, they found, and all of the babies with signs of syphilis were identified, not more than 2 percent of the rest would develop the disease. Such a small number could not justify the current practice of placing all healthy babies on artificial feeding, a practice that had turned the foundling home into a "slaughterhouse for poor abandoned children."

Following Count Isolani's protest over the councilor's use of "slaughterhouse" to describe the foundling home, the session was called to a close. A week later, at its third session devoted to the report, its recommendations were put to a vote and approved. The foundlings would once again be nourished at the breast.

Over the previous years, hundreds of babies had died because of Amalia's lawsuit. Yet, over those same years, dozens of young peasant women owed their health and the lives of their children yet to be born to the woman from Vergato.

In retrospect, the drama that swirled around the unlikely figure of Amalia Bagnacavalli appears as the last crisis of an age that was nearing an end. The pumping out of huge numbers of abandoned babies from the cities to families in the countryside had marked

Italian society for centuries. The end of papal rule and the erosion of the old norms forcing unwed women to abandon their babies would soon begin to reduce this flow. And even more dramatically, the terrible choices that foundling home officials had faced — weighing the fate of the babies against that of the women who nursed them — would soon disappear. With the revolution that would come with the introduction of pasteurization and the discovery in the 1920s of an infant formula that would more closely resemble the content of mother's milk, consigning newborns to bottle-feeding would no longer mean condemning most of them to an early death.

CHAPTER 22

Aristocrats, Lawyers, Doctors, and Peasants: Amalia Looks Back

W HILE COUNT ISOLANI, Dr. Murri, Giuseppe Barbanti, and the members of the provincial council were arguing over what to do about the syphilitic wet nurses, Luigi and Amalia were back in Oreglia with their new baby. In the home that they had once shared with Luigi's large family, there now remained only his mother, who did her best to help with the house and the baby. Luigi's father had died the previous year, and his remaining brother had married and moved out.

With the weakened Luigi the only man in the household and the frail Amalia and her elderly mother-in-law the only women, it was hard to keep the farm going. Before long, their landlord informed them that they would have to leave.

Unable to find another landowner willing to let them have a farm, Amalia and Luigi had to move into a dirt-floor dwelling in another parish of Vergato. There the couple, the baby, and Luigi's mother all shared a single room. Somehow, between the occasional day's work that Luigi found as a laborer and the charity provided by the town office, they survived. Amalia once again found herself pregnant, and in August 1905 she gave birth to another girl, whom they named Marcellina.

Oddly — for multiple marriages between peasant families were not common — in the mid-1890s Amalia's younger brother, Quintilio, had married another of Luigi's sisters, Emilia. Amalia's two brothers, in short, had married Luigi's two sisters.

Although Amalia's father had himself begun life at the Bologna foundling home, her mother's family had owned their farm in Vergato. As a result, the Bagnacavallis were better-off than the Migliorinis. But while relatively well-off among the peasantry of the mountains, the Bagnacavalli brothers did not hesitate when a chance came to escape their arduous farmwork. Just before the turn of the century, Alfonso found a job as a railway clerk in the small town of Pracchia, which lay on the train line just across the regional border into Tuscany, and he soon found a job for his brother as well. The two brothers and their families were joined by their widowed father.

When his mother died, Luigi and Amalia and their two daughters had no one left in Vergato. For years Amalia herself had little reason to want to stay. For a time she had been viewed as something of a maverick, at least among the women of Vergato, a woman willing to fight for the rights of the peasants, the rights of exploited women. But after she ended up with even less than she had had before, she was at best the object of her neighbors' charity. And having everyone know about her syphilis must have hurt her pride, the shame lessened only slightly because all knew how she had gotten the disease.

There is good reason to believe that neither Amalia's brothers nor Luigi's sisters were eager to see the couple join them in their new town. Amalia and Luigi's notoriety had, it seems, been one of the reasons they had all been so eager to leave Vergato and start a new life, freed from the embarrassing associations of the Bagnacavalli name. But there finally came a time when Amalia wore down Alfonso and Quintilio's resistance and when Luigi's pride, too, must have given way to his desperation. The brothers, it seems, insisted on one condition for helping them make the move. Amalia was not to let anyone in their new home know that she was the infamous Amalia Bagnacavalli of Vergato. Instead, she would tell everyone that she was from another province altogether, from Modena, and she would use not her own name but her husband's. She would be related to them not as their sister but as their sister-in-law. It is hard to see how else her listing in the annual parish census of Pracchia could be explained. From the time she moved there in 1916, she was Amalia Migliorini, born in Modena.

When they moved to Pracchia, Maria was fifteen and Marcellina, ten. That she had been able to have children who could help share her burdens and brighten her life was Amalia's one consolation. Yet she had ample reason to worry about their future. As poor as she and Luigi were, they could offer the girls no dowry to speak of, and without a dowry it would be difficult to find them decent husbands.

Amalia must have been relieved when Maria told her one day of a young man she had met, Torquato Venturi. True, he came from a poor family of agricultural day laborers, but Amalia knew that she could not hope for any better. On December 30, 1920, the twenty-year-old Maria married Torquato. Fourteen months later she gave birth to a healthy boy, Franco, Amalia's first and (as it would turn out) only grandchild. But this brief period of happiness in Amalia's life came to an end three years later when Maria, perhaps as the result of an ill-fated pregnancy, got sick and died. Four years later, at twenty-two and still without a husband, Marcellina also died. What she died from is unknown.

For the first time in their lives, Amalia and Luigi lived alone. They could survive only because Amalia's brothers had found Luigi a job as a custodian at the train station where they worked.

When a new priest in town made his first Lenten visit to bless her tiny apartment and to take the annual parish census, he found it odd that Amalia gave her husband's last name as her own. Looking over the previous years' listings, he saw that ever since she had come to Pracchia she had used Luigi's surname. He insisted that — as church practice required — she give him the name she was born with.

Amalia's imagination was clearly limited, for the name she gave the priest was Cavalli. Although to her neighbors she was known simply as Amalia, or Amalia wife of Migliorini, for the remaining days of her life she would appear in the parish records as Amalia Cavalli.

By this time Amalia and Luigi were both getting on in years. Decades earlier, few would have guessed that they would have lived so long. They had been lucky, for they had escaped the degeneration of the nervous system that many syphilitics suffered and the madness and death that came with it. Although Luigi was not well, the people at the railway station had taken pity on him and kept him on the payroll. Each day he would go in and sweep the halls and the platform and wipe the glass at the ticket counter. A few times a day the train from Bologna pulled into the station, stopping briefly on its way to Pistoia and then on to Florence.

Two days after Christmas, 1936, Luigi Migliorini — seventy-nine years old and infirm, but still listed in the parish census as a railway custodian — received the last rites and died. Amalia was now alone.

As the old woman reflected on her long life with Luigi, her thoughts would turn to those strange and terrible times when her life had been so radically changed. Along with the painful memories of little Adele's death and the deaths of her other newborns were the memories of her physical suffering and of Luigi's. She must also have recalled her first train ride to Bologna and all the others that followed.

If she thought back to the lawyer whom she had seen for so long as her champion, the man who would stand up for her before all those powerful forces that she could never hope to understand, what did she recall? Did she think of the hopes that she had once allowed herself to nurture? Did she wonder what had happened to him and to the others who had been part of that distant life? What became of the doctor from the clinic who had fought for her and then taken so much money? What about the count, who was so angered by her attempt to get what they owed her, or the pompous old doctor, who ran the insane asylum and insisted that Paola couldn't have given her syphilis, that she must have gotten it somewhere else?

Of all the people she must have recalled, the only one whose fate she knew was that of Dr. Dalmonte, a man she would still remember with affection, the man who told her she should not let the foundling home doctors get away with what they had done to her. He had died in 1896, well before reaching old age, battling Vergato's mayor to the end.

She hadn't seen anyone else from that distant life after that sorry day when Barbieri had told them there was no money left, that after ten years of fighting, there was nothing. She had returned to her world, the world that she and her parents and grandparents and ancestors had always lived in. And the city lawyers and the professors and the judges and the count had all gone back to theirs.

If she realized that she, the syphilitic peasant woman on whose survival none of them would have wagered, had outlived them all, she would have taken no comfort from it. Count Francesco Isolani had died in 1906, shortly after his seventieth birthday, still president of the Bologna hospital board, a position that had lasted thirty-two years. Professor Francesco Roncati, four years older than Isolani, had died the same year, still head of Bologna's insane asylum, to which he left his entire estate. The city honored him by naming the hospital to which he had devoted so much of his life the Francesco Roncati Psychiatric Hospital, a name the building still bears today. Ironically, the dusty records of Amalia's legal saga are now inside the asylum's walls, with the archives of the foundling hospital and the hospital board.

Domenico Majocchi had died in 1929. After his decisive role in Amalia's case, his career had continued its upward climb, despite the bad feelings he had left among some of his colleagues in Bologna. Famed for the new methods he developed for using iodine to

treat syphilis and admired for his philosophical and historical erudition, he was repeatedly elected president of Italy's Society of Dermatology and Syphilology. It was a heady time for people like
Majocchi, for in 1905 the pathogen responsible for syphilis was
finally identified through a microscope, and a year later a blood
test was devised for diagnosing the disease. No longer would there
be any uncertainty whether a baby was born with syphilis. The
centuries-long debate over whether a man could transmit the disease to his offspring directly while leaving the baby's mother unaf-
fected was finally over. Doctors now knew that babies could be
born with syphilis only if their mother had the disease. The identi-
fication of the cause of syphilis, a kind of bacterium called a spirochete — not a virus, as the doctors had previously thought — led to
new chemotherapies that would ultimately conquer the disease.
Neither Amalia nor Luigi, though, would live long enough to see
the first truly successful treatment for syphilis, with the introduction of penicillin in 1943.

After seeing Amalia for the last time, Augusto Barbieri wrote
no more treatises on good government, no more tracts championing the rights of the working class and peasantry. He threw himself
into his flourishing law practice, occasionally visiting the farms he
bought up in the countryside. He even tried to enter politics — as a
conservative, having abandoned his youthful enthusiasm for the
left — running unsuccessfully for a seat on the Bologna provincial
council. What it seemed he was best at in his later years was making
money. When he died in the summer of 1916, only fifty-four years
old, he had accumulated a notable fortune and was known to enjoy
the finer things in life. Indeed, he long served as the Bologna chapter president of the Wagnerian Society.

Much had changed in Bologna since Amalia's last visit. If she
were to take the train there now, no wall would stand in her way, for
the city fathers — despite opposition from those who said they were
destroying the city's heritage — ordered the medieval wall that enveloped the city torn down. The gate through which Amalia had

passed in March 1890 had been left standing, but it was now an isolated portal, a mute witness to a wall that was no more. No guards
were left to inspect suspicious bulges in peasants' clothes.

The socialists who had so worried Count Isolani and so alarmed
Dr. Roncati had succeeded in conquering the city, a socialist mayor
and city council being elected in 1911. But just nine years later,
even before Mussolini's minions marched on Rome and his regime
was born, fascists invaded the medieval city government fortress
that Amalia had seen that first day and drove Bologna's mayor and
his town council from its halls. When Luigi died, Mussolini was at
the height of his power and his popularity, fresh from conquering
new colonies in Ethiopia and poised to make his fateful pact with
Hitler.

If Amalia was living amid major changes in Italian society, she
would not have been aware of them. The world of Pracchia was
much like the world she had known as a young woman in Oreglia.

Amalia, who had shared so much with Luigi, did not last long
without him. A few months after standing by his grave in Pracchia,
she herself was buried at his side. Some years later, their remains were unceremoniously removed to make room for others.
Only those families who could afford permanent tombs were allowed to keep their dead in that hallowed ground for any length
of time.

Amalia was survived only by her fifteen-year-old grandson, Franco.
But Franco would prove to be the last of the line. Although he married in 1956, he and his wife never had any children, and he himself
died nine years after his marriage, at the age of forty-three. Some
might attribute his fate to a curse that had been placed on the family decades earlier, when a young woman handed five coins to a
ticket vendor at Vergato's tiny train station and headed for the
big city.

When Amalia and Luigi moved to Pracchia, they vowed never
to tell anyone what had happened to them. Amalia Bagnacavalli,
briefly famous in the hills around Vergato, and whose sorry story

was known to readers of law books in the late nineteenth century —
the protagonist of one of Italy's first major medical malpractice
suits — ceased to exist the day they arrived in that small mountain
town. And even though Franco, her grandson, left a widow, who
is still alive today, it is a good bet that not even she has heard
Amalia's tale.

Recovering Buried History

A MALIA BAGNACAVALLI'S suit against Count Isolani and the hospitals of Bologna was long forgotten when I came upon it unexpectedly while working in the archives of the Bologna foundling home on a history of infant abandonment. That research led to a book, *Sacrificed for Honor,* in which I tried to describe the extent of abandonment in nineteenth-century Italy and to make sense of it. But ever since I came across the first documents describing Amalia's decade-long odyssey from obscurity to public prominence, I couldn't get it out of my mind.

There are many ways to write history, and over the years I have tried my hand at several of them. I've written about kings, popes, prime ministers, and major world changes, and I've also written about the lives and daily dramas of illiterate peasants. Although there were many more peasants than kings, popes, and prime ministers, the poor and illiterate have received comparatively little attention from historians and even less from others who write books of history for broader audiences.

Those who would like to do something about this imbalance face the obvious problem that it is not easy to recover the history of people who wrote no letters, kept no diaries, and about whom few contemporaries left any written accounts. But beginning a few decades ago, historians seeking to unearth this buried evidence have tried to find ways out of this impasse. The "new social history" that was all the rage — at least in academic circles — back in the 1970s took as its mission shedding light on this invisible majority. One of the approaches pioneered back then, which heavily influences my own book, came to be known as microhistory. Books in this tradition bring a dramatic series of events into view, focusing on an obscure cast of characters from the past who represent, despite all their peculiarities, the large unlettered population ignored in history. My own use of a trial as a centerpiece for such a story reflects a technique used by others, most famously by Natalie Zemon Davis in *The Return of Martin Guerre* and Carlo Ginzburg in *The Cheese and the Worms*. The focus on trials in these works is not coincidental. Trials not only offer a drama that makes for an absorbing story. They also leave masses of evidence documenting the fraught encounter between the world of the powerless and that of the powerful. Even more important, trials provide precious written records — often voluminous — of the daily lives of the illiterate people of the past.

While I use this method of microhistory, I supplement it with another of the techniques used in the now no longer so "new" social history. If peasants did not keep records of their lives, various public officials did. Most notably, each remote rural hamlet had a parish priest, who was not only charged with recording all vital events — births, marriages, and deaths — but also required to take an annual household census. Thanks to this practice, we can follow Amalia and Luigi and their families back to a time before either was born and up to their deaths and beyond. Alongside these ecclesiastical records, Italian historians are fortunate to have detailed civil records of this period, for by law each town was required to keep a continuous census of its population, recording births, deaths, marriages, migrations, and changes in who lived with whom. Unfortunately, the records of these events for Amalia's family in Vergato were destroyed by Allied bombing in World War II. The only such records of any use left for me were those of the city of Pistoia, under whose authority the mountain hamlet of Pracchia lies.

One of the great pleasures of doing historical research is making unexpected discoveries in the archives. Work on this book took me to the archives of the foundling home and of the hospital board that oversaw it, where hundreds of relevant documents are to be found, to the state archives of Bologna, where some of Dr. Dalmonte's reports lie buried, and to the Archiginnasio of Bologna — the city's historical library — which houses a wealth of documentation from Amalia's trial. Going to Vergato to see if the parish registers for the late nineteenth century remained — guided and driven by my research collaborator, Giancarlo Dalle Donne — was a pleasurably tense experience. The church that Amalia and Luigi attended, in the tiny hamlet of Vimignano, cannot now support its own priest, so we had to find a time when the priest who served several such churches could meet us. Until we opened the dusty cabinet in which the old church records were kept, neither he nor we knew if the ones we needed would still be there. Fortunately, they were, and we could see the entries for Amalia and Luigi's families, including the entry that the priest made just before Easter 1890, when he visited the Migliorini household and recorded the existence there of a foundling named Paola Olivelli.

Some sources that I found only late in my combing of the archives I should, in retrospect, have known to look for earlier. The notarial records offer a good example. As I neared the end of my efforts in the archives, none of the documents I had seen mentioned anything about Barbieri's use of notaries in his dealings with Amalia. It was only when, taking a shot in the dark, Giancarlo and I decided to pore through Bologna's main notarial archive that we excitedly began to unearth these scattered documents. Together, they detailed the fateful course of Barbieri's financial dealings with Amalia. This opened up a whole other side of the story, one as dramatic in its own way as the medical and legal struggle that I had been focusing on until then.

In casting as wide a net as possible, I happily made a number of other discoveries. While I was looking through the historic archives of Bologna's Museum of the Risorgimento, hoping to find material to flesh out some of the protagonists of the case, the archivists, Mirtide Gavelli and Otello Sangiorgi, mentioned a lawyer from the period who had left his personal archive to the museum. I had no reason to believe that he had anything to do with Amalia's story but began to look through the inventory anyway. The man who had left the archive was Giuseppe Barbanti, and I was surprised — and of course pleased — to find that one major category of documents concerned a duel that he had fought with a young Bologna lawyer named Augusto Barbieri.

The pleasure of archival research comes not only from discovering such documents but from handling pieces of paper that were once in the hands of the people whose thoughts and actions of long ago the historian is trying to reconstruct. A simple listing of the archival sources used — as I provide in the pages that follow — doesn't begin to describe their richness. Readers might note from the hospital board archives, for example, a letter that the prefect of Bologna sent to Count Isolani on a certain date, but they get no notion of all the count's comments — some bureaucratic, but others betraying strong emotion — scrawled in his neat handwriting at an angle in the margins. I can list a register of women admitted to Bologna's syphilis clinic in 1890, but I can't convey the excitement that comes from seeing the comments on the treatment of each woman listed there, comments written by the doctors who were at the same time examining and treating Amalia. Even the list of books and journal articles consulted for the project fails to convey what it was like, for example, to work in the historical library of the Bologna dermo-syphilology clinic, holding in my hands the dusty nineteenth-century Italian and French books on treating syphilis that Dr. Gamberini and Dr. Majocchi themselves once read there.

But none of this research is of much use to anyone else unless it can somehow be translated into a narrative that makes this history come alive, one that allows those not lucky enough to have pored through old documents in Bologna to feel as if they themselves had entered another world. The challenge is to write a drama that surprises, a story that appeals to the heart as well as the mind.

If this book is the story of a struggle involving a woman who long ago was infected by a terrible disease, it is also the product of a more recent struggle as well, my own efforts to wrestle with two sometimes competing desires. As a scholar I am trained to stick to the evidence. This is, after all, a work of history and not of fiction. According to the interpretation of this imperative most common in the scholarly world, it means not making any observation without indicating the primary source on which it is based. There are very good reasons for this stricture. But it comes at a cost, for it ill accords with my second goal in writing this book, the desire to reach beyond the scholarly world, to recount a dramatic story for a wider audience.

I have no doubt that the way I went about reconciling these two competing aims will attract criticism from both sides. Some general readers may find it odd that certain details that they are most curious about are strangely absent from the book. I would have loved to have been able to describe, for example, just what Amalia and Luigi looked like, but other than generic descriptions of their health and later descriptions of their syphilitic symptoms, there is no record of whether they were short or tall, whether Amalia's hair was black, auburn, or red, or whether they smiled a lot or only a little. And how valuable it would be to know what Amalia and Luigi told each other when they first got sick, when they suffered through their painful treatments, when they had to make decisions about their suit against the hospital. But of such conversations no evidence remains, and, alas, these are not details that I could invent.

On the other hand, scholars may be displeased by two elements that distinguish this book from an academic monograph. The first is that I have not separately footnoted every statement of fact in these pages. If I had, the text would have been littered with hundreds of footnotes. The great majority of these — citing individual documents in obscure archives, which is what the book is largely based on — would have been of use to no more than a handful of readers, those who might want to actually go to the archives to check particular documents. As an anthropologist, I can't help but observe that such massive footnoting serves another function, acting as a kind of scholarly holy water that, sprinkled throughout academic texts, helps give them an aura of authority.

What I have done instead is to place at the end of the book a list of all the archival and published sources I have used. Should scholars want to check up on any facet of my account, they should have little trouble finding the documents on which it is based.

This book also trespasses on the norms for the writing of academic history because, in seeking to bring this story alive, I offer minor details of people's behavior that cannot be directly known from the documents left behind. This is clearly a slippery slope for anyone who wants to write serious history. The details I have in mind here, though, are those designed to make the narrative flow. The early pages of the book offer a good example. I know, for example, that Amalia first met her lawyer in Barbieri's office in Bologna in early August 1890 and that it was then that she first told him what had happened to her and asked for his help. The substance of what she told him that day is known from the historical record, but what precisely she said is not and how he reacted to her has to be inferred from a variety of other archival materials and can't be known with any certainty.

How successful I have been in trying to write serious history for a general audience must be left to readers to judge. If I am lucky, readers will be touched by this story and find in these pages glimpses into an unknown and unsuspected past. Yet I also hope that, along the way, they not only peer into a past that seems dramatically distant from the present but consider some disturbing parallels with our world today. Today too we witness the drama of a terrible disease passed between baby and the breast, but now it is infants, not the women who are nursing them, whose lives are at risk, threatened with infection by HIV-positive mothers. Nor is the question of what responsibility doctors and hospitals should have for the damage they do in the course of their duties simply a historical one. Today the kind of legal action that Amalia took, which then had no name, has become so common that it is part of a well-known category, the medical malpractice suit. Yet the kinds of moral and legal questions that the judges had to face in late-nineteenth-century Bologna are, at their core, not very different from those courts confront today. As for the fate suffered by Amalia and Luigi, perhaps all we can say is that back then, as today, when the world of the rich collides with that of the poor, it is rarely the rich who suffer.

ACKNOWLEDGMENTS

NOTES

SOURCES

INDEX

Acknowledgments

Thanks are due above all to Giancarlo Dalle Donne, expert archivist and Bologna historian, who collaborated closely with me on this research, helped identify many archival sources, and offered valuable advice on local history.

This research was greatly helped by the collaboration of many archivists who arranged for access to materials that were not otherwise available or assisted in other ways. These include Ingrid Germani and Carmela Binchi at the Archivio di Stato di Bologna; Anna Manfron at the Biblioteca Comunale Archiginnasio di Bologna; Letizia Bongiovanni at the Archivio Storico della Provincia di Bologna; Monica Biagioni at the Archivio Storico del Comune di Pistoia; and Mirtide Gavelli and Otello Sangiorgi at the Archivio Storico of the Museo del Risorgimento Italiano a Bologna. I would like to thank as well the personnel at the other archives and libraries where I worked for their help.

I am indebted to the parish priests whose willingness to open their historical archives to me made it possible to follow the lives of Amalia and Luigi. These include Don Leonardo Masetti of San Lorenzo di Vimignano (along with Angiolina Cortini, who offered help there), Don Giorgio Pederzini of Sacro Cuore di Gesù di Vergato, and Don Maurizio of San Lorenzo di Pracchia (and Leida Vivarelli for her help).

At Brown University, my academic home for the past decade and a half, I would like to thank my talented graduate student and research assistant, Simone Poliandri, and the staff of the Department of Anthropology, Katherine Grimaldi and Matilde Andrade. I would also like to acknowledge all of the help provided by the Paul Dupee Jr. University Professorship of Social Science.

In Bologna, in addition to the people mentioned above, I would like to thank Arturo Parisi and Anna Piga for hosting my wife, Susan, and me in their home for many of the months we were in Bologna while I was working on this project. I'd also like to thank other colleagues at the University of Bologna for their advice, including Pier Cesare Bori, Giovanna Endrici, Andrea Lollini, and Massimo Nobili.

For their encouragement of my belief in the value of this unorthodox book project, I thank Janet Silver of Houghton Mifflin and my literary agent, Ted Chichak. For advice as I wrestled with how to go about writing this book, I thank my friend Jonathan Harr and my editor at Houghton Mifflin, Webster Younce. For her excellent work editing the final text of this book, I thank Luise Erdmann. For comments on earlier drafts of the book, in addition to Webster, thanks to Giancarlo Dalle Donne and Giovanni Pizzorusso, to my daughter and expert editor Molly Kertzer, and to my old friend Nancy Egan, who in her many years of practice in dermatology has seen a lot but never had a patient who contracted syphilis the way Amalia did.

Notes

2. The Fateful Day

1. Francois Mauriceau, *The Accomplisht Midwife*, quoted in Fildes 1986b, 101.

3. The First Signs

1. In 1888 the law governing prostitution was replaced with a new law that abolished the forcing of infected prostitutes into syphilis clinics. The move was opposed by most physicians, who regarded it as a public health disaster, and a new law in 1891 partly reinstated the old practices (Gattei 1984; Lelli 1988).
2. Buret 1891, 13.

4. Suing the Count

1. The quote is from a 1780 letter by Boncompagni to Pallavicini, Cardoza 1982, 28.
2. Sarti 1896.
3. Raymond 1892, 70.
4. Quoted in Bulkley 1894, 171. See also Fournier's (1878, 8) discussion on the subject.
5. Rollet 1887, 24.
6. Baldwin 1999, 355; Raymond 1892, 115.

7. Bulkley 1894, 161–62; Ransel 1988, 280.
8. Crissey and Parish 1981, 80–81; Paci 2004, 369; Musti 1998, 23–24.
9. Hayden 2003, 25–31.
10. Griffini 1868, 486.

5. The Mercury Treatment

1. Crissey and Parish 1981, 360.
2. Baldwin 1999, 470. This curiously echoes a belief found today in parts of Africa regarding the most effective cure for AIDS.

7. Disputing the Doctor

1. Fournier 1878, 23.

8. The Parade of the Syphilitic Peasants

1. Proni 2006, 53–54.

10. The Miserly Syphilologist

1. P. Gamberini, *Trattato teorico-pratico delle malattie veneree* (Milan: Brigola, 1872), 19–23; discussed by Forzoni 2003, 70.

13. The Tribunal Decides

1. Forzoni 2003, 19; Paci 2004, 368.

15. The Loan

1. Sen. Conforti, December 3, 1868, quoted in Santor 1996, 97.

17. Mixed News from the Supreme Court

1. *Giurisprudenza Italiana,* 5th ser., 48 (Turin: Unione Tip.-Editrice, 1896), 19–21.
2. Gabba, C. F. 1895. "Commento." Il Foro italiano. Raccolta generale di giurisprudenza civile, commerciale, penale, amministrativa, volume XX — Anno 1895.
3. Pasi 1998, 740.

20. Amalia's Lawyer Submits His Bill

1. We know what Amalia looked like in 1898 thanks to a court-ordered physical examination performed on May 13 of that year by Celso Pellizzari, the head of the University of Florence Department of Dermo-Syphilology.

Sources

I. Documents from the Trial of Amalia Bagnacavalli v. Hospitals of Bologna and Count Isolani

A. *Archiginnasio di Bologna.*

R. Tribunale Civile di Bologna. *Causa Bagnacavalli-Spedali di Bologna.* Bologna: Soc. Tip. Azzoguidi, 1891. Brief by Avv. Barbieri, proc. #233–262.

R. Corte d'Appello di Bologna. *Bagnacavalli contro Spedali di Bologna di un caso di sifilide per allattamento. Svolgimento delle Conclusioni nell'interesse dell'appellante Bagnacavalli.* Bologna, 27 novembre 1893, Avv. Augusto Barbieri. Bologna: Soc. Tip. Azzoguidi, 1893, #85–125.

R. Corte d'Appello d'Ancona, in sede di rinvio. *Causa Bagnacavalli-Spedali di Bologna. Memoria defensionale nell'interesse di Bagnacavalli Amalia.* Ancona, 25 aprile 1896, Avv. Augusto Barbieri, est.; Avv. Domenico Pacetti. Bologna: Soc. Tip. Azzoguidi, 1896, proc. #44–84.

Regio Tribunale Civile di Bologna. *Causa Bagnacavalli Amalia contro Amministrazione degli Spedali, anno 1893. Comparsa Conclusionale per l'Amministrazione degli Spedali.* Bologna, 12 giugno 1893. Avv. Pietro Baldini; Avv. Odoardo Ferrari, proc. #126–145.

R. Corte d'Appello di Bologna (Presidenza Maielli). *Causa Spedali di Bologna contro Bagnacavalli, Udienza 17 maggio 1892. Comparsa Conclu-*

sionale per l'Amministrazione degli Spedali. Studio, 15 aprile 1892. Avv. Pietro Baldini; Avv. Odoardo Ferrari, proc. #146–162.

Suprema Corte di Cassazione di Roma. *Ricorso della Amministrazione degli Spedali di Bologna contro Bagnacavalli Amalia. Preteso risarcimento di danni da infezione sifilitica. Denuncia la sentenza fra le parti della Corte d'Appello di Bologna 6–24 aprile 1894.* Avv. Pietro Baldini, #163–168.

Corte d'Appello di Bologna. *Difesa per l'Amministrazione degli Spedali di Bologna contro Bagnacavalli Amalia in punto a pretesa riforma di Sentenza di Tribunale di Bologna 20 luglio-8 agosto 1893, Comparsa Conclusionale.* Bologna, 18 marzo 1894. Avv. Pietro Baldini; Avv. Odoardo Ferrari, proc. #169–191.

Sullo stato di Salute dei Coniugi Bagnacavalli-Migliorini contagiati da sifilide dalla esposta Olivelli e sulle possibili conseguenze derivanti da questo contagio pel Prof. Domenico Majocchi. Bologna: Soc. Tip. Azzoguidi, 1894, #192–196.

Perizia Giudiziale del Dott. Giuseppe Ravaglia nella Casa Bagnacavalli contro l'Amministrazione degli Spedali di Bologna. Bologna: Monti, 1893, #197–209.

Dopo la Sentenza. Note Critiche del Dott. Giuseppe Ravaglia nella Causa Bagnacavalli contro l'Amministrazione degli Spedali di Bologna. Bologna: Monti, n.d., #210–219.

R. Corte d'Appello di Bologna. *Sentenza nella Causa Civile promossa da Bagnacavalli Amalia contro Ospedali di Bologna* (a redazione dell'-Ecc.mo Consigliere Cav. E. Angiolini). Bologna: Azzoguidi, 1894, #220–232.

R. Corte d'Appello di Ancona in sede di rinvio. *Sentenza nella Causa Bagnacavalli contro Spedali di Bologna.* Bologna: Azzoguidi, 10 gennaio, 1896, #36–43.

R. Corte d'Appello di Bologna. *Causa Spedali-Bagnacavalli. Note dopo la discussione* (Augusto Barbieri), n.d.

Gamberini, Pietro. 1893. *Parere . . . nella causa Bagnacavalli.* Bologna, Cart. I n. 24.

Santopadre, Temistocle. 1894. *Sifilide ereditaria: Sintomi e riflessioni sopra una sentenza della Corte di Appello di Bologna.* Forlì: Tip. Lit. Democratica, Cart. III n. 32.

Pinzani, Ermanno. 1894. *A proposito della sentenza della R. Corte d'appello di Bologna . . . Bagnacavalli-Spedali.* Forlì, Cart. III n. 65.

B. Archivio Storico, Provincia di Bologna, Corpo Amministrativo Centrale degli Spedali di Bologna, titolo 13 (Ospizio Esposti)

Presidente della consulenza Legale al Presidente del Corpo Amm.vo Centrale degli Spedali di Bologna, 25 ottobre 1890.

Estratto dal Verbale dell'Adunanza Tenuta dalla Consulenza Legale l'8 dicembre 1890.

Estratto del Verbale della Seduta tenuta dal suddetto Corpo Amministrativo nel dì 10 dicembre 1890.

Presidente del Corpo Amm.vo Centrale degli Spedali di Bologna al Prefetto di Bologna, 24 dicembre 1890.

Amministrazione centrale degli spedali di Bologna. Ufficio Legale al Presidente. Bologna, 9 maggio 1892.

Estratto Verbale della Seduta tenuta dal suddetto Corpo Amministrativo nel dì 11 maggio 1892.

Presidente degli Spedali al Prefetto di Bologna, 14 maggio 1892.

Prefetto di Bologna al Presidente dell'Amme, 15 maggio 1892.

Corte d'Appello di Bologna, 31 maggio 1892. *Sentenza nella causa civile formale di appellazione promossa dall'Amministrazione degli Spedali di Bologna in persona del suo Presidente Conte Francesco Isolani . . . Contro Bagnacavalli Amalia in Migliorini.* In punto ad appello della sentenza del Tribunale di Bologna 27 luglio–4 agosto 1891.

Perizia Giudiziale del Prof. Francesco Roncati nella causa Bagnacavalli — Spedali ordinata dalla R. Corte d'Appello con Sentenza del 13 Giugno 1892, 4 agosto 1892.

Amministrazione Centrale degli Spedali di Bologna. Ufficio Legale al Presidente. Bologna, 16 luglio 1892.

Capo Contabile degli Spedali al Presidente, 28 luglio 1892.

Estratto Verbale della Seduta tenuta dal suddetto Corpo Amministrativo nel dì 6 agosto 1892.

Ufficio Legale degli Spedali di Bologna al Presidente, 11 novembre 1892.

R. Tribunale Civile di Bologna. *Nella causa formale promossa da Bagnacavalli Amalia . . . Contro L'Amministrazione degli Spedali di Bologna per*

SOURCES

l'Ospizio Esposti in persona del suo Presidente, Sig. Conte Cav. Francesco Isolani, rappresentata dal Proc. Avv. Odoardo Ferrari. In punto a pretesa liquidazione di danni ed ora ad ammissione di prova testimoniale e peritale per l'Amministrazione. Comparsa Conclusionale (da Pietro Baldini e O. Ferrari), n.d.

R. Tribunale Civile di Bologna. Causa Bagnacavalli — Spedali di Bologna. Bologna: Soc. Tip. Azzoguidi. Comparsa conclusionale, Augusto Barbieri, 18 aprile 1893.

Lettera del perito Giudiziale Signor Prof. Francesco Roncati [al Chiarissimo Sig. Avvocato Pietro Baldini] in risposta al parere del Signor Prof. Domenico Majocchi il 24 di maggio 1893.

R. Tribunale Civile di Bologna. *Causa Bagnacavalli Amalia contro Amministrazione degli Spedali, in punto a pretesa emenda di danni, 12 giugno 1893. Comparsa conclusionale per l'Amministrazione degli Spedali* (Pietro Baldini e Odoardo Ferrari).

R. Tribunale Civile di Bologna. *Causa Bagnacavalli — Spedali di Bologna. Note aggiuntive alla comparsa conclusionale e Lettera del prof. Domenico Majocchi in risposta al perito prof. Roncati*, 15 giugno 1893 (Augusto Barbieri).

Il R. Tribunale Civile e Penale di Bologna (Sezione Prima). *Sentenza nella causa civile iniziata con rito formale da Bagnacavalli Amalia, assistita ed autorizzata dal suo proprio marito Luigi Migliorini . . . contro Amministrazione degli Spedali di Bologna, in persona del suo presidente conte cav. Francesco Isolani,* 20 luglio 1893.

Corte d'Appello di Bologna. *Difesa per l'Amministrazione degli Spedali di Bologna contro Bagnacavalli Amalia in punto a pretesa riforma di Sentenza del Tribunale Civile di Bologna 20 luglio–8 agosto 1893. Comparsa Conclusionale nell'interesse dell'Amministrazione degli Spedali,* 18 marzo 1894 (Pietro Baldini e Odoardo Ferrari).

R. Corte d'Appello di Bologna. Sezione Prima. *Sentenza nella causa civile sommaria in grado d'appellazione promossa da Bagnacavalli Amalia . . . contro Amministrazione degli Spedali di Bologna, in cui è concentrato l'Ospizio Esposti, in persona del Presidente conte cav. Francesco Isolani . . . in punto ad emenda di danni, in appello dalla Sentenza del Tribunale di Bologna 20 luglio–8 agosto 1893,* 24 aprile 1894.

Avv. Pietro Baldini. *Se il Medico di un Ospizio possa dirsi un Commesso a sensi dell'art. 1153 del Codice Civile.* Alla Ecc.ma Corte di Cassazione in Roma. Causa Amministrazione degli Spedali di Bologna contro Bagnacavalli Amalia. Bologna: Regia Tip. 1895, 18 febbraio 1895.

R. Corte di Cassazione di Roma. *Udienza,* 22 febbraio 1895.

Ufficio Legale al Presidente. Bologna, 23 febbraio 1895.

Presidente del Corpo Ammvo al Cancelliere presso la R. Corte d'Appello in Bologna, 29 aprile 1895.

Pietro Baldini al Presidente, 26 giugno 1895.

Nota spese ed onorari per la causa in Cassazione, Amministrazione degli Spedali e Bagnacavalli, 26 giugno 1895 (P. Baldini).

Suprema Corte di Cassazione di Roma. *Ricorso della Amministrazione degli Spedali di Bologna contro Bagnacavalli Amalia. Preteso risarcimento di danni da infezione sifilitica,* n.d.

Regia Corte di Cassazione in Roma. *Ricorso dell' Amministrazione degli Spedali di Bologna, in persona del suo Presidente signor Conte Cavaliere Francesco Isolani . . . in confronto di Bagnacavalli Amalia, e di lei marito Lujgi Mjgliorini, residenti nel Comune di Vergato. Denuncia la sentenza fra le parti della Corte d'Appello di Bologna 6–24 aprile 1894, notificata il 1° maggio successivo,* n.d. (Pietro Baldini).

Ufficio Legale al Presidente. Bologna, 13 febbraio 1895.

Corpo Amministrativo Centrale degli Spedali di Bologna, Moto d'Ordine, Bologna, il 26 novembre 1895, Economo, fondo per spese di Pietro Baldini.

Prefetto al Presidente degli Spedali. Bologna, 23 gennaio 1896.

Archivio del Protocollo del Corpo Amministrativo Centrale degli Spedali di Bologna.

Prefetto di Bologna al Presidente dell'Amme. Bologna, 1 marzo 1896.

Presidente al Prefetto. Bologna, 3 marzo 1896.

Corte d'Appello di Ancona. *Sentenza nella causa civile di rinvio iscritta al N. 1 del ruolo di Spel. add. 10 gennaio 1896 e difesa nell'udienza del 10 giugno 1896 tra Bagnacavalli Amalia e l'Amministrazione degli Spedali di Bologna,* 18 luglio 1896.

Pietro Baldini al Presidente, 25 luglio 1896.

Corte d'Appello di Ancona al Presidente dell'Amme. Spedali Bologna, 20 agosto 1896.

Presidente degli Spedali al Cancelliere della R. Corte d'Appello di Ancona, Bologna, 12 settembre 1896.

Estratto del Verbale della Seduta tenuta dalla Consulenza Legale il 10 settembre 1896.

Estratto del Verbale della Seduta tenuta dal suddetto Corpo Amministrativo nel dì 19 settembre 1896.

Estratto del Verbale della Seduta tenuta del giorno 19 settembre 1896, approvato nella Seduta del 7 ottobre 1896.

Baldini al Presidente, 7 ottobre 1896.

Presidente al Prefetto di Bologna, 11 ottobre 1896.

Gattoni al Presidente, 14 ottobre 1896.

Estratto del Verbale della Seduta tenuta dal suddetto Corpo Amministrativo nel dì 24 ottobre 1896.

Capo Contabile degli Spedali di Bologna al Presidente Corpo Amm.vo Centrale degli Spedali, 24 ottobre 1896.

Prefettura della Provincia di Bologna. Foglio di trasmissione all' Amm.e Centrale degli Spedali, Bologna. Autorizzazione a ricorrere in Collezione contro sentenza della Corte di Appello di Ancona nella causa promossa da Amalia Bagnacavalli, 24 ottobre 1896.

Economo, moto d'ordine, Bologna, 9 novembre 1896, fondo per Pietro Baldini per la causa Bagnacavalli.

Bagnacavalli Amalia in Migliorini, chiedente giudizialmente un'indennità per sifilide, che dice contratta nell'allattamento di un'esposta. Anno 1897.

Cancelliere della Corte di Appello di Ancona al Presidente degli Spedali, 8 gennaio 1897.

Presidente degli Spedali al Cancelliere di Corte d'Appello di Ancona, 19 gennaio 1897.

Corte di Cassazione di Roma. Sezione Civile. *Sentenza nella causa tra l'Amministrazione degli Spedali di Bologna, in persona del suo Presidente Conte Francesco Isolani . . . e Bagnacavalli Amalia,* 28 aprile 1897.

Baldini al Presidente Amme, Bologna, 26 maggio 1897.

Augusto Barbieri al Presidente, Bologna, 17 giugno 1897.

Baldini al Presidente, 19 giugno 1897.

Cancelliere, Corte d'Appello di Ancona, al Presidente, 28 giugno 1897.

Estratto del Verbale della Seduta tenuta dal suddetto Corpo Amministrativo il 10 luglio 1897.

Ufficio Legale al Presidente. Bologna, 5 febbraio 1898.

Corpo Ammvo. Centrale. Estratto del Verbale della Seduta, 10 febbraio 1898.

Presidente al Prefetto. Bologna, 23 febbraio 1898.

Ufficio Legale al Presidente. Bologna, 4 luglio 1898.

Baldini al Presidente, 14 luglio 1898.

Ufficio Legale al Presidente. Bologna, 18 novembre 1898.

Baldini al Presidente, 11 ottobre 1899.

Legale di Uffizio al Presidente. Bologna, 8 marzo 1900.

Estratto del Verbale della Seduta tenuta dal suddetto Corpo Amministrativo nel dì 21 marzo 1900.

Legale d'Uffizio al Presidente. Bologna, 23 aprile 1900.

Estratto del Verbale della Seduta tenuta dal suddetto Corpo Amministrativo nel dì 25 aprile 1900.

Cancelliere Berti (Corte d'Appello di Ancona) al Presidente. Ancona, 29 maggio 1900.

Presidente al Cancelliere Berti. Bologna, 2 giugno 1900.

Estratto del verbale dell'adunanza tenuta dalla Consulenza Legale il 18 giugno 1900.

Baldini al Presidente, 18 giugno 1900.

Il Mondo, compagnia anonima d'assicurazioni. Bologna, il 15 giugno 1900.

Al Avvo. Barbieri aderendo alla sua domanda le significo che il capitale corrispondente ad una prestazione . . . di L 360 . . . a cominciare dalli trentunesimo 31 anno di età.

Estratto del Verbale della Seduta del giorno 28 giugno 1900 approvato e firmato da tutti gl'intervenuti.

Presidente al Prefetto di Bologna. Bologna, 10 luglio 1900.

Presidente al Cancelliere Berti. Bologna, 23 luglio 1900.

Cancelliere Berti di Ancona al Presidente. Ancona, 24 luglio 1900.

Corpo Ammvo. Centrale degli Spedali di Bologna. Moto d'Ordine, 25 luglio 1900.

Ricevuta, Amministrazione del Demanio e delle Tasse sugli Affari. Bologna, il 25 luglio 1900.

Dichiarazione, Luigi Migliorini, 25 luglio 1900.

Dichiarazione, Avv. Barbieri, 27 luglio 1900.

Legale d'Ufficio al Presidente. Bologna, 30 luglio 1900.

Presidente al Cancelliere di Ancona. Bologna, 31 agosto 1900.

Cancelliere della Corte d'Appello di Ancona al Presidente. Ancona, il 26 settembre 1900.

Presidente al Canceliere della Corte di Appello di Ancona. Bologna, 29 settembre 1900.

Estratto del Verbale della Seduta tenuta dal suddetto Corpo Amministrativo nel dì 21 novembre 1900.

Estratto del Verbale della Seduta del 26 dicembre 1900 tenuta dalla Consulenza Legale.

C. Archivio di Stato di Bologna

Prefettura di Bologna AA.GG. Serie I, Cat. 15, b.1, 1891. Lettere da Questura di Bologna e Prefettura di Bologna

Tribunale Civile di Bologna, "Perizie, esami, verbali," 1894, vol. II.

Tribunale Civile di Bologna, "Perizie, esami, verbali," 1897, vol. II.

Tribunale Civile di Bologna, "Perizie, esami, verbali," 1898, vol. I.

Tribunale Civile di Bologna, "Perizie, esami, verbali," 1899, vol. II, testimonianza, Bagnacavalli-Ospedale.

D. Archivio Notarile di Bologna

ANDB, Notaio Pietro Polami, 17 agosto 1890. Procura alle liti estesa anche ad negotia, delli coniugi Amalia Bagnacavalli e Luigi Migliorini nell'Ill.mo signor avvocato Augusto Barbieri di Bologna. Repertorio Registro n. 8056. Repertorio Notarile n. 1606.

ANDB, Notaio Alberto Pallotti, 1 maggio 1894. Repertorio N. 572 — Mat. N. 250. 1894, 1 maggio — Cessione di ragioni ereditarie fatta dalla Sig.ra Amalia Bagnacavalli in Migliorini al Signor Nono Veggetti con revoca di mandato e nuovo mandato fatti dalla suddetta Signora Bagnacavalli nell'Encomiato Sig. Veggetti.

ANDB, Notaio Alberto Pallotti, 1 maggio 1894. Repertorio N. 572 — Mat. N. 250. 1894, 1 maggio — Cessione di ragioni ereditarie fatta dalla Sig.ra Amalia Bagnacavalli in Migliorini al Signor Nono Veggetti con revoca di mandato e nuovo mandato fatti dalla suddetta Signora Bagnacavalli nell'Encomiato Sig. Veggetti.

ANDB, Notaio Alberto Pallotti, 6 gennaio 1898. Repertorio N. 1063 — Mat.

N. 391. 1898, 6 gennaio — Mandato speciale della signora Amalia Bagnacavalli in Migliorini nell'Ill.mo signor Riccardo Orlandi.

ANDB, Notaio Alberto Pallotti, 7 gennaio 1900. Repertorio N. 1396 — Mat. N. 460. 1900, 7 gennaio — Cessione di ragioni ereditarie fatta dalla signora Amalia Bagnacavalli in Migliorini agli ill.mi signori cav. prof. avvocato Augusto Barbieri e cav. prof. Domenico Maiocchi ed alla tipografia Azzoguidi.

ANDB, Notaio Alberto Pallotti, 26 giugno 1900. Repertorio N. 1477 — Mat. N. 478. 1900, 26 giugno — Procura della signora Amalia Bagnacavalli moglie a Migliorini Luigi e del detto Migliorini nel signor cav. prof. avv. Augusto Barbieri.

ANDB, Notaio Alberto Pallotti, 29 giugno 1900. Repertorio N. 1480 — Mat. N. 479. 1900, 29 giugno — Vendita fatta dai signori cav. avv. Augusto, capitano Aldo, Gilberto e Giulia in Genco fratelli e sorella Barbieri e dal signor Antonio Montanari loro zio al signor Desiderio Veronesi e cautela ipotecaria prestata da quest'ultimo a favore del suddetto signor Montanari.

ANDB, Notaio Alberto Pallotti, 28 agosto 1900. Repertorio N. 1499 — Mat. N. 482. 1900, 28 agosto — Dichiarazione di collaudo ed approvazione emessa dai signori coniugi Amalia Bagnacavalli e Luigi Migliorini a favore dell'ill.mo sig. cav. prof. avv. Augusto Barbieri per esercizio di procura tenuto da quest'ultimo.

II. Documents related to other cases of syphilitic wet nurses and to statistics regarding foundlings and wet nurses at the Bologna foundling home

A. *Archivio Storico, Provincia di Bologna, Archivio del Protocollo del Corpo Amministrativo Centrale degli Spedali di Bologna, titolo 13*

Anno 1883. Rub. n. 15. Posizione N. 1. Informazioni chieste dalla Provincia intorno a casi d'infezioni sifilitiche contratti da balie di esposti.

Anno 1884. Rub. n. 15. Diffusione della sifilide per mezzo di esposti poppanti.

Anno 1886. Rub. n. 15. Statistiche.

Anno 1887. Rub. n. 11. Nutrici di esposti colpiti da sifilide.

Anno 1889. Rub. n. 19. Posizione N. 1. Puccetti Domenica.

Anno 1889. Rub. n. 19. Posizione N. 2. Bonetti Amalia.

Anno 1890. Rub. n. 20. Statistiche.

Anno 1890. Rub. n. 21. Posizione N. 1. Bagnacavalli Amalia in Migliorini chiedente giudizialmente una indemnità per sifilide che dice contratta nell'allattamento di un'esposta.

Anno 1890. Rub. n. 21. Posizione N. 2. Puccetti Domenica.

Anno 1892. Rub. n. 4. Nutrici di una esposta colpite da sifilide.

Anno 1892. Rub. n. 9. Posizione N. 1. Puccetti Domenica. Chiede indennità per aver contratto la sifilide.

Anno 1892. Rub. n. 9. Posizione N. 3. Mancini Lucia.

Anno 1893. Rub. n. 9. Posizione N. 1 (Ventura Erminia), 2 (Ghermanti o Grimandi Adele), 3 (Monti Maria), 4 (Magelli Rosa), 6 (Fiorini Stella). Tutte donne che sono nutrici sifilitiche di una esposta.

Titolo 13, Anni 1896–1900. Busta 6.

Rub. 4, pos. 10 (1896). "Oggetto: Tonelli Caterina in Elmi già nudrice sifilitica di un'esposta. Concessione di un sussidio."

Rub. 15 (1896). Statistiche.

Rub. 3, pos. 2 (1897). "Oggetto: Matteuzzi Argia in Dazzani già nudrice sifilitica di un'esposta. Concessione di un sussidio."

Rub. 3, pos. 3 (1897). "Oggetto: Guernelli Luigia chiedente giudizialmente un'indennità per sifilide, che dice contratta nell'allattamento di esposti."

Rub. 3, pos. 4 (1897). "Oggetto: Masi Maria in Landi già nudrice sifilitica di un esposto. Concessione di un sussidio."

Rub. 3, pos. 5 (1897). "Oggetto: Caselli Giuditta in Mazzetti già nudrice sifilitica di un esposto. Concessione di un sussidio."

Rub. 7 (1897). Esposti all'allattamento artificiale. Bambini sifilitici da assoggettarsi all'allattamento artificiale.

Rub. 12 (1897). Statistiche. Statistiche del Baliatico e della Maternità relativa al 1896.

Rub. 13 (1898). Statistiche. Statistica del Baliatico relativa al 1897.

Rub. 14 (1899). "Oggetto: Nudrici di esposti colpite da infezione sifilitica." Pos. 1: Bertozzi Domenica in Cadmi già nudrice sifilitica di un esposto. Concessione di un sussidio.

Rub. 5 (1899). Statistiche. Statistica della Maternità relativa al 1897.

Rub. 8, pos. 1 (1899). "Oggetto: Ispezioni e sorveglianza sugli esposti."

Rub. 15 (1899). "Oggetto: Allattamento degli esposti per parte delle madri."

Pos. 1: "Concessione di sussidio alle madri per l'allattamento dei figli senza il riconoscimento legale."

Rub. 7 (1900). Statistiche.

III. Documents relating to the Bologna Provincial Council investigation into the foundling crisis, 1900–1914

A. Archivio storico, Provincia di Bologna

Deputazione Provinciale di Bologna in Archivio Generale, b. 1369, tit. 7, Rub. 2, fasc. "Esposti," 1900. Verbale adunanza del 2/1/1900, oggetto: "Commissione per i studi sugli Esposti."

Archivio Generale, b. 1369, tit. 7, Rub. 2, fasc. "Esposti," 1901. "Commissione per i studi sugli Esposti": Consiglio Provinciale di Bologna-Sessione Straordinaria.

Estratto del Verbale dell'Adunanza del 22 giugno 1901: "Relazione della Commissione per i studi sugli Esposti."

Estratto del Verbale dell'Adunanza del 28 giugno 1901: "Relazione della Commissione per i studi sugli Esposti."

Regolamento per l'Ospizio degli Esposti e l'Asilo di maternità in Bologna, modificato in base a deliberazioni prese in proposito dal Consiglio Provinciale ed accettate dal Corpo Amministrativo degli Spedali, Bologna, 1901.

Provincia di Bologna, *Studi e proposte pel mantenimento degli esposti e degli illegittimi assistiti dal Brefotrofio di Bologna. Relazione della Commissione nominata dalla Deputazione Provinciale,* Bologna, 1914.

IV. Documents related to Dr. Carlo Dalmonte and public health in Vergato

A. Archivio di Stato di Bologna

Sottoprefettura di Vergato, b. 78, fasc. 13. Verbale del Consiglio Comunale di Vergato, 28 dicembre 1874, nomina del medico chirurgo condotto di Bologna.

Sottoprefettura di Vergato, "Sanità pubblica," b. 37, fasc. 1, Carlo Dalmonte, 30 ottobre 1880, "Alcune considerazioni sugli esposti lattanti nel Circondario di Vergato."

SOURCES

Sottoprefettura di Vergato, "Sanità pubblica," b. 37, fasc. 1, Lettera del Prefetto di Bologna al Sottoprefetto di Vergato, 28 ottobre 1887.

Sottoprefettura di Vergato, "Sanità pubblica," b. 37, fasc. 1, Verbali di seduta del Consiglio sanitario del Circondario di Vergato, seduta del 28 novembre 1887.

Prefettura di Bologna, Serie 1 (Atti generali), Cat. 15, 1891, b. 1, fasc. "Carteggio del Medico Provinciale per affari sanitari in Provincia di Bologna." [7 Dalmonte letters dated 1891]

V. Admissions and medical treatments provided to women in the Bologna syphilis clinic

A. Biblioteca Istituto Clinica Dermosifilopatica, Facoltà di Medicina, Università di Bologna, Archivio storico

Sifilicomio di Bologna, Ospedale Sant'Orsola, [Registro] Donne 1888–89–90.

VI. The duel between Augusto Barbieri and Giuseppe Barbanti

A. Museo del Risorgimento di Bologna, Archivio.

Fondo Barbanti Brodano Giuseppe, fasc. 28. Duello dell'Avv. Barbanti con l'avvocato Barbieri, 1889.

VII. Parish and communal records of the lives of Amalia Bagnacavalli, Luigi Migliorini, and Augusto Barbieri

A. Chiesa Parrocchiale di S. Lorenzo di Vimignano (Vergato, prov. Bologna)

Libro dei Battezzatti, dal 19 dicembe 1878 al 18 maggio 1901.
Libro de' Matrimoni, 1865–.
Libro dei Morti, [1880–1911].
Status Animarum: 1873; 1881; 1885; 1890; 1897.

B. Chiesa Parrocchiale di Vergato (prov. Bologna)

Libro dei Battezzati, dal 1904 al 1909.

C. Parrocchia di San Lorenzo di Pracchia (prov. Pistoia)

Registro dei Battezzati, 1899–1910.
Documenti di Matrimoni dal 1920 al 1923 incluso.

Libro degli Atti di Morte [1936].
Stato dell'Animo: 1904; 1911; 1917; 1921; 1934.

D. Archivio storico Anagrafe del Comune di Bologna (population register documentation for the family of Augusto Barbieri)

E. Archivio storico Anagrafe del Comune di Pistoia (population register documentation for the family of Luigi Migliorini)

F. Archiginnasio di Bologna, "Fondo Ridolfi" (biographical documentation on the family of Augusto Barbieri)

VIII. Francesco Isolani and the Bologna city council

A. Archivio Storico del Comune di Bologna

Atti del Consiglio Comunale di Bologna (1886–1900)

PUBLISHED

Andreoli, Aldo. 1962. "Francesco Roncati." *Strenna storica bolognese*, pp. 7–13.
Angeli, Aurora. 2001. *Esposizione e baliatico a Imola nei secoli 18 e 19*. Bologna: Clueb.
Antonini, C., and M. Buscarini. 1985. "La regolamentazione della prostituzione nell'Italia postunitaria." *Rivista di Storia Contemporanea*, n. 1, pp. 83–114.
Arbizzani, Luigi. 1975. "Barbanti-Brodano Giuseppe." Pp. 161–163 in Franco Andreucci and Tommaso Detti, eds., *Il movimento operaio italiano. Dizionario biografico, 1853–1943*, vol. 1. Rome: Editori Riuniti.
Augagneur, V. 1879. *Etude sur la syphilis héréditaire tardive*. Lyon: Chanoine.
Babini, Valeria. 2004. *Il caso Murri*. Bologna: Il Mulino.
Baccarini, Alfredo. 1907. *Discorsi Politici 1876–1890*. Bologna: Zanichelli.
Baldwin, Peter. 1999. *Contagion and the State in Europe, 1830–1930*. Cambridge: Cambridge University Press.
Banca Popolare di Credito in Bologna. 1907. *In memoria . . . Francesco Isolani*. Bologna.
Banti, Alberto Mario. 1995. "Italian professionals: Markets, incomes, estates

and identities." Pp. 223–54 in Maria Malatesta, ed., *Society and the Professions in Italy, 1860–1914*. Translated by Adrian Belton. Cambridge: Cambridge University Press.

Barbieri, Augusto. 1886. *Lo Stato ed il Comune nella questione della tutela amministrativa della nomina del Sindaco*. Bologna.

Barbieri, Augusto. 1888. *Elementi di Scienza dell'Amministrazione*. Bologna: Zanichelli.

Barnes, David S. 1995. *The Making of a Social Disease: Tuberculosis in Nineteenth-Century France*. Berkeley: University of California Press.

Barrucco, Nicolò. 1894. *Breve compendio teorico-pratico sulla sifilide e sulle malattie veneree*. Bologna: Treves.

Bernabei, Giancarlo, and S. Cagnoni. 1984. *Bologna moderna, 1860–1980*. Bologna: Pàtron.

Bernardi, Giovanna. 1992. *Vergato: pagine della memoria*. Vergato: Editoriale Nueter.

Berti, Giovanni. 1885. *Relazione di un confronto fatto nello stabilimento esposti di Bologna fra bimbi a latte di donna e a latte di bestia*. Bologna: Gamberini e Parmeggiani.

Berti, Giovanni. 1886. "Ricerca fatta sulla mortalità nel 1° anno di vita dei bambini allattati dalle madri nella campagna bolognese." *Bullettino delle Scienze Mediche*, anno LVII, serie 6, vol. 17, pp. 353–60.

Berti, Giovanni. 1887. "Ancora sulla mortalità dei bambini legittimi allattati dalle madri, nel 1° anno di età, nella campagna bolognese." *Bullettino delle Scienze Mediche*, anno LVIII, serie 6, vol. 20, pp. 45–50.

Berti, Giovanni. 1888. *Considerazioni pratiche d'igiene intorno alla sifilide da allattamento fatte in seguito alla circolare ministeriale del 5 novembre 1887*. Naples: Tip. Dell'Unione.

Bettini, Ulisse. 1891. *Per la pretura di Vergato. Il Mandamento di Vergato al Consiglio provinciale*. Bologna: Gamberini e Parmeggiani.

Bianchi, Adanella. 1989. "'L'elemosina di un bambino.' Pratica e controllo dell'abbandono all'Ospedale dei Bastardini (secc. XVI-XVIII)." *Sanità, Scienze e Storia* 2:35–54.

Bianchi, Adanella. 1990. "La 'famiglia' dell'ospedale tra XVI e XVIII secolo." Pp. 39–52 in *I bastardini: Patrimonio e memoria di un ospedale bolognese*. Bologna: Edizioni Age.

Bignardi, Agostino. 1956. *Dizionario biografico dei liberali bolognesi (1860/ 1914)*. Bologna: Bandiera.

Boutry, Philippe, ed. 1991. *Enfance abandonée et société en Europe, xiv–xix siècle*. Rome: Ecole Française de Rome.

Breda, Achille. 1887. *Manuale pratico di malattie veneree e sifilitiche*. Padua: Draghi.

Brugia, Raffaele. 1907. *In memoria di Francesco Roncati: cenni necrologici*. Reggio Emilia: S. Ferraboschi.

Bulkley, L. D. 1894. *Syphilis in the Innocent*. New York: Bailey.

Buret, Frédéric. 1891–1895. *Syphilis To-day and Among the Ancients*. 3 vols. Philadelphia: Davis.

Cardoza, Anthony. 1982. *Agrarian Elites and Italian Fascism: The Province of Bologna, 1901–1926*. Princeton: Princeton University Press.

Cavazza, Francesco. 1906. *In morte del conte commendatore dottor Francesco Isolani*. Bologna: Zamorani e Albertazzi.

Cesena, Davide. 1890. "Studio clinico chimico sul modo di comportarsi di alcuni rimedi mercuriali nella sifilide." *Giornale italiano delle malattie veneree e della pelle* 25:156–74.

Cherubini, A. 1990. "Sifilide (e prostituzione)." Pp. 179–217 in A. Cherubini and F. Vannozzi, *Previdenza di malattia e malattie sociali dall'Unità alla prima guerra mondiale*. Rome: Iims.

Cicero, Salvatore. 1890. "Patogenesi ed etiologia della sifilide congenita." *Giornale italiano delle malattie veneree e della pelle* 25:321–28.

Club Alpino Italiano. Sezione di Bologna. 1881. *L'Appenino Bolognese*. Bologna: Fava e Garagnani.

Commissione di Indagini scientifico-pratiche della Associazione Medica Lombarda. 1890. *Studio sul modo di funzionare del nuovo Regolamento sulla prostituzione in Italia e sugli effetti ottenuti dalla sua applicazione*. Summary in *Giornale italiano delle malattie veneree e della pelle* 1890 25:92–96.

Concetti, L. 1891. "Della sifilide ereditaria nei brefotrofi considerata in rapporto alla nuova legge sulla polizia sanitaria dei costumi." *La Riforma Medica* 6:397–423.

Consiglio Comunale di Bologna. *Atti*, 1886–1900. Bologna.

Crissey, John T., and Lawrence Charles Parish. 1981. *The Dermatology and Syphilology of the Nineteenth Century*. New York: Praeger.

Cristofori, Franco. 1978. *Bologna: immagini e vita tra Ottocento e Novecento.* Bologna: Alfa.

Dadà, Adriana, ed. 2002. *Balie da latte: istituzioni assistenziali e privati in Toscana tra 17. e 20. secolo.* Rome: Morgana Edizioni.

Dalle Donne, Giancarlo, Anna Tonelli, and Cristina Zaccanti. 1987. *L'Inchiesta sanitaria del 1899.* Milan: Angeli.

D'Amato, V. 1901. *La cura pratica delle malattie veneree, sifilitiche e della pelle.* Rome: Forense.

Da Molin, Giovanna, ed. 1994. *Trovatelli e balie in Italia.* Bari: Cacucci.

D'Attorre, Paolo. 1986. "La politica." Pp. 69–112 in Renato Zangheri, ed., *Bologna.* Rome: Laterza.

Della Peruta, Franco. 1980. "Sanità pubblica e legislazione sanitaria dall'Unità a Crispi." *Studi storici* 21:713–60.

De Napoli, Ferdinando. 1911. *Il mercurio nella sifilide e le sue vicende attraverso i secolo (1496–1911) a proposito delle frizioni mercuriali.* Bologna: A. Gherardi.

Di Bello, Giulia. 1989. *Senza nome né famiglia. I bambini abbandonati nell'ottocento.* Florence: Manzuoli.

Di Clemente Ghigi, Eutimio. 1882. *Relazione al consiglio comunale di Vergato, 22 agosto 1882.* Persiceto: Tip. Guerzoni.

Diday, Paul. 1854. *Traité de la syphilis des nouveaus-nés et des enfants à la mamelle.* Paris: Masson.

Diday, Paul. 1866. *Il pericolo delle malattie veneree nelle famiglie.* Milan: Wilmant.

Diday, Paul. 1886. *La pratique des malades veneriennes.* Paris: Asselin, Houzeau.

Di Lorenzo, G., and G. Ciaramelli. 1884. "Resoconto statistico-sanitario della Clinica Dermosifilopatica dello stabilimento dell'Annunziatella di Napoli, dal 1 Gennaio 1883 al 30 Giugno 1884." Reviewed in *Giornale italiano delle malattie veneree e della pelle* 1885 20:241–44.

Direzione Generale della Statistica. 1886. *Risultati dell'inchiesta sulle condizioni igieniche e sanitarie nei Comuni del Regno,* 3 vols. in 2. Rome: Ospizio di S. Michele.

Dogliani, Mario. 1989. "La avvocatura dei poveri." *Movimento Operaio e Socialista* 3:275–90.

Ferrovia transappenninica (La). 1986. *Bologna Incontri* 11.

Fildes, Valerie. 1986a. *Breasts, Bottles, and Babies: A History of Infant Feeding.* Edinburgh: Edinburgh University Press.

Fildes, Valerie. 1986b. *Wet Nursing: A History from Antiquity to the Present.* Oxford: Blackwell.

Forzoni, Alberto. 2003. *Prostituzione e sanità ad Arezzo: il sifilicomio degli Spedali riuniti, 1863–1888.* Montepulciano: Le Balze.

Fournier, Alfred. 1878. *Nourrices et nourrissons syphilitiques.* Paris: Delahaye.

Fournier, Alfred. 1886. *La syphilis héréditaire tardive.* Paris: Masson.

Fournier, Alfred. 1891. *L'hérédité syphilitique.* Paris: Masson.

Fournier, Alfred. 1912. *Syphilis héréditaire de l'âge adulte.* Paris: Masson.

Franceschini, G. 1903. *Il patrocinio gratuito nel diritto giudiziario civile.* Turin.

Frascani, Paolo. 1996. "I medici dall'Unità al fascismo." Pp. 147–89 in Maria Malatesta, ed., *Storia d'Italia. Annali* 10: *I professionisti.* Turin: Einaudi.

Fuà, R. 1915. *Sulla diagnosi precoce della sifilide ereditaria nel lattante.* Ancona: Commercio.

Fuchs, Rachel G. 1984. *Abandoned Children: Foundlings and Child Welfare in Nineteenth-Century France.* Albany: SUNY Press.

Gabba, C. F. 1895. Commenti critici sulla decisione Bagnacavalli-Spedali di Bologna nella corte d'appello di Bologna." *Foro italiano* vol. 20, parte 1, pp. 32–46.

Gamberini, Pietro. 1864–1888. *Rapporto politico-amministrativo-clinico della prostituzione di Bologna.* Bologna: Gamberini e Parmeggiani.

Gamberini, Pietro. 1880. "Statistica delle malattie veneree, sifilitiche e cutanee accolte e curate nella Clinica di Bologna nell'anno 1879 dal Prof. Gamberini. *Giornale italiano delle malattie veneree e della pelle* 15:143–47.

Gamberini, Pietro. 1881. "Decimonono rapporto politico-amministrativo-clinico della prostituzione in Bologna." *Giornale italiano delle malattie veneree e della pelle* 16:104–13.

Gamberini, Pietro. 1881. "Sulla pretesa incurabilità della sifilide." *Giornale italiano delle malattie veneree e della pelle* 16:1–11.

Gamberini, Pietro. 1883. "Ventunesimo rapporto politico-amministrativo-clinico della prostituzione in Bologna." *Giornale italiano delle malattie veneree e della pelle* 18:104–13.

Gamberini, Pietro. 1884. "I sifilografi e dermatologi bolognesi." *Giornale italiano delle malattie veneree e della pelle* 19:1–16.

Gamberini, Pietro. 1884. "Ventesimosecondo rapporto politico-amministrativo-clinico della prostituzione in Bologna." *Giornale italiano delle malattie veneree e della pelle* 19:65–74.

Gamberini, Pietro. 1885. "Ventesimoterzo rapporto politico-amministrativo-clinico della prostituzione in Bologna." *Giornale italiano delle malattie veneree e della pelle* 20:65–74.

Gamberini, Pietro. 1885. *Statistica clinico-terapeutica delle malattie veneree e cutanee accolte nella clinica universitaria di Bologna diretta dal prof. Pietro Gamberini nell'anno 1884*. Naples: Jovene.

Gamberini, Pietro. 1886. "Ventesimoquarto rapporto politico-amministrativo-clinico della prostituzione in Bologna." *Giornale italiano delle malattie veneree e della pelle* 21:65–74.

Gamberini, Pietro. 1887. "Studi teorico-clinici relativi alla sifilide ereditaria specialmente tardiva." *Giornale italiano delle malattie veneree e della pelle* 22:321–28.

Gamberini, Pietro. 1887. "Ventesimoquinto rapporto politico-amministrativo-clinico della prostituzione in Bologna." *Giornale italiano delle malattie veneree e della pelle* 22:65–71.

Gamberini, Pietro. 1889. "Studi e proposte intorno alla sifilide per allattamento in relazione specialmente cogli stabilimenti che raccolgono i trovatelli." Reprinted from *Giornale italiano delle malattie veneree e della pelle*, fasc. 1, marzo 1889. Milan: Prato.

Gamberini, Pietro. 1889. "Studi e proposte intorno alla sifilide per allattamento in relazione specialmente cogli stabilimenti che accolgono i trovatelli." *Giornale italiano delle malattie veneree e della pelle* 24:7–15.

Gamberini, Pietro. 1889. "Ventesimosettimo rapporto politico-amministrativo-clinico della prostituzione in Bologna." *Giornale italiano delle malattie veneree e della pelle* 24:5–6.

Gamberini, Pietro. 1889. *Sintomatologia della sifilide ereditaria infanzia*. Bologna.

Gamberini, Pietro. 1895. *Gravidanza, parto e mali sifilitici*. Bologna.

Gamberini, Pietro. 1896. *La sifilide ereditaria, congenita ed accidentale, specialmente dei neonati*. Bologna.

Gargiulo, Francesco Saverio. 1888. *Corso elementare di diritto giudiziario civile*. Naples: Marchieri.

Gattei, Giorgio. 1984. "La sifilide: medici e poliziotti intorno alla 'Venere politica.'" Pp. 739–98 in *Storia d'Italia, Annali*, vol. 7, *Malattia e medicina*. Turin: Einaudi.

Gemma, Anton M. 1883. "Un caso di sifilide per allattamento pel contagio di una bambina." *Giornale italiano delle malattie veneree e della pelle* 18:294–49.

Gibson, Mary. 1986. *Prostitution and the State in Italy, 1860–1915*. New Brunswick, N.J.: Rutgers University Press.

Gorni, Mariagrazia, and Laura Pellegrini. 1974. *Un problema di storia sociale. L'infanzia abbandonata in Italia nel secolo XIX*. Florence: La Nuova Italia.

Greco, Giovanni. 1998. "Controllo sociale e postriboli nella vecchia Bologna." *Il Carrobbio* 24:221–38.

Griffini, R. 1868. "Sul progetto di regolamento organico dell'ospizio degli esposti e delle partorienti." *Annali universali di medicina* 206:465–563.

Guarnirei, Patrizia. 2006. *L'ammazzabambini: Legge e scienza in un processo di fine Ottocento*. Rome: Laterza.

Guidotti, Paolo. 1985. *Vergato: centro politico e di osservazione della montagna bolognese dal Medioevo all'Unità d'Italia*. Bologna: Nuova Alfa.

Guidotti, Paolo. 1991. *Strade transappenniniche bolognesi*. Bologna: Clueb.

Hayden, Deborah. 2003. *Pox: Genius, Madness, and the Mysteries of Syphilis*. New York: Basic Books.

Hughes, Steven C. 1998. "Men of steel: Dueling, honor, and politics in liberal Italy." Pp. 64–81 in Pieter Spierenburg, ed., *Men and Violence*. Columbus: Ohio State University Press.

Hunecke, Volker. 1989. *I trovatelli di Milano*. Bologna: Il Mulino.

Il Resto del Carlino. 1 gennaio 1916. "La morte dell'avv. Augusto Barbieri."

In memoria del conte dottore commendatore Francesco Isolani Lupari. 1907. Bologna: Stab. Poligrafico Emiliano.

Italia. Direzione Generale della Statistica. 1894. *Statistica della assistenza dell'infanzia abbandonata, anni 1890, 1891, e 1892*. Rome: Tip. Elzeviriana.

Jullien, L. 1881. *Trattato pratico delle malattie veneree*. Naples: Sese.

Kertzer, David I. 1993. *Sacrificed for Honor: Italian Infant Abandonment and the Politics of Reproductive Control*. Boston: Beacon Press.

Kertzer, David I. 1999. "Syphilis, foundlings, and wetnurses in nineteenth-century Italy." *Journal of Social History* 32:589–602.

Kertzer, David I. 2000. "The lives of foundlings in nineteenth-century Italy." Pp. 41–56 in Catherine Panter-Brick and Malcolm Smith, eds., *Abandoned Children*. Cambridge: Cambridge University Press, 2000.

Kertzer, David I. 2004. *Prisoner of the Vatican: The Popes' Secret Plot to Capture Italy from the New Italian State*. Boston: Houghton Mifflin.

Kertzer, David I., Heather Koball, and Michael J. White. 1997. "Growing up as an abandoned child in nineteenth-century Italy." *History of the Family* 2:211–28.

Kertzer, David I., and Wendy Sigle. 1998. "The marriage of female foundlings in nineteenth-century Italy." *Continuity and Change* 13:201–20.

Kertzer, David I., Wendy Sigle, and Michael J. White. 1999. "Childhood mortality and quality of care among abandoned children in nineteenth-century Italy." *Population Studies* 53:303–15.

Kertzer, David I., Wendy Sigle, and Michael J. White. 2000. "Abandoned children and their transitions to adulthood in nineteenth-century Italy." *Journal of Family History* 25:326–40.

Kertzer, David I., and Michael J. White. 1994. "Cheating the angel-makers: Surviving infant abandonment in nineteenth-century Italy." *Continuity & Change* 9:451–80.

Lancereaux, Etienne. 1868. *A Treatise on Syphilis, Historical and Practical*. London: New Sydenham Society (series), vol. 38. Originally published as *Traité historique et pratique de la syphilis* (Paris: Baillière).

Lelli, Bianca. 1988. "Prostituzione e prostitute a Bologna nella seconda metà dell'Ottocento." *La Padania*, anno 2, n. 4, pp. 157–78.

Lesser, E. 1887. *Manuale delle malattie cutanee e venereo-sifilitiche*, parte 1. Third ed. Milan: Vallardi.

Luccini, Gaetano. 1893. *Relazione statistica dei lavori compiuti nel distretto della Corte d'Appello di Bologna nell'anno 1892*. Bologna: Tip. Militare.

Maioli, G. 1937. "Tattini Isolani Lupari Letizia," *Dizionario del Risorgimento nazionale*, vol. 4. Milan: Vallardi.

Manservigi, Salesio, Giuseppe Ferrari, and Danilo Di Diodoro. [1890] 1983. *Memoria in ordine al Manicomio di Bologna, desunta dagli atti esistenti nell'archivio dell'amministrazione degli spedali di Bologna.* Bologna: Clueb.

Massarenti, Carlo. 1876. *La Clinica Ostetrica in Bologna ed il Prof. Carlo Massarenti il direttore di essa dalla fondazione.* Bologna: Soc. Tip. Azzoguidi.

Mauriac, Ch. 1890. *Syphilis tertiaire et syphilis héréditaire.* Paris: Baillière.

Miretti, Monica. 1998. "L'amministrazione della giustizia a Bologna nell'- Ottocento." Pp. 37–50 in Giovanni Greco, ed., *Criminalità e controllo sociale a Bologna nell'Ottocento.* Bologna: Pàtron.

Montroni, Giovanni. 1995. "Aristocracy and professions." Pp. 255–75 in Maria Malatesta, ed., *Society and the Professions in Italy, 1860–1914.* Translated by Adrian Belton. Cambridge: Cambridge University Press.

Morrow, A. 1889. *Atlas of Skin and Venereal Diseases.* New York: Wood.

Mortara, Lodovico. 1887. *Manuale della Procedura Civile.* Turin: Unione Tip.- Editrice.

Musti, Maria Rosaria. 1998. "L'ospedale di S. Giobbe in epoca moderna." Pp. 123–60 in Giovanni Greco, ed., *Criminalità e controllo sociale a Bologna nell'Ottocento.* Bologna: Pàtron.

Nabarro, D. 1954. *Congenital Syphilis.* London: Arnold.

Nacciarone, U. 1888. *Trattato pratico delle malattie veneree.* Milan: Vallardi.

Nitti, G. P. 1963. "Alfredo Baccarini," *Dizionario biografico degli italiani* 5:4–8.

Onger, Sergio. 1985. *L'infanzia negata. Storia dell'assistenza agli abbandonati e indigenti a Brescia nell'Ottocento.* Brescia: AIED.

Paci, Piero. 2004. "L'antico ospedale San Giobbe per sifilitici." Pp. 365–77 in *Strenna storia bolognese.*

Paganella, Veronica. 1998. "Postriboli e megere nella vecchia Bologna." Pp. 81–122 in Giovanni Greco, ed., *Criminalità e controllo sociale a Bologna nell'Ottocento.* Bologna: Pàtron.

Pasi, Antonia. 1998. "'Come d'autunno cadono le foglie'. L'allattamento nei brefotrofi italiani del XIX secolo." Pp. 721–50 in *Storia d'Italia, Annali* vol. 13, *L'alimentazione.* Turin: Einaudi.

Peli, Giuseppe. 1907. "In memoria di Francesco Roncati." Bologna: Gamberini e Parmeggiani. Reprinted from *Bullettino delle scienze mediche,* serie 3, v . 7.

Pellizzari, C. 1882. *Della trasmissione accidentale della sifilide.* Milan: L. Bortolotti & C.

Pellizzari, C. 1888. *Prostituzione e profilassi pubblica della sifilide.* Florence.

Pellizzari, C. 1891. *Dell'azione del mercurio nella sifilide.* Naples.

Pinzani, Ermanno. 1894. *A proposito della sentenza della R. Corte d'appello di Bologna . . . Bagnacavalli-Spedali.* Forlì.

Plazzi, Mirella M., and Angelo Varni, eds. 1993. *Alfredo Baccarini: il liberalismo romagnolo alla prova.* Bologna: Il Nove.

Poli, Marco. 2002. *In nome del progresso, 1902–1904: l'abbattimento delle mura di Bologna.* Bologna: Costa.

Profeta, G. 1888. *Trattato pratico delle malattie veneree.* Palermo: Vena.

Proni, Eleonora. 2006. *Bologna: La nascita dell'Ordine degli Avvocati e Procuratori.* Bologna: Fondazione Forense Bolognese.

Provincia di Bologna. 1901. *Studi e proposte di riforma per l'Ospizio degli Esposti di Bologna. Relazione della Commissione.* Bologna.

Putegnat, Joseph Dominique. 1854. *Histoire et thérapeutique de la syphilis des nouveau-nés et des enfants à la mamelle.* Paris: Baillière.

Quercioli, Giuseppe. 1979. *L'ospedale psichiatrico provinciale Francesco Roncati di Bologna: 1867–1979, centododici anni di storia e di vita manicomiale.* Bologna.

Quétel, Claude. 1990. *History of Syphilis.* Translated by Judith Braddock and Brian Pike. Baltimore: Johns Hopkins University Press.

Ransel, David L. 1988. *Mothers of Misery: Child Abandonment in Russia.* Princeton: Princeton University Press.

Ravogli, Augusto, and Enrico Rasori. 1880. "Resoconto clinico degli ammalati curati nella Clinica e Dispensario Dermo-Sifilitico della R. Università di Roma per gli anni scolastici 1877–78, 1878–79." *Giornale italiano delle malattie veneree e della pelle* 15:205–11.

Raymond, Paul. 1893. *La syphilis dans l'allaitement.* Paris: Rueff.

Renzi, Renzo. 1974. *Il processo Murri.* Bologna: Cappelli.

Rollet, J. 1887. *De la transmission de la syphilis entre nourissons et nourrices.* Paris.

Roncati, Francesco. 1894. *La decadenza della moralità ed il contagio morale.* Discorso inaugurale del prof. Francesco Roncati alla solenne apertura degli studi nella R. Università di Bologna, 1894–1895. Bologna.

Roversi, Giancarlo. 1985. *Le mura perdute: Storia e immagini dell'ultima cerchia fortificata di Bologna.* Bologna: Banca Popolare di Bologna e Ferrara.

Rydell, Robert W., and Rob Kroes. *Buffalo Bill in Bologna: The Americanization of the World, 1869–1922.* Chicago: University of Chicago Press.

Sabbatani, L. 1906. *Alla memoria del prof. Francesco Roncati: discorso letto da L. Sabbatani al Consiglio provinciale di Bologna nella seduta delli 13 ottobre 1906.* Bologna.

Sani, Sebastiano. 1922. *Bologna di ieri.* Bologna: Zanichelli.

Santoro, Marco. 1996. "Le trasformazioni del campo giuridico. Avvocati, procuratori e notai dall'Unità alla Repubblica." Pp. 81–144 in Maria Malatesta, ed., *Storia d'Italia. Annali* 10: *I professionisti.* Turin: Einaudi.

Sarti, Telesforo. 1896. *Il Parlamento subalpino e nazionale: Profili e cenni biografici di tutti i Deputati e Senatori.* Rome: Tip. Pintucci.

Scarenzio, Angelo. 1880. "Sifilide congenita per diretta influenza paterna. Immunità della gestante. Contagio infettante nella puerpera per opera del neonato." *Giornale italiano delle malattie veneree e della pelle* 15:16–20.

Scarenzio, Angelo. 1893. *Parere del Prof. Cav. Angelo Scarenzio . . . nella causa Bagnacavalli contro l'Amministrazione degli Spedali di Bologna.* Pavia.

Scarenzio, Angelo. 1896. *Sulla cura della sifilide congenito.* Florence: Tip. Niccolai.

Siegrist, Hannes. 1994. "Profilo degli avvocati italiani per 1870 al 1930." *Polis* 8:223–43.

Simoncini, Adriano, and Mauro Bacci. 1983. *Il crepuscolo della civiltà contadina: costumanze e tradizioni della montagna.* Loiano: Cassa Rurale ed Artigiana.

Società Medica Chirurgica di Bologna. 1901. *Adunanze pubbliche. Governo degli Esposti, allattamento nei brefotrofi, sifilide negli Esposti.* Bologna.

Società Medica Chirurgica di Bologna. 1924. *Primo centenario della Società Medica Chirurgica di Bologna (1823–1923).* Bologna.

Stefanizzi, Daniela. 1998. "L'Ospedale di San Procolo o dei 'Bastardini' di Bologna." Pp. 161–70 in Giovanni Greco, ed., *Criminalità e controllo sociale a Bologna nell'Ottocento.* Bologna: Pàtron.

Storia di Pistoia. Florence: Le Monnier.

Sull'esercizio delle professioni di avvocato e di procuratore. Legge 8 giugno 1874, n. 1938. Milan: Tip. Pirola.

Sussman, George D. 1982. *Selling Mother's Milk: The Wetnursing Business in France, 1715–1914.* Urbana: University of Illinois Press.

Tagliavini, Annamaria. 1985. "Francesco Roncati, direttore del manicomio," *Sanità scienza e storia,* n. 1, pp. 85–107.

Tartenson, James. 1880. *La syphilis: son histoire et son traitement (méthode anglaise).* Paris: Baillière.

Tassinari, Oriano. 1987. *Terra e gente di Vimignano.* Bologna: Parrocchia di Vimignano.

Testoni, Alfredo. 1972 (1930). *Bologna che scompare.* Bologna: Cappelli.

Titomanlio, A. 1890. "Sull'aumento della sifilide ereditaria nell'Annunziata di Napoli, in rapporti ai nuovi ordinamenti sanitari." *Riforma medica* pp. 278–79. Reviewed in *Giornale italiano delle malattie veneree e della pelle* 1891 26:109–12.

Turno, Michela. 2003. *Il malo esempio: donne scostumate e prostituzione nella Firenze dell'Ottocento.* Florence: Giunti.

Valenzi, Lucia. 1995. *Poveri, ospizi e potere a Napoli 18–19 secolo.* Milan: Angeli.

Valenzi, Lucia. 2000. *Donne, medici e poliziotti a Napoli nell'Ottocento: la prostituzione tra repressione e tolleranza.* Naples: Liguori.

Varni, Angelo. 1993. "Alfredo Baccarini tra Romagna e Stato nazionale." Pp. 11–18 in Mirella M. Plazzi and Angelo Varni, eds., *Alfredo Baccarini: il liberalismo romagnolo alla prova.* Bologna: Il Nove.

Weil, A. 1880. *Presente stato della dottrina dell'eredità della sifilide.* Naples: Vallardi.

Zambonini, G. 1881. "Monografia sulle condizioni agrarie del Circondario di Vergato." Pp. 735–52 in *Atti della Giunta per l'Inchiesta Agraria e sulle condizioni delle classi agricole,* vol. 2, fasc. 3. Rome.

Index

abandoned infants (foundlings)
  as carriers of syphilis, 34–35, 58, 64
  certification of maternal health and, 37–38, 56, 75
  as foundling home workers, 15
  infant mortality and, 148, 158, 161, 176–77
  Italian society and, 177–78, 181
  rural wet nurse system and, 4, 12–14, 34, 54
  surnames and, 17–18
  See also artificial feeding; Bologna foundling home; Olivelli, Paolina
Adriani, Adriano, 154–55
Altieri, Emilio. See Clement X
Amour, Alessandro, 76
Ancona, Italy. See Court of Appeals of Ancona
animal milk, 57, 143
  See also artificial feeding
archival sources, 191–93, 195

aristocracy, 2–3, 31–32, 33
  See also Isolani, Count Francesco
artificial feeding
  Bologna foundling home policy and, 118, 143–46, 148, 149, 176–77, 178–80
  experimentation with, 143–44
  infant mortality from, 57, 118, 148, 158, 161, 176–77, 178–80
  pasteurization and, 181
artistic elites, syphilis among, 36–37
Azzoguidi Publishing House, 62, 129, 167

Baciocchi, Felice, 48–49
Bagnacavalli, Alfonso, 183
Bagnacavalli, Amalia
  change in name of, 184–85
  daughters who lived and, 173, 183, 184
  death of, 188
  deaths of children of, 44–45, 106, 136, 184